11/98

Jim,

Just

of our sincer[...]

& love.

Richard & JoAnne

D0394846

Jack Buck

"That's a Winner"

Jack Buck
Rob Rains
Bob Broeg

SAGAMORE PUBLISHING
Champaign, IL 61820

©1997 Jack Buck
All rights reserved.

Book design, editor: Susan M. McKinney
Dustjacket design: Michelle R. Dressen
Front cover photo: David Stradal

ISBN: 1-57167-111-0
Library of Congress Catalog Card Number: 97-65484

Printed in the United States.

This book is dedicated to all those who ever hired me in Columbus, Ohio; Rochester, NY; St. Louis or New York City. And also to all those who ever fired me, because it always turned out well. A thank you to all those who ever tuned me in or turned me off—I hope you consider me a friend.

Contents

Acknowledgments

Thanks to all those lucky enough not to be mentioned elsewhere in this book. If I needed a favor, I'd call some of these people:

Joe Arndt, the doughnut man
Al Baroni, the river man
Allen Baroucke, the travelin' man
Tom Barton, the never had a bad day man
Brian Bartow, the stat man
Buddy Bates, the Illini man
Chuck Bauer, the quiet man
James Bauer, the take over the booth man
Bob Baum, the sailing man
Jim Bayens, the former everything man
Benedetto, the "mama's in the kitchen" man
Margie Bequette, the do-it-all lady
Vince Bommarito, the five-star man
Bill Brestan, the spotter man
Matt Brewer, the little man
Dr. Jack Carmody, the housecall man
Joe Carter, the 100-year-old man
C.J. Cherre, the travel man
Billy Choate, the minstrel man
Jerry Clinton, the beer man
John Cooper, the nervous man
Gerry Creedon, the Pittsburgh parrott
Mike Cremins, the premium man
Frank Cunetto, the egg nog man
Dr. E.J. Cunningham, the Fighting Irish man
Joe Cunningham, the good humor man
Russ David, the piano man
Doris Davis, the straighten-it-up lady
Hal Dean, the dogfood man
Father John Ditenhafer, the road to Heaven man
Dominic, the hill man
Jack Donnelly, the "I don't care" man
Jack Fette, the whistle man
Bernie Fox, the detail man
Jan Fox, the answer lady

Art Friedman, the agent man
Bruce Froemming and the umpires, the "We get no respect" men
Gene Gieselmann, the "There they go" man
Charlie Gitto, the info man
Bob Goalby, the Masters man
Dr. Kevin Groth, the "It won't hurt at all" man
Bill Hall, the Ritz man
Tom Hanlon, the ride man
Marty Hendin, the trinket man
Colin Jarrette, the "It's not my fault" man
Rich Koster, the writing man
Mark Lamping, the boss man
Larry Legrand, the money man
Dr. Stan London, the "You'll be OK" man
Dorian Magawitz, the carat man
Martin Mathews, the banquet man
Denny McDaniel, the share-it man
Les Miller, the boat man
Angelo Oidani, the toasted ravioli man
Tony Ponturo, the Bud Light man
Jay Randolph, the sans-a-belt man
Harold Rasmussen, the plastic man
Herb Rosenberg, the link to home man
Liz Shepard, the sweet woman
Leland Smith, the nickel man
Charlie Spoonhour, the Arkansas man
Norm Stewart, the Shelbyville man
Pastor Rodney Stortz, the Bible man
Gilbert Tate, the helper man
Lee Thomas, the MadDog man
Jim Toomey, the "I remember" man
Steve Uline, the contract man
Norma Wallner, the guard lady
Dr, William Wright, the pacemaker man
Butch Yatkeman, the little big man
Rod Zimmerman, the bottom-line man

Foreword

"The Mighty Buck"

by Bob Broeg

John Francis Buck, i.e., Jack Buck, couldn't have done more to amuse, entertain, inform and satisfy millions over 46 years than when the broadcaster finally sat still long enough to put one word after another in this autobiography.

I was amazed how many things I *didn't* know about a dear friend and a great talent. I thought I knew more than most about the silver-haired, silver-tongued septuagenarian who has won more awards and decorations than a Mexican general, including being in many Halls of Fame—baseball's, pro football's, and radio's.

Happily, I rode shotgun next to Rob Rains as the young sports author persuaded Buck to tell it all. Among the things I didn't know was that the Buck family lineage goes back to the days of the Mayflower. Francis Cooke of Nottingham was a far-sighted Britisher listed as 17th to sign the Mayflower Compact.

The first Buck, named Isaac, came over quickly, too, "transplanted for refusing to take the oath of conformity," indicating an obstinacy occasionally displayed about the principled person about whom Rains and I write, about whom you've heard and hopefully will read about here. Isaac Buck, a hard-nosed blacksmith, helped turn back native Americans at Scituate, Massachusetts, in 1676. He lived to the ripe old age of 95.

Jack Buck was proud and impressed by the research of brother Earle, ferreting out the family's past in an intermingle of the Schuylers, the Blakes, the Foxes and the Moynihans. As Jack mused, with a light touch of irreverence, "I might have been named Schuyler Blake Buck."

To Buck, humor is second only to cleanliness, if not godliness. Commented Jack with his contagious cockeyed grin, "my father, a Buck, married my mother, a Fox and they had a deer— actually seven deer."

By the time Jack opened his baby blues in 1924, his immediate family was financially hard-pressed, prompting him, as he relates, to work hard before, during and after school. Despite the traditional warming tale of success achieved by the mighty Buck, he turned down a prestigious national award, named for Horatio Alger, the fictional rags-to-riches cliché. Jack honestly felt the connotation wasn't fair to his hard-working parents, most certainly his dear mother. His father's early death took away a personal hero as well as vital family support.

The assortment of Buck's jobs, crafted here, are almost as impressive as they are humorous in his recollection. He paints the picture of a man satisfied after having mastered so many other things, mostly in sports.

Take my word that this Hall of Famer of baseball, football, and microphone could have been many things. Listening to the words flow, flavored with wit, warmth and wisdom, I can see him performing Clarence Darrow as a lawyer, basically defending and not prosecuting because he always was—and still is—for the underdog in fact and finances.

Aware of his appreciation for the good things and for God, I could see John Francis in the pulpit, too, interspersing his moral philosophies with an occasional funny. After all, facing slim pickings as a kid and unfriendly bullets as a soldier, Jack Buck learned to take life seriously, but not himself.

Never really "on stage" in life or in these pages, Buck had to be persuaded to write an autobiography. It is really the first-person recollections of a third-person guy. If it is an oxymoron, the man is a liberal conservative, meaning one who is proud to have lifted himself and encourages others, yet remains soft and sentimental. He would probably cry at the National Anthem or, as he cracked, when cutting the ribbon at a supermarket opening. I do know that when he softly sings "Danny Boy" and, by the way, so well, everyone else is crying.

Above all with his time, talent and money linked with so many charities, Jack Buck is just about the biggest tipper I ever saw. Not for ostentatious reasons, but because every buck Buck gives is a reminder of how tough it was to get one that matched his surname. He has made many a day or night for a doorman, bellman, waiter, waitress or any other service person he figures underpaid or overlooked.

Like collaborator Rains, I think Jack's greatest gift is to his listeners any time, most especially in baseball, where the daily broadcast means so much to so many, including the elderly, handicapped and those who can't get to the ballpark. They rise and fall with his exhilaration or worry-wart fear of defeat. Many a night like me—and I say for shame on both of us—he finds sleep elusive after the bottom has dropped out for the home team, but he is—as his book demonstrates—a sensitive man.

For Rob Rains' tape, Buck recalled poems he had dashed off on plane trips or in hotel rooms. The one here about "The Last Cowboy"—singer-actor-frustrated sportsman Gene Autry—is excellent. So, too, is the one written in angry remorse from the bottom of a soldier's grave at Normandy, where too many gawking cemetery visitors talk rather than walk. Bitter, wishful, melancholic, dynamite!

Over the years I have been amazed at the sparkling wit of Buck, the best emcee I ever heard. I have learned he has the precious gift defined by dictionary's Mr. Webster as "mnemonics," the art of training or improving the memory. For those of us who think we can *remember* better, none can *retain* in memory better than this party of the first part who lives with third-person modesty.

Partly through mnemonics, Jack Buck is linguistic with little effort because of that ability to retain what he has heard. He not only can speak Spanish well enough to warm the homesick hearts of young tongue-tied Hispanics, but he also can do well enough with German, French and—ah, yes!—English.

With a throat golden until later illness, Buck used grammatical, glowing phraseology with knowledge and reserved detachment until he let it all hang out with, "Go crazy, folks, go crazy!" his tribute to Ozzie Smith's first-ever left-handed home run that won a pivotal game in the 1985 League Championship Series. And, of course, the signature that became the subtitle of this frank self-analysis.

"That's a winner" sums up the man as well as his lingo and the life he has led. In this tell-it-as-it-is tale, you will find nuggets of news, know-how, nostalgia and the plain-vanilla philosophy of John Francis Buck.

The mighty Buck—Jack Buck.

1

Lucky Me

"Good morning, Mr. Buck. It's 7:30 and it's 17 below zero."

Now that's a wake-up call. Those words greeted me on the morning of the 1967 NFL championship game in Green Bay, Wisconsin, between the Packers and the Dallas Cowboys. I was there to televise the game for CBS along with Frank Gifford, Tom Brookshire and Ray Scott.

If I had taken the time that morning to reflect on my life, I know I would have considered myself fortunate. I was already a successful sports announcer working for the St. Louis Cardinals in addition to broadcasting professional football. That day I was about to take part in one of the most historic football games ever played, "The Ice Bowl." Sure, it was early in the morning and yes it was cold, but it's easy to get out of bed when you do the sort of work I was doing.

As a dirty-necked kid growing up in Holyoke, Massachusetts, and later in Cleveland, Ohio, I dreamed of what I wanted to do with my life—become a sports announcer. By the 1960s, those dreams had come true, and even better times were ahead.

With the help of a lot of people and good timing, my career would blossom over the next three decades. On that frigid morning in Green Bay, I had no idea that I would become a member of the broadcasters' wing of the Baseball Hall of Fame, or receive the Pete Rozelle Award from the Pro Football Hall of Fame.

I was yet to tell people to "Go crazy, folks" after Ozzie Smith hit a game-winning home run for the Cardinals in the 1985 play-offs against the Los Angeles Dodgers. I hadn't yet screamed, "I don't believe what I just saw!" after a hobbled Kirk Gibson came off the Dodgers' bench in the 1988 World Series and hit a game-winning home run against Oakland.

I didn't know that later in my career I would turn down an offer to become the first play-by-play announcer on the Monday night football telecasts, or turn down an offer to move out of the broadcast booth and become the general manager of the Cardinals.

I did know a lot of things, however, that morning as I had breakfast with Willie Davis of the Packers.

I knew I had gone further in my career than one of my professors at Ohio State had expected. After my first play-by-play broadcast, a basketball game between Ohio State and DePaul in 1949, he advised me "to find something else to do for a living."

I knew was lucky I wasn't killed in World War II.

Lucky? I had become an announcer for the St. Louis Cardinals and worked for Anheuser-Busch, CBS TV, and KMOX Radio, the best radio station in the country. I had a loving family, healthy children and a work ethic that I was proud of.

During an airplane trip in 1976, I reflected on all the good things that had happened in my life. I jotted down these words:

I don't know exactly what it is
  It's almost always been that way
No matter where I am, or who is there
  I know exactly what to say
But there are times I draw a blank
  and take on a certain air
Disinterested, or ill-equipped, I find I just don't care.

When I feel good, elevated, just right
  and those around me don't
I should adjust, be as they are
  I try to, I'd like to, but I won't
After all my years I've concluded
  that those about me could be included
know my thoughts, my mood, my feelings
  but to let them in would just be stealing.
So until there's nothing there
I'll exist with a particular air
  It could have helped or hurt if they had known
But they, like I, are on their own.

In the end, we're all compelled to deal with our own destiny. It was true on that morning in Green Bay, and it's as true now as I sit in my living room in St. Louis.

Whether we're happy or sad, whether we have too much or too little, we each have to live our own life. Some never get to climb the mountain. Others soar to the top. Everyone is on their own.

If a person is healthy, he or she can select his or her own direction. One can be a success or end up in the penitentiary; be lazy or energized; educated or not. In this nation of ours, you can do whatever you wish. Everyone is on their own.

I've always felt that I could take care of myself. I believe we're put on this earth to work, to help others and to find time for enjoyment. This I have also done. I've tried to teach my children what I believe. I think my kids have learned from the example I've set, and I am proud of all eight of them.

My first wife, Alyce and I had six children—Beverly, Jack Jr., Christine, Bonnie, Betsy and Danny. After Alyce and I divorced, I married Carole and we had two kids, Joe and Julie.

Beverly is my oldest daughter. A teacher at Harris-Stowe College, she is married with two boys. Her husband, Mike Brennan, is a teacher at Chaminade High School and a counselor at St. Joseph's High.

Jack Jr. sells home mortgages. He has five kids; four girls and a boy, Jack Buck III. Christine now does part-time work on KPLR-TV, and is married with two sons. Her husband, David Mason, is an architect. Bonnie is the only one of the eight kids living out of town. She's news director at WMAQ Radio in Chicago and has a daughter, Rita.

Betsy is married to Joe Bueckman, the son of one of my best friends, the late Bo Bueckman. Joe runs a Ford dealership, and they have one child, Sara.

Dan is an engineer and has his own home inspection business. He has no children. Julie works at Y-98-FM. She's on the air and also does personal appearances for the station. She was married to Jeff Brooks, an attorney, in December, 1996.

Joe Buck has become well-known for his work on KMOX, with the Cardinals and the Fox network. He and his wife, Ann, have a daughter, Natalie.

My father, who died at 49, would never believe the things that have happened in my lifetime. Sometimes I don't believe it either. Michael Burke, a former executive with the Yankees and CBS, wrote a book a few years ago called *Outrageous Good Fortune*. I wish I could have used that title for this book.

I wouldn't change a thing about my life. My childhood dreams came true.

2

Growing Up

When I was a 10-year-old kid in Holyoke, Massachusetts, I lived across the street from a drugstore. It was a special place to me, because that's where I went to talk and learn about baseball. The country was still in the throes of the Depression. Fenway Park and Boston were 90 miles away. For me, they might as well have been on the moon. In 1934, 90 miles was a very long way away.

I followed the Red Sox and my idol Jimmy Foxx. I listened to Fred Hoey broadcast the games on the radio, imagining what the Green Monster looked like, painting a picture in my head of the green grass and the players whose names I can still recite to this day.

Never in my wildest dreams did I think I would get to see a game there in person, but it happened. Three guys I knew from the drugstore knew that I was a baseball fanatic, and they took me to Boston for a doubleheader between the Red Sox and Cleveland Indians one day in 1934. I still remember the pitchers that exciting day—Lefty Grove and Fritz Ostermueller for Boston; Mel Harder and Willis Hudlin for Cleveland.

My father, Earle, was an accountant with the Erie Railroad. The railroad was based in Hoboken, NJ. He commuted on weekends between New Jersey and our home in Holyoke. When the railroad headquarters moved to Cleveland, Ohio, my father went with them. After he moved to Cleveland, I wrote him and told him I was going to Fenway Park in Boston. He sent me five dollars. My mother went berserk that he had five dollars to send me during those Depression days. She took three of it; so I went to Boston on that summer Sunday afternoon with two dollars.

I insisted on buying my own ticket because my father had sent me the money and because it was my first big league game. The ticket cost $1.25, which left me with 75 cents. I remember Boston won both games, and I also remember going to an elegant restaurant when the twinbill was over.

One of the main reasons my friends had gone to Boston in the first place was to have dinner after the game. They told me to order steak or lobster or whatever I wanted, but I only had 75 cents in my pocket, so I ordered a cheese sandwich. I told them I didn't want to eat because I was upset because Cleveland had lost both games. I had switched my allegiance to Cleveland because my father had moved there and some day the rest of the family would be moving there also. When one of the men picked up the check and paid for it all, I could have died. Man, was I hungry! As we drove those 90 miles back to Holyoke I relived my first big league day— a cheese sandwich and a doubleheader, the awesome ballpark with the high leftfield wall known as the Green Monster, sitting behind the first base dugout, a close-up look at big-league ballplayers, including my idol, Jimmy Foxx. When I got home, my mother relieved me of the 75 cents I had left.

It always meant a lot to me that I bought my own ticket, and the memory of that day remains one of the highlights of my childhood; even though I often kicked myself afterward—a cheese sandwich—I could have ordered my first steak.

Those men at the drug store helped me write a letter to Joe Cronin, the manager of the Red Sox, suggesting a particular lineup. One day when I arrived at the store, the pharmacist had a surprise for me—Cronin had answered my letter! About three days later, I was listening to the broadcast and the Red Sox used the lineup I had suggested, and won the game! That thrilled me, but I was even more impressed that he took the time to answer my letter. Later, when he was president of the American League, I met him and told him the story; he got a kick out of it. Cronin was a wonderful man who got along well with everyone, with no phoniness about him.

When I wasn't listening to the Red Sox games or talking about baseball, I was playing it. When my friends and I started each day, if there were two of us we played catch; if we had three, we played Indian ball. When eight guys showed up, we chose up sides and started a game. It didn't take long before we had 30; 15 on a side. Man, it's tough to get a hit with 15 guys playing defense.

We all played baseball every spring and summer day. I bet I've played more baseball than half the people I'm watching now in the major leagues. We measured ourselves by the game. You played and found out how good you were and where you belonged, whether you were going to be an athlete or not, whether you could fight or not. Could you run as fast as the next guy? Could you catch the ball or hit it? We settled everything among ourselves, and we did it through sports. That's the essence of sports. You learn who you are, what you can do and where you belong.

When your team puts you in right field batting 12th, you knew you weren't very good. If you played first base and hit fourth, you'd say to yourself, "I'm better than the others." That's what life is—a series of competitions. You stay in the middle, fall back, or rise to the challenges. I've always joked that when my father first saw me play baseball, he traded me for a son to be born later.

There were always empty fields to play in, and that's one of the big differences between my generation and today's kids. There aren't many empty lots anymore. That's why mom has to drive them to the park and they only play two days a week. They only play in games and never practice or play on their own. I've flown across this country hundreds of times, seen thousands of baseball fields, seldom with anyone playing on them. What we would have given as kids to have fields like that available to us!

My father used to commute from New Jersey on the New York-New Haven and Hartford Railroad. He also was the manager of the Erie baseball team, and when he came home, he always had a ball or a bat with him. My brothers, Frank and Earle, and I were always anxious to see him after the long week of being away.

My dad was a great baseball player. He pitched and played first base, and hurled a perfect game for Holyoke High School. Later he had a tryout with the New York Giants. He never told us exactly what happened, but he and manager John McGraw had some sort of disagreement and that was the end of his professional dream.

We were always scratching for equipment, and it boggles my mind now when I watch home runs fly into the bleachers and people throw the balls back onto the field, I can't get over it. We'd have done anything for a new baseball. We played with a nickel rocket wrapped with friction tape. The ball cost a nickel and exploded the first time you hit it. The longer we played, the more tape we used, and the ball became heavier and heavier. We had two gloves in the neighborhood—one for the catcher and one for the first baseman.That's all. The bats were cracked and nailed and taped up. When you hit that taped-up baseball, your hands hurt so much your feet couldn't move. That was all we had, and we made the best of it.

I was the third oldest of seven kids. My mother's name was Kathleen. Her sisters were Bridget, Josephine, Eileen, Mame, and Lillian, and her only brother was John Francis Fox. I was named after my Uncle John. My mother's parents had emigrated from Dingle in County Kerry, Ireland. My mother and her siblings all ended up in an orphanage when their parents died at an early age. My mother was the youngest and answered to the name of "Tot." She was a beautiful woman with a lot of wonderful attributes; tough, smart and loving with the usual Irish temper.

My brother Frank was the oldest child in my family, and also the wildest. One time he was summoned to the principal's office to be punished, and when the principal hit him with a ruler, Frank popped him. He was out of school for about a month.

Along came Earle Jr., and he was the opposite—a great student who never caused any problems. When I came along next, they kept a wary eye on me, especially the teachers. I guess I turned out to be somewhere in the middle. Then there were three girls, Kathleen, Mary and Barbara, and last was the baby of the family, my brother Bob.

We lived in a house on Longwood Avenue in Holyoke, owned by my uncle, Dan Hickey, and his wife, Josie. Our family with those seven kids lived downstairs, and my aunt and uncle had five kids living upstairs. It was a busy house.

Holyoke was a great town. Located at the foot of the Berkshire Mountains on the Connecticut River, it was really a pretty place. I loved the white birch trees and hiking in the mountains. The birch is still my favorite tree.

At one time, Holyoke was the largest paper manufacturing city in the world. It was an ethnic town, with Polish, French and Irish people. The Polish people lived on the river in the flats and were flooded out of their homes by the river every spring. They would move right back in when the water receded. It's like some people now in some of the suburbs of St. Louis. People get drowned out almost every year and keep going back. Why?

As I said, I grew up during the Depression, and it seems most of the stories and incidents I remember as a child were connected with the fact our family didn't have much money, even though my dad and mother were always working. We always were trying to squeeze out an extra nickel or dime anywhere we could.

That was the reason my brother Earle and I started singing in the choir at Holy Cross Church. They had a drawing for a nickel after practice each week. When the choirmaster's nephew won the nickel two weeks in a row, we thought we were getting ripped off and quit warbling.

In our basement, we had a gas meter that operated only when you put a quarter in the box. When the gas ran out, you couldn't get more until you inserted another quarter in the meter. When we didn't have money to put in the meter, we would put a slug in there, and it worked. When the meter man came to collect the money from the meter, we all managed to be out and about.

During the summer, my brother Earle and I used to gather newspapers, soak them with water, roll them into balls and let them dry in the coal bin, so when the weather would start to turn in the fall, we could build a fire in the furnace with the paper and warm the house without burning any coal. My mother used to play penny ante poker, and Earle and I used to tend that fire when my mother and her cronies were playing. They would start getting chilly, and would pull on their sweaters or coats. My mother would yell "Jackie, Earle—get that fire going!"

We'd throw some of the papers in the furnace and soon those gals would be sweating and doing a striptease as the flames shot out of the chimney. Then they'd cool off and have to put their clothes back on. This went on all night.

Once they were playing cards and I tried to get Mom's attention. "Shut up Jackie," she said. "But Mom," I tried again. "Shut up," she said once more.

Soon my mom and her poker buddies gave me their full attention. They could smell the smoke. We had a closet where Mom kept reeds for caning chairs, and somehow I had taken a match to the reeds and started a fire.

The fire brigade went to work with pots, pans and cups of water. The ladies squelched the fire as the pennies lay on the dining room table. The next fire erupted on my rear end, started by a leather belt. I learned my lesson; I haven't started another fire since. I still say, though, they shouldn't have been gambling anyway.

❧

Our diet was simple; cereal for breakfast, soup for lunch, and bakery leftovers for dinner. My brother Frank liked Cream of Wheat, so that's what we had to eat. He was the oldest so he got his choice. I *hated* that stuff. Why couldn't he like oatmeal like everybody else? For lunch we'd come home from school and have canned soup.

Then at dinner time, either Earle or I had to go and wait for the bakery truck to come back to the bakery. Sometimes it came back empty; that meant we didn't have dinner. Then we'd have a slice of bread with some mustard or maybe sugar sprinkled with water on it. That was dinner.

If the bakery truck came back with leftovers, our dinner would be whatever hadn't been sold, donuts or rolls or Danish. Once in the dead of winter with snow on the ground I waited in bitter cold for the truck and I got a dime's worth of baked goods in a paper bag. It was still snowing, and the bag kept getting wetter as I walked home, and soon the bag broke. I went home crying. I had lost the baked goods. Minutes later, my mother sent me back to pick them up out of the snow with a fresh paper bag. That was our evening meal.

Every Saturday night we had wieners and beans and baking powder biscuits. That was a feast. Sunday night it was leg of lamb because that was the cheapest meat you could buy. You couldn't sell me a leg of lamb today on a bet. Many people don't know what it was like in those days. Believe it or not, sometimes we didn't have toothpaste and brushed our teeth with table salt. The first time I went to the dentist, at age 15, I had five teeth pulled.

An incident years later reminded me of those good old days. The Cardinals were flying from Los Angeles to San Francisco, which is just an hour and a half flight. Leo Ward, the traveling secretary, asked me what we should have to eat on the trip

I said, "How about wieners and beans and hot biscuits?" He said that was a terrific idea. Do you know what happened? The players boycotted the meal. They let the stewardesses serve the meal, then none of the players touched it. I thought, "What a spoiled bunch this is." Most of them didn't come from affluent families. Bob Gibson was on that plane, and he titled his own book *From Ghetto to Glory.* They wouldn't eat the wieners and beans. How do you figure that?

They should have been with us in the Depression, or later in the Army. In the Army we went a couple of days without anything to eat, including rations. The ballplayers' behavior shocked me. The stewardesses cried as they picked up the trays. I wouldn't do that to anybody. Leo Ward and I enjoyed the meal.

Our relatives who lived upstairs, the Hickeys, had a restaurant, a small grill, in downtown Holyoke. We went to the movies at the Globe Theater for a dime—to see "Rin Tin Tin" and all the cowboy movies. You could get in for a nickel if you brought a crate to sit on. Then they'd put you right down in front of the first row. Sitting there looking up at the screen, Rin Tin Tin looked like an elephant to me. The movie always ended with the dog leaping at some bad guy. I would sit there and feel like this huge animal was going to land right in my lap.

On our way back home from the movie, we'd walk through the alley and try to get into my uncle's restaurant to get something to eat. I say try, because if he saw us coming, he would close the restaurant. He'd lock the door, pull the shades—"look out, here come the Buck kids."

My best memory of my Uncle Dan was when there would be a heavyweight championship fight. We didn't have a radio. Dan had a crystal set, with one pair of earphones. Whenever there was a big event, like a title fight involving Jack Sharkey or Jimmy Braddock, all the kids would gather round. Uncle Dan would listen on the headphones, then relay the information to the 12 kids. I tell people now he was the first play-by-play man I ever knew.

Uncle Dan smoked—Marvels—and he coughed a lot. Boy, did he cough. And he cried when he coughed. He coughed so much he could hardly light the next Marvel; the match shook. The problem was whenever there was a knockdown or a knockout, that's when he coughed. It was really irritating. But what could we do? He had the only radio and he smoked.

After the fights, I would take off for the newspaper building, the *Holyoke Transcript*, to pick up the extra editions. Extras were a big deal in those days because there weren't many radios and no TV. I would pick up the papers for two cents apiece and sell them for a nickel. If I was the first kid to get back to the neighborhood to sell the papers, I could turn a dime into a quarter, which I gave to my mother.

Selling those extras helped develop my voice. "Extra, extra read all about it! The mayor re-elected," or I would shout out the results of the big fight. I was blessed with a particular kind of voice, but I think selling newspapers then and later, plus the time I spent as a drill instructor in the Army, did a great deal to make my voice sound the way it did when I became a broadcaster. Smoking Camels for 40 years also affected my voice.

I would do anything for money when I was young. I used to make a quarter a week for walking a kid to school. He was a skinny little guy who used to get picked on all the time and beat up. His parents gave me a nickel a day to walk him to school so nobody would pick on him. I wasn't double-tough, but I didn't mind fighting and I could take care of myself.

Jackie Moffett was a kid who lived across the street, and one day we had a fight. I don't remember what started it, but it was a good one. The older kids in the neighborhood broke it up, then charged everybody a penny to watch and had us fight again. I was a professional fighter at age nine, except I didn't get any of the money.

The only time I ever went to a camp as a kid was one summer when some neighbors sent me to Holy Cross Camp in the Berkshires, just outside of Holyoke. They had boxing there, and I remember one fight where I really whipped a kid. I knew at that moment, however, that I didn't have the killer instinct. I went back to the barracks after the fight crying. I told everybody I hurt my thumb and that's why I was crying. I really felt bad that I hurt him.

I was banged up a lot when I was a kid, including one time when the lady next door said she would pay me a nickel to go to the store and pick up some milk. That seemed like easy money to me, but it started raining as I was walking home. I was standing on the curb barefoot, balancing myself, and I fell — I must have been a graceful kid. The bottle, with that thick glass, shattered and I had deep cuts in my wrist. It was bleeding like hell. The lady's husband was a fireman, and he dressed the wound. He did a heck of a job, leaving only one scar, an inch and a half long. The lady gave me the nickel anyhow.

One other time my mother was visiting my father in New Jersey and I was visiting a friend who had a swing in the backyard. He was sitting down and I was standing on the same swing and we were pumping. We were really flying. I said, "That's enough. I'm getting tired and I can't hang on any longer." He said, "We're not stopping."

He snapped the swing, and I flew off like a bird, hitting my head on the brick corner of the house. I had a brain concussion and a big hole in my head. When I got to the hospital a doctor dumped alcohol directly on the wound. That hurt worse than the injury. I had a bandage on my head like a turban. I'll never forget the look on my mother's face when I was waiting for her as she got off the streetcar.

Once as a kid I was hit in the head with a baseball bat. I was ragging a player and he said if I said another word he was going to throw the bat at me. He wasn't kidding. I said something and he let it loose. I couldn't get out of the way of the bat, it was whirling so much. They carried me home, and my mother sent my brother Earle back to get even. He beat Earle up. Then she sent Frank after him, and he beat Frank up. The only way he would have lost was if my mother went after him. She almost did.

※

The boys in our family used to get three pairs of shoes a year. We'd get a pair of dress shoes at Easter, a pair of tennis shoes in the summer and a pair of high top boots for the winter. It was tough to make a pair of tennis shoes last for the entire summer. Soon the soles came loose and started flapping. You had to walk like a drum major to keep the flapping sole under your foot. We really needed the boots too, because the winters in Holyoke were long and cold with a lot of snow. We shoveled sidewalks for a dime; a quarter to shovel the driveway.

I never heard of this anywhere else, but the way the city let everybody know if school was called off because of the snow was by blinking the streetlights. They did it at 7:30 a.m. At that time there were no kids on the street, but once they blinked those streetlights, if you walked out the front door you were sure to get nailed by a snowball. We had some great snowball fights. Sometimes if we didn't like a kid, we'd put a rock in the middle of the snowball.

When we went ice skating, it cost a nickel to check your shoes. Not many had a nickel, so we used to skate with our shoes tied around our neck. You could check your shoes for free, but then everybody had access to them. Times were hard; people would take a better pair of shoes than they had checked, or take a pair when they hadn't checked any. Sometimes you went skating with a pair of shoes size nine and you left with a pair size seven. It was better to keep them with you.

The Shriners used to hold conventions frequently in Holyoke, and they would throw nickels and dimes out of the hotel windows and watch us go scrambling for them. Then they'd throw buckets of water on us. They thought it was funny. Other times they would heat the pennies and throw them down, and watch and laugh as we'd burn our fingers picking up the red-hot pennies.

Every year after Christmas, we collected thousands of discarded trees. The big guys would haul them to the empty cemetery lot and the little guys would pull them up to the top of the pile. Then we'd get a permit from the fire department, and crank case oil from the gas stations around town.

On New Year's Eve, we lit the trees and had a bonfire the likes of which you've never seen. The flames reached the sky. A big crowd always came out to watch, and that's when we took up a collection. We called ourselves the Riff-Raff, and we used the money we collected to buy kelly green and black jackets. I'd put on that green jacket with the black trim and the Double R's and thought I was king.

In the summer, I would walk or hitchhike the eight miles to the Mount Tom Golf Course, where I was a B caddie. A caddies made 65 cents for a round, B's got 55 cents with no tipping. We're talking about a real ugly economy now, aren't we?

My mother would make me an egg salad sandwich to have for lunch. Some days I'd sit there all day and never get to caddie. I'd go home and tell her I didn't get out all day, so I didn't bring home any money. Sometimes she didn't believe me. "BS, let me have the money," she'd say. "Mom, I didn't get out," and she'd give me a hug. She was a good hugger.

One time the caddies went on strike. The caddie master was a little Scotsman and he chewed us out. Then he turned and looked at me and said, "And you! You little bastard! You're the leader of the B's. And you'll pay for this." I didn't know what the hell he was talking about, I wasn't the leader of anything. It made me feel good, though. I'd finally been recognized for something. He was wrong, but I'd been recognized.

¿a

The greatest scourge of my generation was polio. We used to go to the swimming pool, and they had a guard inspect everyone. You had to take a shower, then they made certain you were clean enough to get into the pool. I used to get sent back two or three times to clean my feet. You wouldn't believe how dirty I used to get. I had the dirtiest neck any child ever had. Polio was transmitted through the swimming pools. One day you would be a normal healthy youngster, and the next day find yourself in an iron lung. Dr. Jonas Salk, who discovered the vaccine to prevent polio, is one of my lifetime heroes.

In the fall we'd hike up to Amherst to watch college football games, but in the summer we'd go eight miles the other direction, down the railroad tracks to Springfield, where the Washington Senators had their Triple A farm team. We usually sneaked into the park, but once in a while we'd buy a ticket. I used to go early to watch them hit fly balls to the outfielders with a fungo. It was like looking at a Picasso. The rhythm, beauty and the power of the game intrigued me. It still does.

We were still living in Holyoke in 1938 when a hurricane hit the Northeast. They blinked the streetlights that day to signal no school. Holyoke got the edge of the storm, but that was bad enough. Of course we didn't stay inside, but stood in the empty lot of the cemetery and watched trees get uprooted and coffins thrown all over the place. What stands out to me to this day is that the furthest thing from our minds was to loot those caskets. Today, I'm afraid it would be the first thing people might do. Morals have changed considerably in this country.

୬

The hardest part of my childhood was that my father was away from our family so much. When we all moved to Cleveland in 1939, we were excited that we were going to be a family again.

My oldest brother, Frank, graduated from high school in 1937 and went to work for the railroad with my father. Earle and I were in high school and our family bought the first home we ever owned. Things looked great, but my father had high blood pressure and his eyesight was failing. I read him the sports news out of the *Cleveland Plain Dealer* every day. Just when we thought everything was going to fall back into place for the family, my dad went into the hospital.

I remember the phone call in the middle of the morning informing us he had died. His high blood pressure caused uremic poisoning, which they couldn't treat then as they do now. He was only 49 years old. He was buried back in Massachusetts next to his sister Lola. I was 15.

I was at the funeral parlor, and the first two men who walked through the door to pay their respects were black men who worked in the office with my dad. That told me something, that he was a kind man and nice to those with whom he worked. The two men were very complimentary about him, and that has always stayed with me as a reminder about the way I should try to live my own life.

My father's death meant the family was hurting for money again, so we all pitched in and did what we could. My mother got a job in a sewing machine factory. It's a wonder with all the things that happened to her—seven kids, World War II, and working—that she lived as long as she did. She died of a heart attack when she was 66. There's such a bond between mothers and children; losing a mother is usually the hardest thing in life. My mother was a happy person with a hearty laugh, who loved to sing and tell jokes. She taught all the good things like honesty, respect and how to listen to your conscience.

ک

As a teenager, I enjoyed working and I still do. I like to be busy, and I like to pack everything I can into the day. Three days a week, in the mornings before school, I delivered the *Shopping News*, running up to the door and hanging the paper with a rubber band on the doorknob.

After school I worked at the Franklin Ice Cream Shop jerking sodas, then went down to the basement and packed ice cream orders. By that time the afternoon newspaper was out, and I delivered the *Cleveland News* door-to-door. Then, I sold the *Cleveland Press* on the corner of Detroit and Warren Road in Lakewood on the west side of Cleveland. I used to hop on the streetcar, sell the papers and hop out the back door. "Get your final *Press*, stocks and sports." Man, could I yell. I was a fixture at that intersection. My evening job was at a drive-in restaurant, Jack Kraw's, in Rocky River, a suburb of Cleveland. I'd get home at midnight during the week and 2 or 3 o'clock in the morning on weekends.

I did a variety of jobs at the drive-in; one night I did the dishes, the next night I worked the grill, and another night I'd take care of the soft drinks. I also worked the dining room and ran the curb. They used to let us do everything except touch the cash register. They were smart.

One night I was on curb duty. That's where I made the most tips. A fellow pulled up wearing a tuxedo and ordered a cup of coffee on his way to a dance.

There are two kinds of trays at a drive-in, one that can be hooked inside the car window or outside, depending on the weather. In this case, it was an outside tray, where the window has to be all the way down to hook it on. As I put down the tray, the customer raised the window and the hot coffee spilled all over his tuxedo. Today he probably would have sued me and the restaurant.

It was his fault, but he was ticked. He got out of his car and started to chase me, and we ran clear across the Hilliard Bridge, a very long way. He chased me about half a mile before he stopped and waved me back. He went back to the drive-in and ordered a hamburger, then went home. He said he didn't want to go to the dance anyway. He even gave me a big tip.

We had about 20 guys working at the drive-in who each kicked in 50 cents a week, for a total of $10, and we bought a Model T Ford. We had about five of them, two or three of which would be in working order at any one time. After work on Saturday nights, we went down in the valley in Rocky River and played tag with the Model T's. We'd run into each other, trying to get away through the trees and down the riverbed. It was harmless fun really, except for one night.

I was wearing moccasins, white slacks and a T-shirt. As we got into the car I said, "Let me sit in front so in case we get hit, I won't get hurt." On the way to the valley, we stopped at a traffic light. I looked in the mirror and saw a speeding car. I knew we were going to get hit. I put my hands on my head, and he hit us and knocked us 55 feet through the intersection. The impact blew the rear window out of our Model T, and a lot of glass flew into the back of my head. I was the only one who got hurt, and I had picked the front seat.

The driver of the other car backed up and was trying to drive away, but his steering column was broken. He drove around in a circle and ran into a steel telegraph pole. He got out of the car, wandered into a field, collapsed and died, because nobody knew where he had gone.

The accident occurred about five miles away from my home in Lakewood, but the ambulance they called had to take me a half hour away to a Cleveland hospital. I was lying on a table and the doctors were picking glass out of my head, pitching it into an enamel pan. I heard one of the doctors say, "I don't think he's going to make it. He's lost too much blood." Somehow they got the bleeding stopped, patched me up and told me I could go home. They had no rooms at the hospital.

I had to go home by cab. I had lost my T-shirt, my slacks were covered with blood, and I'd lost one moccasin and I had a huge bandage around my head. I arrived home about 8 o'clock in the morning and saw my mother sitting in the window smoking a cigarette, still waiting. Can you imagine the sight of me getting out of that taxi cab? That was my first brush with going to Heaven early. There would be others.

を

One of the people who frequented our drive-in was Oscar Grimes, a reserve infielder with the Cleveland Indians and he was the first major-league player I ever met.

Baseball was my great love, and I listened to as many games and announcers as I could. Jack Graney did the Indians games, and I remember the way he re-created the game on opening day in 1941 when Bob Feller threw a no-hitter in Chicago. Ironically, years later, after Graney retired he moved to Bowling Green, Missouri, and I used to get notes from one of his daughters telling me that he was living in a nursing home and enjoyed listening to me on the Cardinals' broadcasts. How ironic—I grew up listening to him while dreaming of big-league baseball. I relied on him to be my eyes and ears at the ballpark. Later he relied on me—that's the beauty of what I do.

There were other announcers I tuned in, like Bob Elson in Chicago, Harry Heilman and Ty Tyson in Detroit, Mel Allen and Red Barber on the Yankees and Dodgers. I even listened to games broadcast in Spanish from Cuba late at night. I had the names and information about the teams from *The Sporting News*, and I knew enough about the game that I could follow the rhythm of the broadcast and make out what was happening. Frequently my mother would come downstairs in the morning and find me asleep on the floor, static on the radio. I always loved the game.

Early on I was practicing to be a broadcaster and didn't really know it. Back in Holyoke, we'd be playing baseball and I would say things such as, "There's a fly ball to Buck. He drops it. Two runs score."

Later, after moving to Cleveland, my brother Earle and I would take the streetcar to the Indians games as often as we could and sit in the bleachers, either at League Park or at giant Municipal Stadium. As we sat there, I would be talking, either practicing announcing or just talking about the game. Earle would yell at me, "Shut up!" or he would move to another section of the bleachers.

I think radio and television have made a big difference in the way kids view players today. Youngsters today see a player like Ozzie Smith walk out of the clubhouse, and they feel like they know him personally, and they shout, "Hi Ozzie, Hi Ozzie!" When I was a kid, was I going to say "Hi Joe" to Joe DiMaggio? First of all, you couldn't get to him; secondly, I wouldn't call him Joe, and thirdly, I'd probably be too excited to even talk. We were just much more in awe of our heroes then, and not to mention more respectful.

Earle and I were in the bleachers for the 1935 All-Star game in Cleveland. We were still living in Holyoke, but my dad got tickets and we came out by train. My hero, Jimmy Foxx, hit a home run that landed a few seats away from us.

Many years later I met Foxx, when he came to St. Louis to celebrate Stan Musial's retirement. He was drunk at the dinner, and it tore my heart out. It proves you never really know the people you admire from afar. What a let down, what a lesson. It reinforced my philosophy that you have to be your own hero; you can't count on anybody else to be your guiding star. You've got to do it yourself. Everyone is on his own.

Earle and I were also in the bleachers the night the Indians stopped Joe DiMaggio's record 56-game hitting streak in 1941. Pitchers Al Smith and Jim Bagby got the credit, but it was really two great plays by Ken Keltner at third and one by Lou Boudreau at shortstop that ended the streak. DiMaggio has always treated me very kindly.

1941 was the year I thought I should quit high school and get a full-time job, so I could help support the family. I would have quit except for a teacher, Edna Kleinschmidt. She went crazy when I told her I was leaving school. She even went to my house to talk to my mother. She stomped her foot, and nobody stomped their foot at my mother. My teacher said, "He is not quitting school," and I didn't. I never had much time for homework and I wasn't much more than a C student, but if I hadn't finished high school, my whole life would have been different.

A few years ago I went back to be inducted into the Lakewood High School Hall of Fame, and I told this story to my wife. Carole said, "Why don't you call her?" and I did. She didn't remember me, but I told her who I was and what I did, that I had been broadcasting for the Cardinals, and that she had kept me from quitting high school. I said, "You've made my day by being able to talk to you." She said, "You've made my year."

之

The father of my friend, Howie Nunn, was an undertaker, and I used to hang around his house after school when I wasn't working, which wasn't often. We used to go down and watch people being embalmed—what an education that was. Howie had a St. Bernard, and there was a dog in the neighborhood that used to come into his yard and bother his dog. One day I was there and the other dog came into the yard. I'll be darned if Howie didn't reach into the closet, pull out a bow and arrow, fire one shot and kill the intruder. He brought it into the funeral parlor and cremated it. Only the two of us ever knew what happened to the dog.

When I wasn't hanging around there, I was at the home of another buddy, George Reed. After high school, he got a job working on an ore boat for the Cleveland Cliffs Iron Co. That seemed exciting, and soon I was to do the same.

While still at the drive-in, I was working one Sunday morning in December 1941, a month before my high school graduation. The radio was on but nobody paid much attention until the announcer broke in with those stunning words: "We interrupt this broadcast for a special news bulletin."

The bulletin on that morning, of course, was that the Japanese had bombed Pearl Harbor. Nobody knew where Pearl Harbor was in 1941. All of us working at the drive-in that morning knew that our lives had changed. The older ones would be in the military in a flash. Until the war, the world was made up of tiny cocoons of people who had their own environs and stayed there. You didn't get into your car and drive to California, didn't fly to Florida for the weekend, didn't get on the train and go to Texas. People were not mobile.

I'm still surprised when I go to the airport now and see people traveling with all their kids. It's a way of life I never knew when I was young. World War II changed everything in this country.

Pearl Harbor Day also changed my life. After graduation in the winter of 1942, I followed my buddy George Reed and landed a job on one of the ore boats on the Great Lakes. I was 17 years old, stepping out on my own.

3

Life on the Lakes

There are moments in everyone's life when emotions really run high. Take a bit of excitement, add a touch of fear, combine it with a little sadness and a whole lot of uncertainty, and you end up more than a little confused and anxious.

I was filled with all of these emotions in March, 1942. Wearing an overcoat two sizes too big and carrying a Gladstone bag borrowed from my neighbor, I got off the train in Chicago from Cleveland, ready to start my new life on the Great Lakes.

I had never been on the water before and had no idea what I was getting into. Climbing the 60-foot ladder to the deck of the J.H. Sheadle, docked on the Calumet River, it was impossible to imagine what would happen in the next two years and how my life would be changed again.

People in this country have no idea how important the Great Lakes are to their daily lives and the activity that takes place on the Lakes. Most probably can't name the lakes. Huron, Ontario, Michigan, Erie and Superior. An easy way to memorize them is that the first letter of each spells the word h-o-m-e-s. They constitute the largest body of fresh water in the world, and are the main thoroughfare by which products are brought from west to east. Traveling in the other direction, east to west, ships and boats transport coal and manufactured products.

Freighters built to accommodate the iron ore trade, coal and grain represent the greatest development in cargo handling this country has ever seen. The total freight tonnage passing through the lake port of Duluth on Lake Superior in 1941 was more than 67 million tons.

The activity on the Lakes at that time was more important than ever, because the war effort was gearing up. Japan or Germany could have crippled the United States if they had been able to bomb the locks at Sault Ste. Marie.

The Sheadle was a 700-foot steamer, one of several boats operated by the Cleveland Cliffs Iron Co. Ore boats spent about nine months out of the year on the Lakes carrying iron ore, coal, or wheat. Some of the ports I visited included Superior, Wisconsin; Duluth, Minnesota; Escanaba and Marquette, Michigan; Port Arthur, Ontario; Buffalo, New York; and in Ohio, Conneaut, Ashtabula, Cleveland, Lorian, and Toledo.

My job as a porter was to keep the galley clean, do the dishes, peel potatoes, help the cook, serve the meals—pretty much anything and everything I was asked to do. It was also my job to help load the supplies, which we always took on in Buffalo.

One day after leaving Buffalo, traveling past Detroit, we were on Lake Huron, and I had been below taking a nap in my bunk. I decided to go up to get a glass of milk. We had loaded 50 gallons of milk, in 10-gallon cans, all tied down with a heaving line in the walk-in refrigerator along with gallons of mustard, ketchup and pickles. I untied the line and thought to myself, "Why is this all tied down?" I left it untied, got my glass of milk and left.

Then came the first storm I encountered on the Lakes. We were tossing and bouncing and rolling all over the place, and I quickly learned why those milk cans had been tied down. Forty gallons of milk spilled in that refrigerator, splashing around so badly that milk was dripping down into the spotless engine room. Everything on the boat was spotless, and the engineer came up to the galley looking for the cook with murder in his eyes.

They opened the refrigerator, and there were 40 gallons of spilled milk with pickles floating across the floor, and mustard everywhere. There was only one 10-gallon can of milk that hadn't spilled. It looked like a Salvador Dali painting.

Guess who had to clean up the mess by himself?

Shortly after that, another storm caused me to be seasick for the first time. The fact that I was frying pork chops didn't help. I asked the cook to take over but he said I was doing just fine with frequent trips to the railing.

I was promoted to night cook and baker when it turned out the guy who had the job was gay and was put off the boat in Detroit. I was responsible for feeding the crew of 30 all night and baking either pies or cakes every day. The food was terrific–all the crew members got as much as they wanted to eat. I once fried 24 eggs for one of the engineers. He started with four, and the cook called him a pig. Then he ordered four more and kept going. I kept frying them, the cook kept swearing at him, and he kept eating them.

I made more money as a night cook. My two older brothers, Frank and Earle, were both in the Army, but mom had four more kids at home and her job in the factory didn't pay all the bills, so I mailed my weekly paycheck to her. I didn't need much money because most of my time was spent onboard the boat.

Once I sent cash home instead of sending a check. I mailed it in Detroit, and the letter never made it to Cleveland. To the day she died, my mother never believed that I sent that money. I don't know exactly how much it was, but it was a couple of hundred dollars. That taught me never to send cash through the mail. My mom and I always kidded each other after that. "I sent the money, Mom," I would say. "Baloney!" she would answer.

The boats operated as late into the winter as possible, until it got so cold the Lakes froze over usually in December. We made one last trip to Duluth, loaded the iron ore, and took it to Buffalo. We unloaded 14,000 tons of ore, and the last of it had to be shoveled out by hand. Then we had to clean the holds so they were spotless. Then we picked up a load of coal in Toledo, took it to Milwaukee, and had to clean the boat again. Then we picked up a load of wheat in Port Arthur and brought it back to Buffalo, where they layed the boat up and stored the wheat for the winter.

One of the other boats owned by Cleveland Cliffs was the Cadillac. It tied up for the winter in Cleveland, and I needed a job, so I signed up to paint that boat.

There I was, using a 10-foot pole with a six-inch brush, painting the boat with black lead paint on the shore of Lake Erie in January. What a miserable job! I had paint in my eyes, my ears, my nose, my mouth, everywhere. That job lasted about a month.

Thirty-five years or so later, I went back to Cleveland to broadcast a football game. My wife Carole was with me, and after we got back from dinner we realized she had left her purse in a taxi. The cab company found it, and we went to the office to get it. The office was in an area of town called the flats, along the Cuyahoga

River near the lake front. As we passed by the river, I saw the Cadillac, still painted green and black, the colors of the Cleveland Cliffs line. "I painted that damn thing!" I told Carole. It still looked good, too.

In the winter of 1942, I worked at the National Carbon Co. in Cleveland, and the next spring I went back to work on the Sheadle, this time as a deck hand. We went through the locks in March at Sault Ste. Marie, and when they opened the locks, all of the ice came through with the boat. We deck hands had to walk across the top of the locks, pushing a piece of ice with a grappling hook. It was a struggle to see how far you could push the ice out of the lock—usually a few feet—then you would turn around and the ice would come back in. We worked all night to get the boat through the locks.

Once through, we ran aground in the St. Mary's River because the Coast Guard had put the buoys in the wrong place. We were on a very tight time schedule, because we had to get through the Lakes and to Buffalo as quickly as possible. I was in my bunk when we ran aground and came to a screeching stop. I flew out of my bunk, and luckily was not injured.

We couldn't get off the bottom, and a Coast Guard ship came to assess the situation. I was familiar with the heaving line from my experiences the year before, knowing it was used to tie up the ship when we reached port. When the heaving line was thrown to you, instead of trying to catch it, you let it drape over your arm, then pulled on the line, grabbed the cable, and then attached the cable to a piling or a cleat.

When the Coast Guard cutter pulled alongside our ship, it was my job to catch the heaving line and tie it up. There was a wooden ball on the end of the line, called a monkey. It made it easier to throw the line. I had never seen one before, and nobody warned me about it. The crewman on the cutter was about 10 feet away when he threw me the line. I let it drape over my arm, and that ball hit me right between the eyes. I fell over a hatch, and the line went heading down the deck. The Coast Guard ship was going to run aground, just as we had done. Fortunately, I was able to catch up to that line and tie up the cutter.

We were stuck so badly, though, that the Coast Guard didn't have any luck. They had to bring in an empty boat and unload the ore so we would rise up in the water to float free. Our captain was fined $1,000 for the delay that running aground had caused.

☙

The locks at Sault Ste. Marie were protected by anti-aircraft guns and barrage balloons, so every time we went through the locks it was an interesting experience. One time, I wasn't paying attention to where we were, and I stepped out of the galley and threw a bucket of garbage into the lake. When I looked up, I saw we were entering the locks.

Fear of an enemy attack made everyone who worked on the locks very cautious, and they had seen me toss the bucket of garbage overboard. They thought there might be a bomb in the garbage. Sirens blared, and they stopped our boat. The bomb warning flag went up. People came out on a small boat with grappling hooks, and started going through the garbage to see if there was a bomb. All the other boats were being cleared to go around us, and we were stuck there until they finished the search. I had done it again.

None of us ever had a second thought about tossing garbage overboard. It's astonishing when you look back on how we ignored the ecology. We did what we wanted to do, and we didn't consider the consequences. There was no Environmental Protection Agency, and there were no restrictions about what companies could do to our natural resources. We dumped waste into rivers and lakes because it was the easiest way to get rid of it. Lake Erie was misused so badly, that it is just now starting to come back to normal. We took the largest body of fresh water in the world and darn near ruined the whole thing. In fact, at one time it was proposed to bury spent nuclear rods in the salt mines under Lake Erie. Can you imagine that?

When you pass by Detroit and see the pleasure boats off Belle Isle, it's a beautiful sight. It's a great resort area, and there I was 18 years old, leaning on the railing, looking at the yachts. The war was a long way off for those people. Men were fighting and getting killed, and people there were partying on their yachts just as people were dancing at the Chase Hotel in St. Louis or having fun at the Waldorf in New York. It was the luck of the draw whether you had a rifle in your hand or a cocktail. Everyone was on their own.

A person might be enjoying a boat ride outside Detroit simply because he had a punctured ear drum or flat feet, while another was fighting at Guadalcanal. The irony of that situation never left me. Some were fortunate they didn't have to go into the Army and they got a job in production. Others were married with a bunch of kids and they were able to get a defense job. I thought I was lucky with the job I had, being able to spend my time on the water. There were times when I would lean over that railing and say to myself, looking at those yachts, "Someday I'm going to live that kind of life."

I have a very good life now, but one thing I've never done is buy a boat. I would never really have time to take care of one anyway, but you can always dream. Everywhere I go around the country I see yachts tied up. People use them one day a week, or one day a month. I wonder how many people are actually able to use and enjoy their boats. I'll bet it's a very small number. It's smarter to have a friend who has a boat; let him take care of it.

Occasionally we were able to leave the boat for brief periods of time, including once when we were near the iron ore range. A few of us went to Ely, Minnesota, and we were in a bar when a fight broke out. It looked like a western movie; people were throwing chairs and tables, getting knocked over the banister. I kept looking to see if Alan Ladd was in the middle of it. I hid under a table. It was the best fight I ever saw.

ex

My boss was called the deck watch, and he and I didn't get along. We had been in a fight the year before when I threw a pot of tea leaves into the wind just as he came around the cabin. The leaves smacked him in the face. I took off running, but he caught me and beat me up. It's tough to avoid a fight when you're stuck on a boat.

The next year, my boss went ashore one day in Buffalo. The boat unloaded more quickly than he expected, and we started down the Buffalo River. We had just left the dock when he pulled up in a taxi.

He was 10 feet away from us, and we had a 60-foot aluminum ladder laying on the deck. He yelled, "Throw me the ladder." I was a deck hand, and remember I didn't like this guy. I turned to the deck watch on duty, and said, "Do I have to throw him the ladder?" The boat was moving literally two miles an hour. The deck watch told me, "It's your ladder."

I looked at my boss on the dock and told him I thought it would be too dangerous.

"Come on you little SOB, throw me the ladder," he yelled. "I don't want to lose my bonus." The company had a policy that if you stayed on the boat all year, you received a bonus. A lot of transients were working there, and that was one way they tried to encourage people to stay instead of leaving whenever we reached a port.

There are three drawbridges between the steel mill and the lake in Buffalo, and as we got close to the second bridge, there he was again.

"Throw me the ladder," he yelled. "Do I have to throw him the ladder?" The deck watch said, "It's your ladder." I yelled that it was still too dangerous.

We came to the third and final drawbridge before heading out into Lake Erie, and there he was again.

"Throw me the ladder," he said, begging now. "Do I have to throw him the ladder?" I asked. I got the same answer. "It's your ladder." I just waved as we pulled away and there he stood. I haven't seen him since, but if I did and he remembered me, I'm sure he'd try to whip me again. I was a hero with the others on the boat, however. They watched the whole thing, and nobody liked him very much.

It would not have been dangerous to put the ladder out to him, but there could be a lot of danger involved in the use of the ladder on the boat. Once we were in Escanaba, Michigan, pulling away from the dock, and I had to let go of the forward line, run to the stern, let go the aft line, then climb the 60-foot aluminum ladder to the deck.

The ladder should have been hanging alongside the boat, but on this occasion, the top of the ladder was on the stanchion, the bottom on the dock. It was raining, it was cold, and nobody else knew there was a problem.

I was trying to climb hand-over-hand up the ladder, which was twisting. My future lay between the boat and the dock. I knew that if I fell off the ladder I was a dead man. Nobody was paying any attention to me and they would never find me. There was no way I could make it.

At the last moment, I felt a hand from above, pulling on the back of my neck. I weighed 165 pounds and the second mate, Olson, lifted me to the deck with one hand. How he was able to save me, I don't know.

When we reached a port, it was the deck hand's job to go over the side on a bosuns chair to the dock. Someone would throw a heaving line tied to a cable and you had to tie the cable to the piling on the dock. Going over the side was a real kick. Sometimes you were swinging wildly and bouncing off the ore chutes with your feet. You had to be careful not to miss the dock. There were a lot of accidents on the lakes, and a lot of people were killed, usually when a cable snapped.

The dangers of the job didn't keep me from enjoying the time I spent on the water. I loved the water then, and still do. I get goosebumps and the hair stands up on the back of my neck when I'm on the ocean standing on the bow of a ship. I could have stayed on the Lakes forever, except for a fact I learned when I went to get my AB (able-bodied seaman) papers. That's what I needed to become a deck watch and be exempt from the military draft. I learned I was color blind.

I have trouble seeing the difference between greens and browns. They gave me the test where you're supposed to identify the colors inside of various light bulbs, and I couldn't do it. Being color blind changed my entire life.

Over the years I've learned how to adjust to telling the different colors, but I still have trouble. If I put a penny down on a golf green to mark a ball, I have a hell of a time trying to find it. It stands right out to most people, but I have to search until I actually see the penny.

After a baseball game one night in St. Louis, I was trying to unlock my car and the key didn't work. It was because the car belonged to Joe Torre, then the Cardinals' manager. We had identical cars, except mine was green and his was brown. They looked the same to me.

The Army didn't care, however, that I couldn't tell the difference between those two colors, and when they learned I would not be promoted to a deck watch, I became eligible for the draft. We always picked up our mail in Detroit, and I was supposed to receive my draft notice, but it didn't come so I stayed on the boat until we reached Buffalo.

I got off the boat, and a gentleman was standing there waiting for me.

"John Buck?" he said as he approached.

I answered, "Yes."

"FBI," he said, flashing identification. "You're under arrest for draft evasion."

I wish I had a picture of the astonished look that must have been on my face.

We sorted through the problem, and determined I wasn't really trying to evade the draft, but I had not received my notice. He was going to take me back to Cleveland to make sure I reported to the draft board, but I convinced him that wasn't necessary. I had been looking for it and waiting for it ever since I knew I wasn't going to become a deck watch, and I actually wanted to go in the Army. It was June of 1943 and the world was really upside down.

When I look back on it, I wonder what would have happened if the Japanese had waited to attack the U.S. until after Hitler had conquered England. Hitler could have taken all of Europe and moved on to Russia before we would have gotten into the war. Until we were attacked, there were isolationists in this country who wanted no part in what was going on. The Germans were killing the Jewish people and others, like the physically handicapped, and we weren't doing anything to try to stop him.

Some people in this country were just oblivious to what was going on. If we hadn't been bombed by Japan, I believe we wouldn't have become involved until much later and Hitler would have won the war.

We never could have gotten into Europe if the Germans had controlled it all. We never could have landed there, or mounted a big enough force to go across the Atlantic. No wonder the English didn't appreciate us at the time. If I had been English I wouldn't have liked us either.

It wasn't my role to question that at the time. I was headed for the Army, ready to do what I was told.

CHAPTER
4

In the Army

I was drafted into the Army in June of 1943, and suddenly I was no longer John F. Buck. I became a number: 35067459. Talk about losing your identity. I was 19 years old, 5-foot-11, weighed 165 pounds, in good shape from working on the lakes, and not unlike thousands of other eager but anxious draftees, ready to serve my country.

I was inducted at Fort Hays in Columbus, Ohio. There they asked me to select the area where I'd like to be assigned. I indicated transportation, because of my love for the water, knowing they had harbor boats and tugboats under Army command. I don't remember being on any kind of a ship during my three years in the Army except for the Mauritania, the luxury liner on which I shipped over to Europe a year and a half later or the Liberty Ship which brought me back to the States in 1946.

My first assignment was anti-aircraft training, and I was sent to Fort Eustis, Virginia, for basic. Rookie training lasted 13 weeks, learning how to use all sorts of weapons; learning to drill.

After completing my 13 weeks, I joined the cadre as one of the instructors and was given the rank of corporal. Because of my voice, and I was really good at close-order drill. You could hear me all over the area. It was the first time I realized that some adults in this country didn't have a high school education. Many of the trainees coming in for basic training were really dumb, couldn't learn, couldn't march, and didn't care.

Thirteen weeks isn't really a long time to get a soldier ready for combat. Most were leading rather soft lives until they were greeted by the President and drafted. It's tough to get ready to hike 30 miles carrying a full field pack and rifle when you used to sit behind a desk as a student or laid around doing nothing. I was an instructor for three of those 13-week sessions, each of which we ended with a 30-mile hike to Yorktown. In Virginia, it was hot as heck in the summertime and bitter cold in the winter. I was in such good condition I could have hiked forever, but a lot of the trainees kept dropping out and had to be picked up by the meat wagon and taken back to camp.

One time at Fort Eustis, I took a battery of trainees, each carrying a light field pack and rifle, on a 10-mile forced march. We came back in at attention and never lost a man. We hiked the 10 miles in 1 hour, 25 minutes, an average of just more than 8 minutes per mile.

I really enjoyed my job as an instructor, but teaching a recruit how to handle a hand grenade was always a test. You can pull the pin on a hand grenade, press the handle down and hold it forever. But you couldn't convince the jeeps, as we called the trainees. When they finally used a live grenade, we lined up 16 at a time, eight pits to my left and eight to my right. The commands were "pull pin, prepare to throw, and throw." Invariably, after the first command, a grenade or two would come flying out of the pits. So there were the others with live grenades, waiting to get rid of them. Some never could throw the grenade and I would have to crawl into their pit, take the grenade away from them and throw it myself. I always dreaded live grenade day. It was always screwed up.

I also instructed on the 40-millimeter guns. The shells were about 16 inches long. Whenever there was a misfire, someone had to take the shell out of the gun and take it to ordinance. Guess whose job that was?

"Hey Buck, there's a misfire over here. See if you can get this thing out." People cleared out of the way when you carried that twisted shell to the experts, who had to disarm it.

I also instructed on the M-1 rifle, the Browning automatic rifle, the rifle grenade, 30-caliber machine gun, 50-caliber machine gun, both air cooled and water cooled, the 37-millimeter anti-tank gun, the bayonet, the gas mask, and the infiltration course. I also taught the rookies how to march and drill. It was the first time I realized that I could lecture and teach. Frequently in the barracks, we had some of the recruits crying all night. Some crying for their mother, others wet the bed. Some were discharged as section 8s, real wackos.

At Fort Eustis one day I was with a sergeant by the name of Rick. We were in a jeep and he was driving. Those jeeps turned over frequently, and he flipped it. I jumped out, rolled out of the way and didn't get hurt. He was pinned down, with his arm under the jeep. Believe it or not, I was able to lift the front end high enough to free him. The adrenaline was really flowing. He suffered a compound fracture, and was discharged from the Army.

We did a lot of boxing at Fort Eustis. I had fought frequently as a kid, and thought I was pretty good. One night they introduced me, "John Buck from Lakewood, Ohio," then they announced my opponent, "from Oil City, Pennsylvania...." I didn't even hear the guy's name. Oil City, Pennsylvania, was enough to let me know I was going to lose, and I did.

All of this was before President Truman integrated the services in 1945. We didn't have any black soldiers in our units. We had one trainee with kinky red hair and almost pure white skin. They thought he was a Negro, and shipped him out of our outfit. The black outfit shipped him back because they thought he was white. They didn't know what to do with him, so they took the easy way out and discharged him. That's how narrow-minded and stubborn people were at the time. He wasn't white, he wasn't black, he wasn't wanted.

When Truman integrated the services in 1945, it was a huge step forward for this country. It really opened the lines of communication and was the start of some positive race relations. Black people had started to realize the opportunities available in this country, and they longed for some of the good things in life. It was the first time blacks from southern states knew there was another world out there. Radio was well established, and soon television would hit the scene. Improved communication also forced the white population to change its way of thinking, and I felt a lot of progress that began during the war has continued through the years.

During the war, everyone was proud to be an American, and looked for ways they could aid the war effort. It was strange going home on furlough, because very few of your friends were around since most also were in the military. There were stars on the flags in the windows to show how many from that household were in the service. We had three—Frank, Earle and me. My mother was involved, working at the White Sewing Machine Co., making uniforms. The unity that existed in this country was something for everyone to be proud of.

At Fort Eustis, there was an obstacle course that everyone had to traverse as part of basic training. We always told the jeeps to take off their jewelry, but one young fellow decided to leave a ring on his finger. He scaled a wooden fence and his ring caught on a knot in the wood. He let go, and his finger was severed and landed in a pile of sawdust. I retrieved his ring, and the finger was laying there, so I picked it up.

They took the kid to the dispensary, and I took the finger over there, thinking that perhaps the doctors could reattach it. The doctor looked at me and said, "Get that thing out of here." I was 40 years ahead of my time.

That night in the mess hall, I decided to have some fun. I still had the ring in my pocket. I took a piece of asparagus about the size of a finger, slipped the ring on it and rolled it down the table where 10 GIs were eating. They peeled away like fighter planes. I had the table all to myself.

One of my pals at Fort Eustis was Luke Riley, who had played football at Duquesne University. One day we were talking about what was going to happen when we left Fort Eustis, and we decided to go to Officers Candidate School. To qualify, one had to complete the obstacle course in a prescribed period of time. For a while I had the record for the fastest time on the course, and we knew time would be no problem for either of us.

We ran the course, and were both way ahead of the qualifying time when we arrived at the last obstacle. Luke stopped and said, "I don't really want to do this. Do you?"

I said, "I don't think so."

We sat at the wall long enough so we didn't meet the qualifying time. We never became officers. It was probably one of the smartest decisions I ever made. A lieutenant in the infantry didn't last very long in combat.

One day all the non-commissioned officers were assembled, and they asked anyone who had ever played high school or college football to step forward.

"Come on, we'll play football and have some fun," Luke said. He stepped forward.

I also stepped forward, then I said, "I can't play football, I'll get killed," and I stepped back into the ranks.

As it turned out, they didn't want football players. The next day, everyone who had stepped forward was sent to the Rangers to get ready for the invasion of Europe. Luke ended up in the 36th infantry division, the Texas division, and was in combat all through Germany. Little things have a major impact on your life.

Shortly thereafter, I was transferred to Camp Stewart, Georgia, still training troops in anti-aircraft. That was where I saw my first German soldier. They were prisoners of war who had been captured in Africa, and sent to prison camps in this country. We made a special point of drilling troops in front of the POWs and marched by their compound in perfect cadence so they could see what good soldiers we had.

Once at Camp Stewart, we were on bivouac in the Okefenokee Swamp and an officer parked a halftrack. The next morning, all we could see of the halftrack were the barrels of two 50-caliber machine guns sticking out of the quicksand. The halftrack had disappeared. The officer was courtmartialed, convicted and sent to prison in Fort Leavenworth, Kansas. Tough times.

Another friend who also shipped to Camp Stewart was Billy Choate, who now lives in Wayne City, Illinois. Billy was going with a girl named Thelma in Virginia who he planned to marry. When we were sent to Camp Stewart, Thelma came to Georgia and brought a girlfriend along. The morning Billy and Thelma were to be married, both he and I had duty as charge of quarters, and couldn't get off the base. Thelma and her friend were staying at Jack's Motel, just outside Savannah.

We worked it out so we could both get off base the next morning, and the wedding was to take place. Early that morning, I was in my bunk when two cooks who had been out all night stumbled in. They were bragging about how they spent the night with two girls from Virginia, one named Thelma, at Jack's Motel. Billy wasn't around and didn't hear any of this. I was faced with a dilemma: should I tell him or not?

At that time, GI insurance had a value of $10,000. Everybody in the military had a policy. Some women married military men, some of them more than one, so they could collect the insurance if they got killed. All of us were close to being sent overseas, so I decided I had to tell Choate about his future wife.

He took it well. We went to the DeSoto Hotel in Savannah where Thelma, her girlfriend and the minister were waiting. Billy poured the champagne, proposed a toast, then pitched the bubbly in Thelma's face. Sometimes I tell that story at parties and play a game of "Would you have told him or not?" Most of the men say yes, most of the women say no. It all ended well. Billy is happily married, but not to Thelma.

I was at Camp Stewart when the troops landed at Normandy on D-day, June 6, 1944. The war in Europe was going well. Then came the Battle of the Bulge in December. More GIs were killed in that battle than in the entire Pacific war. The brass began scrambling to get more infantry to send overseas, and I was transferred out of anti-aircraft into the infantry and sent to Fort Jackson, S.C. for further training.

They soon sent 250 of us by train across the country to Fort Ord, California. The first day there, they gave us parkas and boots and told us we were going to Alaska, where we were still fighting the Japanese in the Aleutian Islands.

The next day, they took the parkas away and gave us mosquito netting and told us we were going to the Pacific. The very next day, they decided to send all 250 of us to Europe. Back on the train, we headed across country to Fort Meade, Maryland. On Christmas Eve we stopped at Union Station in St. Louis.

The train station was a hectic place, with people trying to get home for the holiday. We had organized a chorus, and sang Christmas songs to entertain the people who were stuck there with us.

Little did I know that I would be living in St. Louis just 10 years later, broadcasting baseball.

ىہ

Boxing was always a big deal at all of the Army bases. At Fort Meade, you got a 24-hour pass if you boxed, whether you won or lost. I boxed frequently, until some troops from the Philippines came through Fort Meade. I was 5-foot-11 and weighed 165 pounds, and when you get a Filipino that size, you've got a man on your hands. I stopped boxing until they shipped out. They weren't fighting for the pass, they just wanted to level somebody.

When I did get a pass, a friend of mine and I used to go to Philadelphia to visit my uncle Phil. Just before we shipped out, my mother came from Cleveland to Philadelphia for a visit. My mother was happy to see me, but my uncle wanted me to leave because we were drinking all his whiskey and eating all his food.

My friend's name was Adams, and he had been a drummer with the Pinky Tomlin orchestra before the war. Tomlin was best known for his recording of "The Object of My Affection." In Philly, Adams had a date with a cousin of mine and I had a date with her friend. Adams drank too much and passed out. It was snowing, and we were running late and had to get back to the 30th Street train station, then to Fort Meade, where we were on alert. There were no cabs around, and I thought we were going to end up in the stockade. A taxi finally came by and I stood in front of it until it stopped. The passenger was a general.

"General, we're on alert and we've got to get back to Fort Meade," I told him.

He let us in the cab to get to the 30th Street Station. Adams was still half-out, but I managed to get him to the bathroom, where he accidentally locked himself inside a pay toilet. I had to crawl in to get him out.

We finally got on the train and made it back to the base on time. He was shipped out, and ended up in the 2nd infantry division, the Indianhead division. I later ran into a fellow from the 2nd at a hospital who knew Adams. He told me Adams had been standing behind a tree when he was shot and killed by a sniper. I did a hell of a job getting him back to the base on time, so he could be sent overseas and killed. I think of him every time I go by that railroad station in Philadelphia. There I am on a bus with a bunch of young baseball players, hooting and hollering and having fun. I look at that railroad station and think of Adams.

ༀ

We shipped out in February 1945 from Camp Patrick Henry, Virginia. We each carried a big dufflebag, not only for ourselves but as replacement equipment for those already in Europe. Each of us was just a number. They wrote your number on your helmet and dufflebag in chalk. They loaded a couple of thousand troops on the Mauritania, a big luxury liner that had been stripped for transporting troops. We went overseas with no escort. The ship could outrun submarines, and the big submarine scare had passed.

We headed for Liverpool, England, and it only took a few days to get there. My bunk was down on the fifth deck, but I quickly looked for a way to get out of there. Almost everyone was seasick, and man did it stink! I smoked cigarettes at that time, so I slipped up to the top deck and made friends with some of the sailors and they let me sleep on the top deck at night. I slept with a life preserver around my neck. If we were torpedoed, I was going to be the first one over the side.

On that trip some GIs crawled into their bunk before we left the states and never got out until we reached England because they were so seasick. They didn't eat, you couldn't make them move; they didn't do anything except throw up. They looked like they had been gassed.

We landed in Liverpool, then crossed the English countryside by train to Northampton, crossed the Channel and landed at Le Havre, France. They put us on another train, then loaded us on trucks, and in a blink we were in Liege, Belgium, in the replacement center called the "repple depot".

I had always wanted to go overseas and go into combat. Once we reached the replacement depot, we were at the front in no time. We were trucked to the front, and I was assigned to K company, 47th regiment, 9th infantry division.

The first night, I went out as a rifleman with a machine gun crew. I had volunteered, and I think I was more excited than scared. I thought about the sergeant who had assigned me to this unit. He had said that one out of every three of us was going to be wounded or killed. I turned to the two guys next to me and thought, "You're in trouble."

The company that we relieved was moving up, and we were placed in reserve. The departing outfit told us we were in a hot spot. The Krauts had the place zeroed in, meaning the first shell would land right on top of us. We dug in, and soon it began. I don't know how long the barrage lasted. It seemed like 12 hours, but it probably was closer to 10 minutes. Trees were coming down, guys were getting hit and yelling for the medics. At the time, I felt so incredibly helpless. We hadn't had time to dig a foxhole, so my face was in the ground with my legs together, and I had absolutely no control of my fate. What am I doing here? What did I do to deserve this? Some SOB is firing at me who doesn't know me or doesn't even know I'm here. More importantly, when will it stop?

Being pinned down by artillery is the worst. When you are in a firefight with a rifle, attacking a house or another target, there usually is some sort of cover you can take. But when you're pinned down and mortars and 88s are being fired at you, there's nothing you can do but hold your breath and pray.

Winning the Battle of the Bulge two months earlier made it certain that the Allies were going to win the war. The only question was how much longer it was going to take. The Germans had almost nothing left, and the Allied troops were beginning to enter German territory. The Rhine is only a short distance behind the border and blocked the way to the Autobahn and the heart of Germany. The Germans were setting up a major defensive line behind the river, which was going to be difficult to cross, because the Germans had destroyed most of the bridges.

On March 7, in the town of Remagen, a group from the 9th Armored Division arrived and found the Ludendorf railroad bridge still intact. It had been wired for demolition, but had not gone down. A gutsy sergeant went across the bridge while under fire and dismantled the charges. It was a historic moment in World War II and hastened the end of the German empire.

On the day the bridge was taken, our outfit hiked 20 miles and reached the bridge at night. No one knew how much longer the bridge was going to stand, because it already had been hit with artillery and was about to collapse. I crawled across that bridge on my hands and knees, with my helmet strap loosened, boots and ammunition belt hanging by only one hook so if I fell in the river there was some chance to get rid of the equipment and make it to shore. If you were weighed down, you surely would drown. I made the long trip safely to the other side.

Across the bridge was a tunnel. The far end of it was blocked, and it seemed like a safe place to go. I don't know how many GIs were sheltered in the tunnel when a colonel came in and yelled, "Everybody out. Saddle up, C'mon, let's go." Nobody moved. The colonel pulled out his .45, and pointed it at one GI. "You're first," he said. That soldier left, and we all followed.

The Ludendorf Bridge finally collapsed, but by then we had built a pontoon bridge over the Rhine and moved troops and equipment across to the other side.

There was a fellow in our company whose last name was Grenier. I never knew his first name. On the 14th of March, he was sitting at the edge of my foxhole watching some German jets try to bomb the bridge to slow the American advance. It was the first time I had ever seen a jet. It was over my head and out of sight before I even heard a sound.

Grenier never dug his own foxhole. He always said, "If we don't get shelled, I won't need one. If we do, someone will get hit and I'll take their hole."

Thump. He was hit in the chest by a .spent 50 caliber slug that fell from the sky, and down he went. It hit just over his heart. I was trying to bandage him, and he reached down and pulled out the bullet, which was about the size of a ring finger. Blood shot everywhere. He broke away, and tried to run toward the road. We caught him, tended to him, until a medic took over. That was the last I saw of him. I don't know if he lived or died. The Army records center is in St. Louis, and I've thought about trying to track him down. I have a good idea if I ever check it out that I will learn that Grenier was killed in action on March 14, 1945. I don't think I'll ever check.

If the Germans had been able to collapse the bridge, the war probably would have lasted another month or so, and the Russians would have had time to occupy more of Germany than they did. The result would have been that post-war West Germany would have been smaller, East Germany larger, bad for NATO and the Western Allies.

Beware the Ides of March. March 15 rolled around, and that was the day I was wounded. It was 5:30 in the morning. I had been made a squad leader, and I was taking out a patrol to bring back some prisoners. I knew the Germans had a particular crossroad zeroed in because of all the shelling the day before. I talked to the squad members and told them to be quiet and not make any noise.

A group of tanks were lined up waiting to join the action. It's my guess that one of the tankers got cold and fired up his engine. As soon as I heard the engine start, I yelled. "Run." I was scrambling for cover when an .88 hit a tree behind me and the shrapnel got me in the left arm and leg. I had a hand grenade hanging on my chest and to this day I don't know how the shrapnel missed it. I just missed losing my left arm, not to mention having my head blown off. I was really lucky.

As I lay there, the first GI who came along took my rations. The second took my grenades. The third was a medic and he put a bandage on the wound. "Stay here," he said. "I'll send a jeep for you."

More shells started to hit, so I got up and got the hell out of there. I started walking down the road to a field hospital and lit a cigarette. One of the tankers yelled at me to put it out because it was still dark. "Screw you," I yelled back. I was angry at them because one of their tanks had started an engine, causing me to get hit.

Another of the tankers yelled, "How's your leg, soldier?" I looked down, and my pant leg was gone. I didn't even know it. Fortunately I just had some superficial wounds on the calf of my leg. I caught up with a jeep and headed for the field hospital behind the lines.

After I came to St. Louis to work for the Cardinals in 1954, I was in the stands watching a soccer game and I recognized the goalie. I knew that I didn't know him from St. Louis, so I talked to him at halftime and we determined that after the war, we had both tried out for the 9th infantry division baseball team. His name was Frank Borghi. He got the job, and I joined the fast-pitch softball team.

In 1975, I was the emcee of a banquet at which Borghi was being honored as the goaltender for the team that beat England 1-0 in the 1950 World Cup game in Brazil. To this day, it's one of the most monumental upsets in World Cup history. We were seated at the head table, and we talked about the 9th infantry division. I asked him what regiment he was in, and he said the 47th. I said I was also. I asked him what company he was in, and he told me he was in K company. So was I. I asked what he did in K company, and he told me he was a medic. I asked how many medics there were in K company after we crossed the Remagen Bridge. He told me he was the only one, because the other medic had been wounded. We determined that he was the medic who bandaged me the morning I was hit. That's unbelievable.

Frank was really involved with the 9th infantry, he saw duty in North Africa, Sicily, Salerno, Normandy and Germany and earned five battle stars. My role in combat pales by comparison.

Another startling coincidence involves a well-known sportscaster, the late Lindsey Nelson. I was playing golf one day in St. Petersburg, Florida with a friend and he started asking about when I was wounded. I asked him why he wanted to know.

"Have you ever talked to Lindsey Nelson about this?" he asked. No, I hadn't, and he said we should talk.

It turned out that Lindsey, who did the Mets and Giants games for years as well as Notre Dame football, also was in the 9th infantry division. He was also wounded at Remagen, at about the same time, and also hit in the left arm.

Lindsey said, "The same SOB got us both."

It's a strange thing about being hit by a bullet or shrapnel. Sometimes it can hit your helmet and bounce off, other times it can hit the helmet and get in between the helmet and the liner and go over your head and exit. Other times it will go straight through everything, including your head. A million stories came out of World War II about this.

I was lucky to have survived. I knew it that day, and I know it now. When the jeep reached the field hospital, they put a different bandage on my arm. While they were taking care of the more seriously wounded, I crawled under a bench and went to sleep. I don't know how long I was out, but when I woke up there wasn't anybody in the room except me and one nurse.

The next stop was an evacuation hospital, where a colonel inspected wounds and made an estimate about how long soldiers would be out of action. If it was 30 days or less, you stayed in Germany. If it was going to be 60 days, you went to France; 90 days to England, and if it was to be longer than 90 days, you were "ZI"ed, zone of the interior, you went home.

The colonel checked me out and asked if I'd rather go to to France or England. England was my choice.

"I don't think you'll be out that long," he said. So they put me in an ambulance, then a hospital train en route to Le Mans, France and the 177th General Army Hospital.

Shortly after my ambulance went across the pontoon bridge over the Rhine, the bridge let loose, and troops, tanks and trucks were swept into the river. They never had a chance. Once again I was lucky.

Because I was more mobile than a lot of the other wounded, they put me on the third deck of the train. Penicillin had just been introduced, and there were two kinds, one red and the other amber. One hurt like a son of a bitch, and I had to get three shots a day for 50 days. That's 150 shots, and they wouldn't give it to you in the butt. Because my left arm was bandaged, they gave me all the shots in my right arm. It ended up hurting worse than the one that was hit by shrapnel.

On the train, the nurse who had to administer the shots could hardly reach up to the third bunk to my arm. It was like she was throwing darts. On the way to Le Mans, we stopped alongside a supply train that was headed toward the front. Some French soldiers were guarding it, and we decided to raid it. They had cigarettes and booze on board. For some reason, the French soldiers never fired a shot.

It took a couple of days to get to the 177th General, and by that time the bandage on my arm was bloody and felt like Plaster of Paris. They couldn't get it off. The nurse was using liquid vaseline when a doctor came by and said "Let me see that." As he said the word "see" he yanked the bandage and ripped it off my arm. I looked up at him and tried to call him a bad name, but I couldn't because I passed out.

When I came to, I looked at my arm and I could actually see the inside of my bicep. I could move my fingers and watch the nerves move at the same time. That's when I knew again how lucky I was. All around me in the operating room, sheets covered those who had died. A lieutenant was getting ready to operate on my arm, and a colonel who had just lost a patient walked by. He looked at me and told the lieutenant, "If you don't mind, I'll do this one." I think he welcomed a change from some of the more serious surgeries, and I didn't mind. I'd rather have a colonel operate on me than a lieutenant any day.

They hit me with sodium pentothal, and I slept for 14 hours. They did a wonderful job on my arm. The wound was five inches by three inches, and I still sport quite a scar. My arm doesn't hurt unless somebody grabs me around the upper arm, then I will go to my knees. Part of the underside of my forearm is dead to the touch, but I don't pay any attention to that.

I was to receive a Purple Heart. In some of the movies about the war, those ceremonies are a lot more dramatic than they actually are, at least that was my experience. All I remember was sitting on my bed and an officer came down the aisle and said, "John Buck?" When I identified myself, he tossed the medal to me, then moved on to the next guy. No big deal.

Everyone reacted to the war and being wounded in different ways. In the same hospital was a fellow named Finnegan, who was from Philadelphia. He had been wounded for a third time. He was a tanker, from the 2nd armored division. Tankers always carried a .45 pistol, and he still had his with him, under his pillow.

He couldn't wait to get out of the hospital to go back to his unit and into combat again. A captain was walking through the ward one day and he said, "Doctor, when am I getting out?" The doctor said he thought it would be a couple more days. That wasn't what Finnegan wanted to hear. He lifted up the pillow and showed the doctor his .45.

He said, "Captain, if I'm not out of here soon, some day somebody's going to walk through that door and I'm going to bring him down." The captain turned to the nurse who was with him and said, "Lieutenant, discharge this man."

Part of my rehab at the hospital was spent on the softball field. I couldn't straighten out my left arm. I was playing first base, and there was a ground ball to the shortstop. He uncorked a high throw, and I had time to think to myself, "Should I catch it or not?" I reached up and caught the ball, and man it hurt. As I was trying to shake off the pain, a loud voice came from behind me.

"Buck, I saw that." It was my doctor, who said, "You're ready to leave."

Believe it or not, when you left the hospital, it took only one day before you were back at the front in combat, getting shot at again. It was like going from St. Louis to Chicago. The morning I was to be discharged, I woke up with tonsillitis, which I used to get twice a year. I had a fever of 103, and they put me in isolation. When I finally was able to leave, they gave me a 48-hour pass before I had to rejoin my unit. I headed for Paris. It was May 7.

Rumors were spreading that the war had ended, but they turned out to be false—for a day. The war did end on May 8, and I was in Paris in the middle of the big celebration. The Glenn Miller Orchestra played at the Red Cross center and Johnny Desmond was the vocalist. I watched Charles DeGaulle speak at the Place d' Opera. I stayed in Paris for a couple of extra days to enjoy the action, then I was picked up for being AWOL and sent back to Germany.

If I had not been in the hospital, I would have been there when my outfit liberated Dachau. I have enough bad memories of that place. I'm glad I wasn't there at that time.

With all of the celebrating at the end of the war, the one person I was thinking about was my brother Earle. My brother Frank had spent the war in a non-combat unit, but Earle was in Germany with the 86th Blackhawk division, and saw a lot of action. He was a lieutenant, and I learned later he was in a battle and wounded, but still led his troops into a town and captured it. He was recommended for the Medal of Honor, and did receive the Silver Star. He and I had always had an instinctual feeling about each other, and I knew when I rejoined my outfit he had either been killed or wounded. There was a letter waiting for me from him. He had been wounded severely and was back in the states.

Years later when my brother Frank died, the family was staying at Earle's home in Cleveland. I asked to see his Army Silver Star citation. It described what had happened in the battle in 1945, and as I finished reading it, his son said, "Uncle Jack, may I see that?" He was probably 35 or so, and he had never seen his father's citation because Earle doesn't like to talk about the war. A lot of people are like that, but it doesn't bother me to talk about it. My combat experience was so brief there's not a hell of a lot to talk about.

Earle ended up making a career out of the Army, and during the Korean War, he was in charge of the Army's payroll. He used to get the money, which was millions of dollars, in cash from an uncle of mine, Bill Ryan, who was the president of the Bank of America in Tokyo. This was the same Bill Ryan who was captured by the Japanese in Shanghai in 1941 and was later repatriated in the Swedish Red Cross liner the Gripsholm. Earle enjoyed his Army career. He was discharged as a warrant officer.

When I rejoined my outfit, I was supposed to be promoted to sergeant and I wanted the stripes. They didn't want to give them to me unless I re-enlisted, and I had no intention of doing that. The officers in charge of our unit wanted me to go back to the states to go to Officers Training School. They were going to give me a 60-day leave so I could go home, and then go to the school and come back as a first lieutenant. Six months later I would have been promoted to captain and would have taken over the company. They couldn't talk me into that either, so I remained a corporal.

After the war, our first assignment was pulling guard duty at Mooseburg, where SS Troops were being held as prisoners. Guard duty was tough. So many GIs had been sent home we were pulling guard duty eight hours on, four off, 16 hours a day. I had to figure a way to get out of that action. Sports was the answer.

The division had a fast-pitch softball team and I ended up playing first base. We had a lot of fun playing teams from other divisions and traveling around Europe. The third baseman on our team was from New Orleans, Gus Taromini. One day, his brother, who was on leave from the quartermaster corps, came by to visit. We were seated on our bunks, batting the breeze, when the brother asked to see Gus' .45 revolver. He pulled the trigger, and it went off. It sounded like a cannon. The bullet went into the floor right between my feet.

I had just gotten out of the hospital. I had lived through the war, and he almost did me in playing with a .45.

On the wall of our quarters in Ingolstadt was a flare gun, with about a two-inch barrel. It was rusted, and periodically people would take it down from the wall and try to open it up and inspect it, or they would pull the trigger and nothing would happen. One night a fellow started fooling around with that flare gun and it went off. It was designed so the flare would shoot about 200 feet in the air, then explode. Instead, it ricochetted around that room for a couple of minutes. It hit every wall three times, the ceiling five times, the floor, it bounced up, it went under the bunks. It caught blankets on fire. People were running into each other trying to get out of the way. It was dangerous, but it got to be so funny you couldn't help but laugh.

There was a small pond outside the building, in our sports complex, and as it warmed up in the summer, the water evaporated. Sitting there in that pond was a 500-pound bomb that had probably been dropped by a B-17. We had been sleeping 30 feet away from that bomb for three months. It was about as big as a pool table, and experts had to come in to defuse it, and I was far away when they did.

Playing on the athletic teams kept me off guard duty. After the softball season, I was the assistant trainer on the football team, where my job was to tape ankles. I made the basketball team. We had some good athletes in our outfit. We played for the European softball championship, and our football coach was Dr. Andy Kerr Jr., the son of the famous Colgate coach. We had a fellow on the football team, Floyd Thomas, who played at Arkansas. Blair Brown, who later played at Oklahoma State, was on the team, as was Jack Mildren, whose son, Jack Jr. played quarterback at Oklahoma, went on to the pros and then became a Congressman.

Even though I could hardly skate, I went out for the hockey team. "I'm a goaltender," I said. We had all the equipment except for the goalie, so I had a baseball catcher's chest protector and my first baseman's glove. Nobody even thought about wearing a helmet or a mask back then.

As a kid when we played hockey on the frozen ponds in Holyoke, we used a tin can for a puck. Later, when I was growing up in Cleveland, I watched the Cleveland Barons play, so I had some idea about what I was doing, but I was way out of my league. During practice a fellow skated in on me, and before I could even move my glove, he fired the puck and hit the inside of my thigh. I thought he broke my leg. My thigh read, "Spalding, Made in USA" for about a month.

Another player fired a puck at me, and it took off before I could react. It hit my chest protector, bounced up and hit me in the Adam's apple. It knocked me back and my head hit the crossbar. They carried me off the ice. The team left for a game in Sweden without me, and lost by a score of 22-1.

While the team was gone, I was staying by myself in a chalet on the side of the mountain in Garmisch-Partenkirchen. I had a jeep, double rations, and I had a good time for about 10 days. Finally, some MPs discovered I was there and came and knocked on the door.

"Who the hell are you?" they demanded. I said, "Am I glad to see you. Here are the keys to this place. I didn't know what to do with them or who to give them to. Here you go."

I went back to my outfit, and the officers wanted to know where I had been. "Playing hockey," I told them.

Part of my job was scheduling games, and I set up a softball game against the 38th Triple A Battalion at Berchtesgaden, Hitler's former home. When we got there, there wasn't any team to play. The 38th didn't show, but I wasn't surprised. I made up the game and got the rations so we could go to Berchtesgaden, and visit Hitler's headquarters. There wasn't any 38th Triple A Battalion. Nice going, Jack.

General Eisenhower had visited the site the day before we arrived, and he had ordered the sign "Field Officers Only" removed. He wanted the GIs to see the place. That was a mistake. The Eagle's Nest was torn apart by soldiers taking anything they could find for souvenirs—shutters, doorknobs, sink handles—anything. I have a picture of me standing on the guard tower. That and my memory of what I saw was enough for me.

One of the Army's strictest rules in immediate post-war Germany was against fraternization. If the MPs caught a GI fraternizing with a German woman, he was put into a labor camp with no questions asked. It didn't make any difference who you were or what you had done. Those camps were awful.

That threat didn't stop some of us. Two others and I were heading back to our outfit one day when we ran into some German girls at an apartment building. We were trying to romance them, and somebody called the MPs. Here they came in a jeep. The three of us rushed to find a place to hide, and the other two were caught quickly. They couldn't find me. The MPs were ready to leave, and the Germans kept telling them, "There's one more, one more."

They looked a little while longer, but still couldn't find me and finally left.

I had climbed my way to safety through a bomb hole in the roof, and was lying on the roof of this three-story apartment building. Now the MPs were gone, and I came down. The Germans were still in the building, laughing about how they had the GIs arrested, and I came down the stairs and started screaming and firing a pistol into the ceiling. I scared the hell out of them, and while they were diving for cover I ran out the door. I never saw the two other guys again, but I know they ended up in a labor camp.

I almost got arrested for simply saying hello to a girl who was working for the Red Cross. She said I was flirting with her. They were serious about that stuff; the officers could do whatever they wished.

There was a fellow in our outfit whom we called Costello. He looked like the fat guy from Abbott and Costello. He told us he couldn't wait to get out of the service, because he was from Brooklyn and was going home to a great job. Later, when I was broadcasting with the Cardinals and we were in Ebbets Field —where the press box was very close to the field—I was in the booth before a game one day and looked down at the guy who was raking the dirt around home plate.

"Hey, Costello," I yelled down. It was him. That was the great job he had waiting for him when he came home.

My last assignment was in Augsburg, Germany, where I moved into an apartment that had been used by a former major-league pitcher while he was there with the 72nd infantry division.

Up the street from the apartment was a camp for displaced persons, "DPs" they were called, people from Hungary, Latvia, Lithuania and Estonia, all of whom were waiting to go back home or, unfortunately, to Russia. The first night I was in the apartment there was a knock on the door, and there stood the best-looking blonde I had ever seen.

She was Estonian, and I started to talk to her in German. She wanted to know where the guy was who had been staying in the apartment. When I told her he had gone home, back to America, she fainted, passed out right in my hallway. She was pregnant. I shut the door and bolted it—I didn't need that kind of trouble. Somewhere in Estonia there's a 51-year-old man who can throw the hell out of a baseball and has no idea why he's able to do it.

Christmas Eve 1945 rolled around and a group of us GIs went to church. We shared the mass with a group of German civilians— they sat on the left side of the church and we were segregated on the right. Their city had been heavily bombed during the war, and there was no love lost between the civilians and the American GIs. However, when the organist played "Silent Night," the Germans started to sing and we did also. It was a moment I'll always remember. Christmas Eve, 1945.

My orders finally came to ship home, in April 1946. We sailed into New York harbor, past the Statue of Liberty. I had climbed to the top of the torch of the Statue of Liberty with my father when I was about eight years old. Seeing it on this occasion was a dramatic moment, and the GIs on the Liberty Ship were very emotional and many happy tears flowed that day.

The rest of the trip back to Cleveland was by train, where I stepped off at the Terminal Tower. My mother and others in the family were there to meet me. I had no idea what the next stage of my life would bring. Like most other former GIs, I didn't have a job. None of us were treated like heroes, because everybody was in the same predicament. Every family had gone to war and been affected by it. It was a scramble, and it was every man for himself.

One of the greatest things that ever happened in this country was the GI Bill, which paid for servicemen to go to college. It changed the standard educational level in this country from a high school- to a college-level, and helped put more women and more blacks into the work force. It was one more example of how the war changed everything in this country.

There are some people who have greatly influenced my life even though I've never met them. One of them was Harry Truman, someone I really would have liked to have met. Years later, Whitey Herzog, the Cardinals manager, who knew Truman from all his years in Kansas City told me I should just have gone over to Independence and Truman would have been very accommodating. I never did, and I regret that. What I would have liked to have known from Truman was, if the war in Japan had ended first, would he have authorized dropping the atom bomb on Germany? From the people I've talked to who did know Truman, I think the answer would have been yes.

Almost 50 years after the war, Carole and I took a trip back to Germany and France and visited a lot of places I had seen during the war. I had missed the D-day invasion. When I walked down the beach at Normandy in 1995, and later saw the cemetery near there, it really got to me.

I was impressed with the youth of the people who were buried at Normandy, and again reminded of how lucky I had been to miss it. I could see myself coming ashore with the others. I was the right age, I could have been there. While looking at the names, and the outfits represented there, I noticed the people who were walking through the cemetery. They were speaking many different languages, and it was clear to me how the world has come together since the 1940s. Some of the visitors were laughing and talking in the middle of the cemetery. I was riding in a car back to Paris with good friends Mike Roarty and Art Pepin and I took out a pen and wrote this salute to those who died at Normandy:

> *They chatter and laugh as they pass by my grave*
> *   And that's the way it should be.*
> *For what they have done, and what they will do, has*
> *   nothing to do with me.*
> *I was tossed ashore by a friendly wave*
> *   With some unfriendly steel in my head.*
> *They chatter and laugh as they pass by my grave*
> *   But I know they'll soon be dead.*
> *They've counted more days then I ever knew*
> *   And that's all right with me, too.*
> *We're all souls in one pod, all headed for God*
> *   Too soon, or later, like you.*

The Lord above had kept me alive during the war. Now I had no idea what I was going to be doing next.

C H A P T E R

5

Getting an Education

My immediate need was to find a job, exactly the same problem as thousands of other servicemen returning home. It was time to go back to work and help support the family. Frank went back to the Erie Railroad and Earle, after going to the railroad for a short time, decided to re-enlist in the Army and as mentioned, made that his career.

I landed a job working in the warehouse at Glidden Paint Co., but that didn't last very long. My job was to load five-gallon paint cans on a sled. Another fellow had to put the clamps on the cans to close them. In order to lift the cans, I had to swing them. When he was putting the clamps on, he skipped a can, and as I was swinging it, it spilled.

Five gallons of white lead paint spilled everywhere. The boss looked at me and said, "You can clean it up, or you can leave." I said, "It's been a pleasure."

My next job was at Midland Steel Co., working on an assembly line riveting automobile frames. I quickly learned that job wasn't for me either. When I put a rivet in the wrong way, they stopped the assembly line, and my co-workers wanted to choke me. They were all on piece work, and I was costing them money. Then I tried another assembly line, making airbrakes. Talk about boredom; it was the worst. You worked all day doing the same thing. Finally I got a good job—oiling on a crane.

Those jobs were tough to get because the union was very strict, but I was able to work on a permit. I had to ride the street car for an hour to get to the job site on the east side of Cleveland. I was learning how to operate the crane and set steel. The iron workers were not very confident in my ability. The length of the boom on the crane was 90 feet, the legal limit at that time. When you got a steel beam swinging, it was difficult to stop it. When the iron workers would see me get into the cab of the crane, they scrambled down like monkeys. They didn't want anything to do with me.

I was also learning to operate a pile driver; that was really hard work. The only good thing about those jobs was the money. Once we went on strike; and I took the opportunity to go back to Holyoke to visit some of my relatives and friends. A lady there, the mother of the fellow who hit me with the baseball bat, asked me what I was doing and what I was going to do.

"I want to go to college," I told her. She said, "Then what are you doing here?"

That stuck with me as I went back to Cleveland after the strike ended and went back to work. Someone had moved the crane that I was operating and they weren't supposed to do it. I told the supervisor, and the union made the contractor write me a check for six days' pay. I said I didn't want the money, but the shop steward was standing there and then went with me to the bank and made certain I cashed the check. That was the way the union operated. Somebody had moved the crane, so they had to pay me.

One September day in 1946, I went downtown to pick up my paycheck and stopped at a bar to cash the check. I ran into Bill Thiel, an acquaintance of mine It was a Saturday and he was depressed because he was leaving to attend classes at Ohio State in Columbus on Monday. He had rented a double room—only to learn his roommate had decided not to go. He was stuck.

"I'm your new roommate," I told him.

I talked it over with my family, and Frank and Earle and my mother were supportive and said they would take care of the rest of the kids. I quit my job and headed for Columbus. I had no GI papers, I didn't have my high school transcript, I didn't have much idea about what I was doing, but on that Monday morning, I became a student at Ohio State.

Sometimes the decisions you make on the spur of the moment turn out for the best. If I had planned it, had waited until I had everything in place and made certain I was making the right decision, who knows how much longer, if ever, it would have been before I enrolled in college.

Even though I didn't have the GI papers, I was able to talk my way into classes. When I tracked down a copy of my high school transcript, I found out I shouldn't have graduated because I was one credit short.

I wanted to major in radio speech, with a minor in Spanish, so I looked at the obligatory subjects like English and science, and made up my own schedule.

There was an overflow of students, many of them ex-GIs, and in a lot of the classes students had to sit on radiators or the floor or a window sill because there weren't enough chairs. There were 50 or 60 in a classroom designed for half that many. Some of the classes were taught in quonset huts. You either paid attention or you didn't. You either wanted to learn or you didn't.

I had more than one professor who questioned me about what I was doing in class without being officially enrolled.

"Who are you?" they said.

"I'm waiting for my papers."

"You can't come in here until you get your papers," they said. "You can't come in this class."

"But I already paid for this class."

That one usually stumped the professors. "I thought you said you were waiting for your papers?" they said.

"I did, but I paid cash while I was waiting."

"Where's the receipt?" they asked.

"It's in the registrar's office," I said.

Luckily for me, the conversation usually ended there and nobody ever checked it out and learned that I was bluffing. I hadn't paid for any of those classes. My papers finally came through and then I became an official student.

Thiel and I didn't work out as roommates. He met a girl and moved in with her, so I was then paired with an engineering student from Cleveland. We were an unlikely couple. I was getting by with bluffing, and fitting in my homework whenever I could while working and by using my imagination and creativity. He was up until 3 a.m. using a slide rule and an abacus figuring out engineering problems. He flunked out.

Even though my schooling was paid for by the GI Bill, Public Law 16, disabled veteran, I still needed money to live on, which meant constantly juggling two or three jobs again. My first job was at the Big Bear Grocery Store, making 75 cents an hour, working in the vegetable department. Then I found a better job, making a dollar an hour at the Standard Oil gas station on High Street in Olentangy Village. It was hard to get any job back then because people wanted to work and needed to work and were glad to get any job they could. It's not like today when you see signs in the window that stores have jobs open and are looking for people to hire. At the same time there are people who are unemployed or choose to remain on welfare rather than get a job. It doesn't make sense to me.

On Saturdays I worked right up until time for the football games, then ran like hell across the campus to get to the stadium in time for the opening kickoff. I didn't have a car. A lot of times I worked an all-night shift at the gas station, starting at 11 p.m. and getting off at 7 a.m. It gave me time to do my homework, and luckily I was never robbed or shot at. That's a job I don't think I would do today. I also waited tables in Reagan's Restaurant, and the best thing about that job was my meals were included.

Running into people now at a gas station or a restaurant reminds me of those days, and the different way people act now. You never hear please or thank you. In some gas stations you don't have to talk to anybody—you pay at the pump and never go inside. In our society today, people are not forced to interact.

Working people in large cities are cold and unfriendly. They will ring up your sale at the cash register and hand you the change and not even look at you, let alone say thank you. The change might be wrong, also. Life should be a series of meeting people and being kind to each other. My parents taught me to say yes sir, no sir, yes ma'am, no ma'am. It was just a natural way of talking. I still talk that way, and I hope I've taught my kids to do that also.

The worst phrase ever spoken is, "Sorry about that." A waitress will spill coffee on you and say, "sorry about that." That's a real irritant to me when people say it so insincerely. In other words, go screw yourself. Using proper language and being nice to other people are a couple of the things I talk about whenever I'm asked to speak to young people. I'm not a high-flying speaker and I can't talk about the solar system, but I can talk about everyday life. I talk about not cheating and not lying, and I talk about saying please and thank you, being punctual and neat in your appearance. It's surprising, but people never talk to kids about things of that sort when they are in school, so where would they learn it if they don't get it at home? In fact, most kids learn the opposite, how to dress down so they can keep up with their peers.

A man stopped in the gas station one night when I was working. He was in the radio business and said, "You have a terrific voice. You ought to be a sports announcer." I thanked him, and said that was what I was studying in school. He said, "Keep it up and you'll do well." He offered me some advice that I've never forgotten, and that I try to pass on to anybody interested in broadcasting as a career—read out loud as much as possible. It's one thing to see a word in print and recognize and understand its meaning. It's another thing to have to say the word. It helps when pronouncing difficult names as well. I've always appreciated people who offered me encouragement and advice of that sort.

We did a lot of writing in my speech classes—dramas, comedies, news programs and the like. During the fall of 1948, when the Indians and the Boston Braves were playing in the World Series, one of my assignments was to write a World Series preview. Part of it read,

> "This is Frank Bennett with a cheery 'good evening' from the Hotel Bradford in Boston, Mass. Boston is the home of Braves Field where the first game of the 1948 World Series will be played tomorrow afternoon. Baseball has really taken over this city. The home for the aged is deserted, the sick have left their hospital beds and four-month-old babies have started to walk, as everybody heads for the ballpark to watch the Cleveland Indians tangle with the Boston Braves. Temperance leaders have lost their temper, barbers in their excitement have cut everything but their prices. Everyone is being carried away by their enthusiasm over the World Series. Everyone, that is, except the Boston Red Sox. The reason for the lack of joy on the part of the Red Sox? Here he is, Manager Lou Boudreau of the Cleveland Indians. . ."

The instructor wrote next to my script, "good stuff." We also had to write quiz shows and other dummy scripts, practical assignments that helped when I actually went on the air for the first time, working at WOSU, the university station, in 1948.

Things were different then. Now people have a lot of practical experience before they ever go on the air commercially. There are broadcasting classes with mock interviews, play-by-play and other assignments. When I went on the air to do a sports show at

WOSU, I had never done a sports show before. When I did a basket-ball game, it was the first time I ever did play-by-play. The same with football. I didn't know how to do those things, I just did them. It was the ultimate example of learning by experience, and I'm glad there were no tape recorders around to immortalize how bad some of those first shows and broadcasts must have been.

The way to improve was to keep doing it, getting as much experience as possible. That's still true today. Other ingredients needed for success in radio and television are luck and timing. You can't get a job until you have experience, and you can't get experience until you have a job.

I was in the WOSU office one day, typing a story, when a fellow walked in and started to talk with my co-worker, Bill Hein. The newcomer told Bill about a job available at WCOL, a commercial radio station in Columbus. I was half listening to their conversation.

After the visitor left, Hein turned to me and said, "He was talking to me. Mind your own business and stay out of this." If he had not said that, I wouldn't have done a thing. But his remark spurred me into action.

When I went to work that night at the gas station, I called WCOL and asked for the name of the program director. His name was Ed Sprague, and they gave me his home telephone number, and I called him. It was 11:30 at night.

"I understand you have a job opening," I said.

"We do."

"May I audition?" I asked.

"Yes you may," he said. "When can you do that?"

"Tomorrow," I said.

"That's fine," he said. "What time will you be there?"

"What time do you get to work?" I asked.

"8 o'clock," he said.

"I'll be there waiting for you."

Looking back on it, I was fortunate he didn't hang up on me. I didn't think about disturbing him at home. I just wanted the job and didn't want Bill or anybody else getting a chance to audition before I did.

I worked at the gas station until 7:30 a.m., and was at the radio station waiting for Sprague when he got to work. I did the audition, went to my classes, and was on the air that night doing a sports show on WCOL. I've seen Bill Hein since then, he was selling insurance in Buffalo, and he never knew he kick-started my professional career.

WCOL was not broadcasting sports at that time, but the general manager decided he wanted to carry Ohio State basketball. Any station that wanted to do the games could get the rights for the university events. There were several others already airing the games, but the GM thought it could be profitable. He wanted me to do the play-by-play, and I did. I didn't know how to do it, but when the game started, I was at the microphone, doing play-by-play for the first time.

Ohio State and DePaul; I'll never forget the starting lineups—Schnitker, Donham, Taylor, Burkholder and Brown for Ohio State; Leahy, Campa, Pavalonas, Vuckovich and Govaderica for DePaul.

Years later, I was at a Super Bowl dinner in New Orleans and was seated next to Ray Meyer, the longtime DePaul basketball coach. I said "Ray, do you know one of your teams I really liked? That 1949 team of Leahy, Campa, Pavalonas, Vuckovich and Govaderica."

"Damn," he said, "How do you remember those names?" I told him why I was able to remember that lineup.

I was still a student at the time, and everyone in our class knew I was doing the game that night. The assignment for everybody else in that class was to listen to me and critique my broadcast the next morning. The professor's name was Dick Mall, who later became the head of alumni affairs at Ohio State.

Both teams used a fast-break offense, and they played about eight minutes before either team called a time out. I said, "DePaul calls time out, thank God." The use of that phrase was one of the criticisms the next morning.

The critiques were honest and helpful, but I'll never forget what the professor said to me: "You'd better find something else to do for a living." I knew he was wrong. I was still chasing my dream. The last time I saw him I was on my way to New Orleans to televise Super Bowl IV for CBS. We both laughed.

I graduated from Ohio State after three years and three months in December 1949 with a BA degree. Then WCOL decided to pick up the broadcasts of the Columbus Redbirds, a Triple A baseball affiliate of the St. Louis Cardinals. Nobody was broadcasting their games at the time, and there wasn't much interest in the team.

We had to get announcer approval from Al Bannister, the general manager of the Redbirds. For the audition, he handed me a copy of *The Sporting News'* baseball guide from 1949. In the back pages was a play-by-play account of the playoff game between the Indians and Red Sox in 1948. I was conversant with both of those teams and knew a lot about each team's history.

Bannister put me in the ticket office, where there was a hand-held intercom microphone. I held the book in one hand, the microphone in the other and recreated the game doing the play-by-play for three innings, also keeping score. The only information in the book was the result of what each batter had done, so I had to imagine the balls and strikes, the details of each play and make it sound like the game was in progress. That assignment was a lot harder than actually broadcasting a game.

After those three innings, I stepped out of the office where Bannister and others were listening. He said, "Keep going."

I went back into the ticket office and did a few more innings, went back out to see what he had to say. This time he said, "Finish the game." I went back into the ticket office and finished the game, and when I walked back out again, Bannister said, "You've got the job."

The job sent me on my first trip to Florida for spring training, to Daytona Beach, where the Columbus and Rochester teams were training at the time.

While I was in college, I had met a girl named Alyce Larson. We had some of the same classes, and we started dating. Previously, I had often asked my mother, "Who do you think will be the first of your sons to get married, Frank, Earle or me?" She always said, "You." I always said "No way," but she was right. With the help of $100 she sent me, Alyce and I ran away to Kentucky and were married in 1948. Our oldest daughter, Beverly, was born 10 months later and the three of us lived in one room in the same house where I had been living. The lady of the house, Dora Soler, was Spanish. She had raised kids of her own and knew all the tricks. She really helped us, because Beverly was a handful. Some babies are calm, others are not. Beverly wasn't calm.

We had very little money when we left for Florida by train. The club was going to pick up the bill for my hotel room, and we were getting a per diem of $8 per day.

No sooner had we arrived in Daytona Beach when Alyce's asthma acted up. The climate didn't suit her at all. She couldn't stay. I put her and Beverly back on the train to Columbus—and handed her a bag of candy bars for the trip home. I didn't have any money to give her. She made the trip from Florida to Columbus with the candy bars and the baby.

The Redbirds were playing a game one day in Sanford, Florida, and I wanted to go down to the bullpen to talk to one of the pitchers. The bullpen was in front of the bleachers. The only way I could get there was to go into the bleachers, which I did.

There was a sign that said "Colored Only" but I paid no attention. I started to talk through the fence to the player, when a sheriff came up and tapped me on the shoulder. "You can't stay here," he said, to which I naturally asked, "Why not?"

He turned and pointed, "Didn't you see that sign?"

This guy was big enough to be a sheriff, and I wasn't cut out to be a hero, so I left, but I was shocked. I was astonished that this sort of segregation was still going on in 1950. We had no African-American players on the Columbus team. I had some friends who were African-American from college, including the daughter of Olympian Jesse Owens. Jesse later became a good friend.

There were still problems with black players and segregation in Florida for several years after that. The black players in the Cardinals' farm system were not allowed to stay in the same hotel as the white players, and that even happened with the big league club for years in St. Petersburg. Gussie Busch put an end to it, finding a hotel where everyone was welcome and made certain that all the players stayed there.

Back in 1950, preparing to do my first baseball season, I asked a lot of questions and sought out as much advice as possible. Rollie Hemsley was the Columbus manager; it was his first managing job. He had been a catcher in the big leagues for a long time, and spent some of his years with the Cleveland Indians, where he caught some of Bob Feller's pitching gems.

Hemsley pondered the question about what I should or shouldn't say during the broadcast, then offered this advice that has always stayed with me: "If somebody doesn't catch the ball, and you couldn't have caught it either, keep your mouth shut. If they didn't catch it and you could have caught it, give 'em hell." It's still a practical philosophy.

One of the things I learned early about being a baseball announcer was that you had more than one boss. You work for the radio station, and you also work for the team. Any time either of them wants you to do something, you have to do it.

One thing Al Bannister wanted from me that spring was an interview with Ted Williams, because the Red Sox were going to stop in Columbus to play an exhibition game on their way north to open the season. That was at a time when Williams was feuding with the press, and he wasn't talking to anybody. I prevailed on the traveling secretary of the Red Sox, Tom Dowd, and explained my situation. I needed an interview, it was my first job, I was an ex-GI—all the sympathetic buttons I knew how to push. Dowd told Williams.

Williams had a routine he followed when he first came on the field. He carried four bats, and flipped them in the air. He would look at the waiting reporters, who were hoping to talk to him, and said "Morning guys, no interviews," and take off for left field. He told Dowd that after he did that one morning, and was safely away from the other reporters, he would take off his cap as a signal for me, and I was to come out and he would do the interview.

The modern small tape recorders had yet to be invented. I had a wire recorder, which was in a big suitcase and weighed about 50 pounds. The morning we set for the interview, I stood there and waited. Williams tipped his cap, and I ran out to the left field corner lugging the wire recorder.

Interviewing was not my strongest suit, but Williams must have felt for me. He talked for half an hour. It wasn't an interview, it was a speech. I recorded it, and came back with the goods.

On another occasion, I was fortunate that a coach I was interviewing was an understanding person. Tippy Dye was the basketball coach at Ohio State, and the team was getting ready to play Minnesota to decide the Big 10 championship. Dye stopped his practice and did a half-hour interview for me with his players. Oh-oh, I forgot to push the record button. We did a half-hour, and there was nothing on the tape. I had to tell him that I blew it.

He said, "I gave you half an hour and there's nothing on the tape? Now you want another half hour?"

He said, "Let's do it," and they gave me another half-hour interview. I don't know how many others would have been that gracious and understanding.

Perhaps Dye had a soft spot in his heart for me because I had tried out for his basketball team as a walk-on player. I was a lefthanded shooter. We were practicing in the tryouts one day and were to run a play where I brought the ball down court, and was supposed to use a bounce pass to get the ball into the pivot. Everybody on defense knew what play we were running. They were sagging and falling off, and I couldn't get the ball in to the center. I shot the ball, and made the bucket.

Dye blew his whistle and stopped play. "You know what we're supposed to be doing here." he said. "Do it again."

I came down court again, and the same thing happened. I couldn't get the ball in to the center because the defense was sagging all around him, so I shot the ball again and made the basket.

He blew his whistle. "That's it," he said, motioning me off the court, ending my basketball career. I wasn't very good anyhow.

There was another interview I'll always remember. One of the shows I did for WCOL was a big band show, which we did live on Saturday mornings from Lazarus Department Store. I opened the show by saying, "Hello ladies and gentlemen from Lazarus Department Store in downtown Columbus, Ohio. Lazarus presents the music of Glen Gray and his Rippling Rhythm Review."

We had bands like Glen Gray, Shep Fields, Jimmy Dorsey, Sammy Kaye and others. There were a hundred big bands. Stan Kenton came to town, and he had developed a new kind of jazz. I had to interview him, and he was not very cooperative. I had a heck of a time trying to comprehend what I was trying to accomplish in the interview and he wasn't any help. It was one of the worst moments of my life. It was so bad I had to ask another announcer who was there to join in the discussion. He did, and together we finished the interview.

Later, I tried to figure out what had happened and why I couldn't do a good job of interviewing Kenton. Now, interviewing people is one of my strengths as a broadcaster rather than a weakness. Before every interview I   conduct, I determine what I wish to accomplish. I think about it long and hard and know what I want to ask. The key is to listen to the interviewee. If one has a prepared list of questions and just reads them off and doesn't listen and respond to what the person is saying, the interview will be a failure. You must pick up on what is said and not have any preconceived idea about where the interview is going. I never know how an interview is going to end, but I always know how I'm going to start it.

One of the pitchers on the Columbus team in 1950 was Harvey Haddix, and I always thought he was going to be more successful in the major leagues than he turned out to be. He was dominating in Triple A, and was one of the reasons we had a good team. We finished third in the regular season, but got hot in the playoffs, upsetting Minneapolis and Indianapolis to win the championship, then went on to win the Little World Series against the champion of the International League, Baltimore.

Triple A baseball at the time was a lot better then than it is today. There were only 16 teams in the major leagues, and that meant that a lot of really fine players couldn't crack the big-league rosters. For example, in 1951, the Yankees' Triple A team was in Kansas City, and they had a lineup that included Mickey Mantle, Jackie Jensen, Bob Cerv, Elston Howard, Vic Power, Moose Skowron and others, and they finished third. That's how good professional baseball was then.

It was obvious Mantle was going to be a terrific player, but one day in Columbus he faltered. He was playing centerfield, and the bases were loaded with two outs, late in the game. There was a fly ball to deep center. Mantle had his sunglasses down, but he dropped the ball and three runs scored. Mickey had a tantrum. He threw his sunglasses over the fence, then his glove, and then his hat went over the fence, too. I don't know what he would have tried to toss over next, but by then the manager got to him and walked around with his arm draped over Mickey's shoulder. He calmed him down, then moved Jensen to center and Mantle to right. That was about the only thing I ever saw Mantle do wrong.

Willie Mays played in that league—briefly—on his way up to the Giants, and there also was something special about his ability that was easy to see. He was in spring training with the Minneapolis team, and one day I was sitting next to Halsey Hall, a newspaper reporter-broadcaster from Minneapolis. He told me before the game, "Jack, you're going to see one of the greatest players who has ever come along in the game of baseball, that kid out there in centerfield, Mays."

During the game somebody hit a ball into left center. Mays ran over, planted his foot in the middle of the wooden fence, caught the ball over his left shoulder, did a somersault off the fence and threw a strike to second base. I turned to Halsey and said, "I believe you." When the Giants called Mays up he was hitting .477.

1951 was the first year I learned how long a baseball season can be when you're working for a lousy team. We lost 101 games and finished 42 1/2 games out of first place. For me the highlight of the year was an exhibition game we played against a semi-pro team at the state mental hospital in Chillicothe, Ohio. I played second base for the Redbirds, and if you want to get technical about it, it was the only time I ever played as a professional. I had a chance or two, but I don't remember whether I got a hit or not, so I probably didn't. The shortstop in that game for the Redbirds was Fred McAlister, who later became the successful scouting director of the Cardinals for a long time. Harry Walker was the manager.

About the middle of a year like that is when you start looking forward to the football season. I did football at WCOL, so I was doing the baseball, football and basketball games, a record show in the morning, a classical music show on Sunday morning, making sales calls and doing public appearances, for $5,200 a year, $100 a week.

I have never cheated on my expense reports. I turned in a report for a football trip one time and it came out to an even $100. The station manager looked at it and said, "Either I'm getting screwed, or you're screwing yourself. No expense account ever comes out to $100 even. Make out a new one."

I made the new one for $99.50. He said, "I thought you'd make it for $100.50." When you're making all that money, $100 a week, 50 cents is not that important.

There was a sports writer in Columbus at that time who turned in an expense report to the newspaper at the same time his expenses were being picked up by the ballclub. He was married, but was involved with another woman. He needed the extra money and didn't think they would catch him. They did, and fired him. Most recently, the UCLA basketball coach was fired for allegedly cheating on an expense account. It's crazy. People lose $100,000-a-year jobs because of a phony $25 taxi fare receipt. Human nature, I guess. It happens all the time.

ề₀

Broadcasting football games was fun. Ohio State had won the Rose Bowl game following the 1949 season, and was trying to go back again as the Big 10 champ. Heading into the final game of the regular season, at home against Michigan, an OSU victory would accomplish that goal.

Michigan is Ohio State's biggest rival, then and now, and more times than not the conference championship and trip to the Rose Bowl depends on the outcome of the game. The night before the game I was in a restaurant and heard somebody was looking for tickets. I had two, which somebody in my family was going to use, but someone offered $100 each for them, the same as a two-week paycheck, so I sold them.

The game was scheduled for 1 p.m., and the weather forecast was OK. Athletic Director Dick Larkin checked the tarpaulin that covered the field at 11 a.m. and everything was in good shape. Two hours later, it was another story.

A big storm blew in, and there was almost a foot of snow covering that tarp, which was now frozen to the ground. Ohio State wanted to postpone the game, but Fritz Crisler, the athletic director at Michigan, wouldn't agree.

The spotting board which I made up for the games indicating the names and positions of the players had some mechanical wheels. You couldn't have the window closed in the broadcast booth because it fogged over, so it remained open, and with the snow blowing in, the little wheels on my spotting board froze and it was useless.

It didn't really matter. The field was covered with so much snow you couldn't see the yard markers and couldn't tell where the sidelines and the endzones were. Nobody ran or passed the ball, both sides punted it back and forth, hoping for good field position. There were 42 punts in the game. Michigan didn't make a first down, didn't complete a pass and didn't kick a field goal and yet won the game 9-3, knocking the Buckeyes out of the Rose Bowl.

Vic Janowicz kicked a field goal to put Ohio State up 3-0, but Michigan blocked a punt for a safety, then blocked another and recovered it in the endzone for a touchdown.

Watching Janowicz play was a thrill. He won the Heisman Trophy in 1950 as a junior. A single-wing tailback, he ran and passed the ball. He was also the punter and placekicker, the kick return man and played safety on defense. I saw Tom Harmon play a few games in college, but Janowicz was the greatest college player I ever saw. After his senior year, he went to three postseason All-Star games. He was the MVP as a quarterback in one of the games, the MVP as a tailback in a single wing in another, and the MVP as a halfback in the third game.

Janowicz played baseball in high school but never in college. He signed with the Pirates after college as a catcher and played a few games in the big leagues before he went on to a career in the NFL with the Redskins.

There was a game at Sportsman's Park when Janowicz was the catcher. A foul ball was hit behind the plate, and he went back and didn't come close to catching it. Another foul ball went up, and a leather-lunged guy familiar with Janowicz' football career yelled, "Call for a fair catch." He dropped that one too.

There were some other Buckeyes who stood out to me, people like Dick Schnitker and Fred Taylor. Schnitker was an All-America basketball player. As the football team prepared for the Rose Bowl after the 1949 season, some of their receivers were injured. The coaches asked Schnitker to play, even though he hadn't played football since high school. He caught some passes, one for a touchdown, and helped the Buckeyes win the game. Taylor was on the basketball team, and we became good friends. He later became the coach there for a long time. Ohio State made the NIT in New York one year, and Taylor had a great game against City College of New York. He was making moves, faking one way, going the other and playing like he was the only one on the court. He had the biggest game of his life. Later he learned several players on the CCNY team had conspired to throw the game.

While working at WCOL they told me to go see a running back at Central High School in Columbus. I went and saw this red-headed kid running all over the field and said to myself, "He'll never do that in college." How wrong I was—It was Howard "Hop-Along" Cassady, another Heisman Trophy winner, in 1955.

It turned out the "Blizzard bowl" game against Michigan was the final game of Wes Fesler's coaching career at Ohio State. There was a big debate about who the school should hire as its new coach, and *The Columbus Dispatch* was endorsing Paul Brown, then coaching the Cleveland Browns in the NFL.

I didn't think the newspaper should dictate who the school should hire, so I editorialized on the radio saying that the university, not the newspaper, should make the choice. Woody Hayes was the coach at Miami of Ohio and Ohio State was interested in him. I didn't know Hayes, but I indicated that I thought he would be a good candidate.

Some of the Buckeye fans didn't like it that I had taken a stand against the newspaper and found out where I lived and threw garbage on my front porch. The *Dispatch* really ran Columbus, and people didn't like it when somebody opposed its view. It wasn't long after that when the Golden Gloves matches were held in Columbus, with the newspaper the main sponsor. I went to the fights and showed my pass, and the guards wouldn't let me in. I bought a ticket, went to the fights, went back on the radio the next night and blasted the newspaper again.

Hayes got the job, and when the football season began in 1951, I needed to learn more about his coaching style so I signed up for a class he was teaching. Most of the students were players on the team.

I had never played football as I had baseball and basketball, and didn't understand the intricacies of the game. I was sitting in the back of the class, a non-football player who was six or seven years older than most of the other students. Hayes spotted me.

"Who are you?" he demanded.

Those in the class expected an ugly confrontation. Hayes' fiery reputation was established, and the football players expected him to come down hard on me.

I told him who I was and explained that I broadcast the games on WCOL and had enrolled in the class "to learn what you are going to try to do."

"TRY TO DO," he yelled back at me.

He paused for a moment, calmed down, and said, "OK, but don't miss a class. If you miss one class, you're out."

That was the beginning of my friendship with Hayes. I worked with him on his radio show, which we taped on Friday nights. This was an era when communication was not as sophisticated as it is now, so after we taped the show, I had 30 duplicates made, wrapped each tape and addressed it and delivered them to the Greyhound bus station.

They went to radio stations in Springfield, Lima, Cleveland, all over Ohio. The stations played the tape before the game the next afternoon. That took care of my Friday nights during the football season—I did all the work, and Hayes got all the money.

One night I was conducting the interview, and I made a rather innocuous statement which I expected him to pick up on. I said something like, "So the teams are rather even and the one that makes the fewest mistakes is going to win."

He said sarcastically, "Very sound deduction."

I said, "Wait a minute. Stop the tape. What are you trying to do? This is your program, not mine, you're getting the money for this."

He didn't understand what I was talking about, so we played the tape back. He said, "Oh yeah, I see what you mean." From that point on we were the best of friends.

Years later, when I was working on the Grandstand show on NBC, Ohio State was getting ready for another trip to the Rose Bowl. The weather was brutal in Columbus, and the team was working indoors in the field house. We went there to do an interview with Hayes for a story, and the cameraman snuck in while Hayes was talking to the players. Soon he had that camera right up in Hayes' face. The coach stopped talking and turned on the cameraman and said, "What are you doing?"

The players expected a tirade, but the cameraman said, "I'm here with Jack Buck." Hayes turned around, and when he saw me, he said very nicely to the cameraman, "OK."

In the Gator Bowl years later, when Hayes took a swing at a Clemson player returning an interception, (the incident that cost Hayes his job), I was able to dismiss it and not let it change my opinion of the man I knew. He was frustrated, and the player got close to the sideline and Hayes took a swing at him. It wasn't as though he shot him, and he later apologized.

It was time for him to leave anyhow. In my opinion, he was the perfect man and the perfect coach, and one of the reasons was that he never compromised. To me the biggest failure people make is when they do compromise—on their character, their principles, their work ethic, their honesty, whatever. Once you start to compromise there's a soft spot in your makeup and it erodes like the bank of a stream. Hayes never compromised. To me, he was almost perfect.

He was always his own man, always the same person. He treated his wife Anne and his family well, and his job and his family were the most important things in the world to him.

ॐ

Baseball, football and basketball made my job fun. The baseball team told me I was doing a good job. We had a radio appreciation night and drew 14,000. That was huge for Columbus. I thought the team was going to come back in 1952, and we wouldn't have to suffer through another 101-loss season.

Then everything changed. I was told the boss at the radio station wanted to see me. Always the optimist, I thought maybe he was going to give me a raise. Wrong again, Jack.

"The station has been sold," he told me. "There will be no more sports. We're going to be a rock-and-roll station. You're fired."

I was 27 years old, with a wife, three kids and a mortgage. Now what?

6

From Television to the Majors

I was unemployed for one day before getting an offer from another Columbus radio station, WHKC. It included a $1,500 a year raise, to $7,000 a year.

It was only a verbal agreement, and when I went back the next day to sign the contract, the general manager of the station said there was a problem. The station was owned by WHK in Cleveland, and the management there would only approve a salary of $6,000.

I asked if I could use the telephone, and dialed the number for WBNS-TV in Columbus.

"Dick Borel, please." I said.

After a few seconds, he answered the phone.

"This is Jack Buck," I said.

He replied, "I've been waiting for you to call." He knew I had been fired.

We set up a meeting. I hung up the phone and turned to the general manager of the radio station and said, "Thank you, I'll not be working here," and left.

The next night I was on the air on WBNS-TV, making $8,000. Another classic case of good timing and good luck. If the boss at WHK hadn't tried to chisel me out of $1,500, I would have stayed on radio, but because he did, I was working in television.

This was 1952, and television was in its infancy. It was not nearly as sophisticated as now, and there weren't many people who had a lot of knowledge about what they were doing. That helped me feel more comfortable, but I think even in those early days of TV, I knew I was going to be the sort of broadcaster who would be better off on radio.

Everybody did a variety of jobs at the station, which aired on Channel 10. My main jobs were a nightly sports show, called "Buck Eyes Sports", a rather clever play-on-words considering my last name and the nickname of the Ohio State teams, and a morning variety show. I also did a lot of commercials, voice over slides.

We had another sportscaster at the station, Earl Flora. Every night, five minutes after my show, he came on and did a sports commentary program called "Flora Scope on Sports." My family and I lived in an apartment that was literally two minutes away from WBNS, and every night I would dash out of the station following my show, zoom home and be sitting in front of the television when Earl came on. That was the routine I followed one night, and as I slumped into the cushions of my couch, I heard the off-camera announcer say, "It's time for Earl Flora, and Flora Scope on Sports. Here substituting for Earl Flora is Jack Buck."

Then I remembered I was supposed to stay there and do his show that night. I could just imagine the scene at the station as people were scurrying around trying to find me, and didn't know what to do.

The announcer said, "one moment please," before he finally said something about technical difficulties and they put some other program on the air. Would I be fired again? Fortunately, the station manager was understanding or they might have ended up with Jonathan Winters doing the sportscasts.

Winters, now one of the most well-known comedians in the world, was just starting out as an announcer at WBNS. He had a five-minute comedy show, and also did a lot of the voice-overs on commercials. That was where he developed some of the characters and voices that made him such a star later on. He is the most hilarious person I've ever met. He can make you laugh so hard your jaws ache.

The problem we had at WBNS was trying not to laugh at what Winters did and said. We had an announcers booth that was six feet square. When we had two 30-second commercials running back-to-back, he would do one and I would do the other. The station had a policy that if anybody laughed while they were on the air, the person who caused him to laugh would get the axe.

I did commercials for Omar Bakeries, and Winters was in my ear the entire time, acting out everything I said.

"When your friendly Omar baker walks up to your house and knocks on the door," I said, while Winters whispered walking and knocking sounds in my ear. "And rings your bell," and Winters would go "ding-dong." I'm telling you it was tough. I knew if I broke up he would get fired. It was hard to keep a straight face and get through those 30 seconds.

We had a ball. His comedy show was sponsored by Gambrinus Beer. They had a pilsner glass they used for commercials. They didn't pour the beer; the glass was painted, and they had a little wad of cotton sitting on top to make it look like foam. One night Winters walked up to the camera and went "poof" and blew the cotton right into the lens of the camera.

"And have a good glass of Gambrinus Beer," he said as everything went to black.

One night he was getting ready to go on the air, and he had no routine and no idea what he was going to say. He said, "Buck give me something to do."

I told him to pretend he was an attendant in a gas station and a car came in that had electric windows. "OK, OK," he said. "That's good."

He went on the air doing a little pantomime. "Fill it up, sir?" and then the driver supposedly raised the windows, pinning Winters' fingers. He was knocking on the windows with his thumbs. You had to be there.

From the beginning you could tell that Winters was unique. He went to New York, where Mickey Spillane, the author of the Mike Hammer books, met him at a cocktail party and became his benefactor, getting him jobs, and Winters' career took off.

A while later we ran into each other. He had a pocketful of checks and $100 bills stuffed in his pockets. He and his wife were snarling at each other, and I knew that he had been caught up in the show business lifestyle. He later had a drinking problem, but received the help he needed and everything turned out well.

Winters was a big baseball fan, a Cincinnati rooter, and we both played on the television station's softball team. Once we played at the state mental institution. I was playing first base, Winters was catching. We were ahead by a run and they had runners on second and third. The batter hit a ground ball to me, and I made a perfect throw home. The ball went through Winters' legs, ran up the screen, two runs scored and we lost the game.

"You dumb SOB Winters," I yelled.

Winters turned to the inmates who were seated in the grandstand behind third base.

"Did you hear what he called me?" Winters said. "He thinks I'm Yogi Berra. Am I Yogi Berra? Noooo."

I thought he was going to start a riot. He had people jumping up and down and yelling at me, pointing at me, and I finally had to clear out of there before something nasty happened.

After he moved to Los Angeles, Winters became a fan of the Los Angeles Rams, who were playing their home games in the Coliseum. I knew where his seats were, and every time I was there doing a broadcast, I would always stop and say hello on my way up to the booth from the field before the game. He was always an entertainer.

There was a large portable hot dog stand set up outside the press gate, and Winters would always go there before the game and wear some sort of costume. Whatever he wore indicated who he was. If he showed up wearing a jacket and cap, he was an English Navy captain for that day and would put on a show. The next week he wore a pith helmet and shorts and acted as if he had just returned from Africa. It was humor that nobody had seen or heard before. There's no one like Jonathan Winters.

A few years ago, the Cardinals were playing in Los Angeles one night and the Dodgers were way ahead. Winters came into our booth, and I introduced him on the air as Whip Willis, a former big-league pitcher, and he went into a routine that cracked up our audience. I never said who he really was, and there might have been some people listening who thought this was really Whip Willis. Twenty years later, we still play that tape at KMOX.

ॐ

Bob Kline was a coach with the Columbus Redbirds. He visited the prisoners at the Ohio State Penitentiary, which was in downtown Columbus. Kline used to take softball teams to play against the prisoners, and I hooked up with him for some of those games, then took over the arrangements when Klein left to become a scout. Some of the inmates got to know me, and they also were familiar with me because of my broadcasts on radio and television.

On Halloween night in 1952, I received a phone call from Ralph Alvis, the warden of the penitentiary. Some of the convicts wanted to talk to me, they had complaints they didn't believe would be heard by anyone else. Alvis indicated the prisoners might be getting ready to riot, so I drove to the prison.

I walked into the prison yard, and selected a group of cons to talk about the problems. They had concerns about meals and yard time. We were having a frank discussion, and I thought I was making some progress when we were interrupted.

My past run-ins with the *Columbus Dispatch* over the Woody Hayes hiring and the Golden Gloves matches, showed me how much the newspaper ran that town. When a reporter at the newspaper learned there was a potential riot at the penitentiary, he showed up and wanted to come into the yard to talk to the inmates. The warden wouldn't let him in, so the reporter, Red Foley, called his publisher, who in turn called the warden. In Foley came.

He walked up to the group, and said the worst thing he could possibly have said: "OK, who's the ringleader?" I knew he had just blown the whole thing wide open. One of the inmates looked at me and said, "Mr. Buck, head for the gate, and take this jerk with you. I'll make sure you both get out."

An hour later the prison was on fire. Four buildings were destroyed, including the hospital and the personnel building, which also housed the commissary. The stained glass windows in the chapel were smashed before that building was set on fire. The National Guard was called out, and order was never really completely restored for several days. Before it was over, one inmate was shot and killed and three others were wounded.

I don't know what would have happened had that newspaper reporter not interrupted our discussion in the yard, but I honestly think had he not shown up I might have helped prevent the riot that night.

When I moved to St. Louis, I knew how much entertainment meant to the prisoners in a penitentiary, so I arranged to occasionally take softball teams down to the Menard penitentiary in Chester, Illinois. Davey Bold, a comedian, and Sammy Gardner, a clarinet player, and others were with us and they would play on the KMOX team and then entertain the inmates with comedy and music. It was always a worthwhile trip.

I chartered the bus and we drove down there and spent the day. One time, one of the inmates beat out an infield hit and one of his pals in the grandstand yelled, "LeRoy, if you could have run like that when the police were chasing you, you wouldn't be in here."

I was at home one night in November 1965 when I received a call from KMOX. A riot had broken out at Menard, and some guards were being held as prisoners. I had become friends with Ross Randolph when he had been the warden there, before he was named the Director of Public Safety in Illinois. He wanted me to come down to see if I could be of any help. KMOX obtained a helicopter and I flew to Menard, landing on the softball field. By the time I arrived it was over. Three guards had been stabbed to death, six had been wounded and two others had been taken hostage but were later released.

I was in the warden's office when he had told some of the families that their husbands or fathers had just been killed. They took the four ringleaders and put them in solitary confinement.

Reporters were arriving from all over Illinois and Missouri, and Randolph said to me, "Is there anything I can do for you?"

I said, "I'd like to interview those guys."

With a couple of goons, inmates who work with the prison guards, I went down to solitary, which they called "the hole."

I did the interview, and those prisoners acted as though nothing had happened. Just two hours earlier they had killed three people. Their pulse rate was the same, and they knew those guards were dead. Those inmates believed that those guards deserved to be killed.

Randolph had always been against capital punishment. There is an electric chair at Menard, and Illinois has the death penalty. At the end of that long night, an exhausted Randolph looked at me and said, "Jack, I would pull the switch myself." That night influenced my feelings regarding capital punishment. One might think he is very much against it, but if that someone's wife or kid is killed, it might be a different story.

Morris Shenker was a well-known defense attorney in St. Louis, and I once interviewed him on KMOX. I said, "Morris, the next time you defend a murderer, and he gets life and gets out in eight years, I'm gonna do you a favor."

He was waiting for what was coming next and I said, "I'm gonna buy that man a house, right next door to you."

It makes a difference, doesn't it? He wanted to help turn a murderer lose, but he certainly didn't want him living next door.

Not doing sports play-by-play in 1952 made me think perhaps I might end up with television as my career, but fate intervened.

The baseball play-by-play broadcaster in Rochester, Ed Edwards, had been speaking at a banquet and told a dirty story. The general manager—a person who would turn out to be a long-time friend, Bing Devine—fired him on the spot, took him to the stadium that night after the banquet and wrote him his final paycheck.

Devine knew Al Bannister from their association with the Cardinals, and he called and asked Al if he knew of any broadcasters who were available. Bannister liked me, and he gave Devine my name. Devine called and asked me to come to Rochester to audition for the job.

I had to do the same thing I had done in Columbus, recreate a game from a box score and play-by-play sheet. I got the job, I got another raise—this time to $10,000—and I needed the money, because by then we had four kids, Beverly, Jack Jr., Christine, and Bonnie. We loaded the four kids in the 1950 Plymouth. I had bought the car new when I was 26 years old; it was the first car anybody in my family ever owned. We headed to Rochester. It was 1953.

The sponsor for the broadcasts in Rochester was going to be Old Topper Beer and Ale, and I was going to be their spokesman. Just before the season started, Anheuser-Busch bought the Cardinals, and the Columbus and Rochester farm teams were included in the deal. Budweiser then became the sponsor instead of Old Topper. That helped me get the tryout for the Cardinals. If Old Topper had been the sponsor that year in Rochester, I don't think that would have happened. The timing was exquisite.

An added assignment was broadcasting the games of the Rochester Royals of the NBA. We didn't travel to the away games, so I recreated them off the Western Union ticker just as we did baseball. I never heard of anyone else re-creating professional basketball games.

When recreating a game, an announcer is totally dependent on the person sending the information over Western Union from the ballpark or arena. Some were good, some were horrible. Bill Seltzer was the Western Union operator in St. Louis, and he knew baseball and was very good. A lot of times, the information was either inadequate or incomplete and that made it really tough. I learned to become very creative.

Sometimes a report would come in, "Jones flied to center. After three, no score," and you knew of only two outs. You didn't know who had batted and what happened, so you had to wait until the next inning to see who led off, then you knew who made the last out. There was a lot of vamping. One thing I learned was never to say that the weather was perfect, because I never knew when the ticker was going to break down or I'd get some bad information, so I was always capable of making it rain. Players developed a lot of cramps that they never actually experienced.

On the air one time I said that catcher Bill Sarni had been hit by a foul tip. I was stalling for time. The trainer came out to check him, and so forth. His wife was listening at home as I re-created the game. She called him that night after the game and said, "How's your finger?" He didn't know what she was talking about. "You got hit by a foul tip," she said. Sarni later confronted me and wanted me to pay for the long-distance call because I was the one who said he had been injured.

Montreal and Ottawa were in the International League then, and you could always count on getting some bad information from those games, because most of the Western Union operators there spoke French and didn't know much about baseball. For some reason, it always seemed to rain a lot when Rochester was playing in Montreal and Ottawa.

Bing Devine knew how valuable newspaper coverage of his Redwings was, how important it was for selling tickets. He was always supportive of the newspaper people and made certain they were treated well and received all of the information they needed. He had the same approach later when he moved to St. Louis and became general manager of the Cardinals, and later when he ran the Mets in New York.

One night I was re-creating a game from Montreal and according to the telegraph operator, the game ended with Tom Burgess making a leaping catch against the fence to preserve a Redwings victory. The next day, Matt Jackson wrote a column in the *Times-Union* newspaper saying that you couldn't believe what you heard on the radio. I had called the catch sensational, and he wrote that it was only an ordinary catch, according to his reporter who was covering the game in person.

When the club came home, some of the players told me it was one of the darnedest catches they had ever seen. They thought Burgess was going to go through the fence. They didn't know how he managed to hold onto the baseball. I asked one more player for confirmation, and he said, "I'll tell you something else. Don't say I told you, but that writer wasn't even at the game. He was with his girlfriend."

During the broadcast that night, I said, "Please stay tuned at the end of this first inning because I have something I want to tell you about the column in the newspaper written by Matt Jackson." At the end of the inning I told the story, ending with the kicker, "So you can't believe what you read in the newspaper."

Bing went nuts. He didn't want his broadcaster picking a fight with a newspaper that he was counting on for support and to give publicity for the team so he could sell tickets. The newspaper fired the reporter. I explained it all to Bing and that was the end of it.

Nobody has ever told me what to say or not to say on a broadcast with regard to the playing of the game. However, one time after I joined the Cardinals, I received a call from Devine after doing a broadcast from Wrigley Field in Chicago. It was a cold, blustery day with the wind whipping off Lake Michigan directly into the broadcast booth. I talked all day about how cold it was.

When Bing called, he said, "I caught pneumonia listening to you this afternoon." He was still trying to promote sales, and he thought that repeating how cold it was would be harmful. He asked me to lay low in talking about bad weather.

Re-creating basketball was harder than re-creating baseball games. It was tough to invent a rain delay. Only the barest of details were provided over the ticker: "Field goal Wamser. Foul. Davies was fouled, shooting two. Miss." You had to make up the rest, and you learned to use your imagination. Bobby Davies, a Hall of Famer, was the star of that Rochester Royals team.

When you work in baseball, in the majors or minors, you learn to relish a day off. The games tend to run into each other, and the days when you don't have to go to the ballpark and can relax with your family are very few.

On one off day in that summer of 1953, we took the kids for a picnic on the beach on Lake Ontario with some friends. Danny Whelan, a trainer who later would go on to work for the Pirates and then the New York Knicks of the NBA, was there. Our daughter Christine was about three, and didn't know how to swim. We had our backs turned for only a moment, and she wandered off and walked into the lake. Whelan was the only one who saw her, and he went into the water and rescued her. If he hadn't seen her, she would have drowned.

After that, when we built a house that included a swimming pool, one of the things we made certain of was that all our kids learned to swim as early as possible. I'm still that way anytime people bring their kids over to our pool. I want to make certain they know how to swim. That incident on Lake Ontario showed me how quickly and easily accidents of that sort can happen.

≈

My work for Budweiser got some notice at the D'Arcy advertising agency in St. Louis, which was responsible for hiring the Cardinals announcers after Anheuser-Busch bought the team. They were trying to decide who to hire to do the games with Harry Caray in 1954, and they wanted to see what I could do so they arranged for me to televise a game between the Cardinals and Giants from the Polo Grounds in New York. It was live back to St. Louis, and it was my audition for the big-league job.

After a night game in Rochester, I took a train for New York and checked into the Commodore Hotel, which is now the Grand Hyatt, arriving there at 5 o'clock in the morning. It was an afternoon game, and I knew if I went to bed I might not wake up in time to get to the ballpark.

I sat in the lobby waiting for the players to come down. Dixie Walker was on the team. His brother Harry was the manager in Rochester. He told Dixie I was coming to New York, and Harry had arranged for him to make certain I didn't get lost and got to the park on time and to introduce me to some players. The first man to come down to the lobby I thought was Dixie Walker.

I introduced myself, "Dixie, I'm Jack Buck from Rochester" as I stuck out my hand. He roared at me, "I'm not Dixie Walker. I'm Enos Slaughter. Now get the hell out of here and leave me alone." Slaughter maintains to this day that he didn't say that, but he did.

Dixie showed up and we went to the ballpark and I did the game. A famous broadcaster at that time, Bill Stern, also was at the ballpark that day doing a taping for an audition, and he had two spotters with him. I knew he wasn't going to get the job if he needed spotters at a baseball game.

Some people think my first Cardinals game was the memorable one in which the Cardinals rallied from an 11-0 deficit and beat Sal Maglie and the Giants 12-11. But that game was in 1952. My broadcast debut wasn't anywhere near as dramatic—the Cardinals won—but what stood out to me that day was how helpful some people were, like the Giants' announcer, Russ Hodges. He gave me all of the information I needed and offered a lot of encouragement.

All winter, I waited to see what was going to happen. I had sent some tapes from my Rochester games to the advertising agency in St. Louis, and all I could do was wait. Finally, the phone call came and I was told I had the job, working with Harry Caray. I told Alyce and the kids, "We're going to St. Louis."

She said, "Wonderful," and then asked about the salary. "I don't know," I said. I had never asked and quite frankly, I didn't care. I was going to be a major-league broadcaster, and that was enough for me. We loaded everybody back into that 1950 Plymouth in the spring of 1954 and headed West.

CHAPTER
7

In the Big Leagues

Before leaving Rochester, I received a tape from Cardinals' vice president Bill Walsingham. It was a recording of Harry Caray broadcasting a game. Walsingham included a note: "This is the way we want you to broadcast."

I listened to that tape, and I knew I was in trouble. I could no more broadcast a game in Caray's style than I could any other announcer's. That's a mistake a lot of young announcers make, trying to pattern themselves after someone like Bob Costas, Vin Scully or Al Michaels. That's the wrong approach; you have to develop your own style and do it your own way. I wasn't going to try to broadcast a game like Caray. If the people in St. Louis didn't like my style, I'd have to go elsewhere.

It didn't take me long to realize that Harry and I not only had different styles of announcing, we had different personalities and lifestyles. Our relationship got off badly because he didn't want me to get the job in the first place. He wanted the Cardinals to hire Chic Hearn, who at the time was a broadcaster in Peoria, Illinois. Hearn didn't want the job and later ended up in Los Angeles, where he became the longtime broadcaster for the Lakers basketball team.

Caray wasn't even assured of keeping his job in 1954. After Anheuser-Busch bought the Cardinals, a year earlier, he was doing the games with Gus Mancuso, and even though Anheuser-Busch owned the team, the sponsor was still Griesedieck Beer. There was a lot of concern among the advertising people at the brewery about what to do with the broadcasts. How would it sound if Caray immediately switched from doing commercials for Griesedieck to Budweiser? That's when the decision was made that Caray would stay and do the games, but another announcer would be hired to do the commercials. That's how I got the job, because I had done the Budweiser commercials during my stint in Rochester.

Milo Hamilton, who has gone on to a fine career with several teams, also joined the broadcast that year and he and I split time on the air. Milo went on the road with Caray for the first half of the season, I did the scoring updates and commercials from the studio. We switched at the All-Star break, and I went on the road, but didn't have a lot to do because the broadcasts definitely were Harry's. I did a couple of innings a game, and that was it.

I was happy to have a job in the big leagues—at that time a rather exclusive club. There were only 16 teams, and most of them were not broadcasting their games on television, so there probably weren't more than 40 people who were major-league announcers. Besides, I was earning more money than I had made in Rochester, $12,000, and as it turned out I did so many commercials they had to give me an extra $4,000 to satisfy the union.

Owning the Cardinals turned out to be one of the best things that ever happened to the brewery, because it forced Anheuser-Busch to use a different style of advertising. When I came to St. Louis, the most popular beer in town was Falstaff. Dizzy Dean and Buddy Blattner were sponsored by Falstaff on the game of the week. Old Milwaukee outsold Budweiser in Chicago. Owning the ballclub forced Anheuser-Busch to create advertising to put on the baseball broadcasts. Their baseball network grew to more than 100 stations across the Midwest and South. Until the major leagues expanded, there was no opposition in any of those areas.

Writing advertising copy, and trying to make it relate to a baseball game, was new to the brewery. Wally Armbruster was the creative director at the D'Arcy agency, and he did all of the work on the commercials. Armbruster was trying to learn as much as he could about baseball, asking how you made the pivot at second base and other questions about the fine points of the game. We learned to work well together, and it reached the point where I would just ad-lib a lot of the commercials. He would set it up, and I had to end the commercial by saying something about what was going on in that particular game.

I went to school at the brewery, learning all of the facets of making and packaging beer. Anheuser-Busch always insisted that their employees know the business inside and out.

Dolan Walsh was with D'Arcy for a long time and was one of the people involved in hiring me. He likes to tell a story that when I got to town, Ray Krings, the advertising manager at the brewery, gave Jack Macheca (the account executive at D'Arcy) his Boyd's credit card and told him to buy me some new clothes. He bought me three suits. I must have been quite seedy when they first met me.

I was poking around Walsh's office one day and noticed a stack of tapes on the floor. "What are these?" I asked. "Those are the tapes of all the people who auditioned for the job you got," Walsh said.

"That's interesting. Let me see who some of these people are," I said.

Do you know whose tape I found in that stack? Mine—the one I had sent from Rochester. All they had done was throw it in the stack with the others. That convinced me I was hired simply on the strength of that one-game telecast from the Polo Grounds.

The most memorable event of my first season in St. Louis came on a Sunday afternoon, May 2, 1954, in a rain-delayed double-header against the Giants. Stan Musial hit five home runs, three in the first game, two in the second, and might have had another with the longest ball he hit all day, but it was to straightaway center and was caught by Willie Mays. Caray was on the air for all five homers, and it was just as well. It used to bother him when he wasn't on the air when something really big happened. As for me, it was just fun to be there.

Harry didn't get along with Milo any better than he got along with me at the time, and we knew he wanted to get somebody else on the broadcasts with whom he was more friendly. The man he wanted—and got—was Joe Garagiola.

Joe was from St. Louis and quite popular in town. He and Harry had become friends when Garagiola was playing with the Cardinals, before being traded to Pittsburgh in 1951, then to the Cubs in 1953. He probably could have played a couple of more seasons, but Harry kept bending his ear about getting into broadcasting. Joe decided to quit baseball and do it. Harry talked the brewery and advertising people into hiring Joe, but that meant one of the other announcers had to go. I don't know if Harry was consulted about that or not, but Milo was fired.

I still had a job, so I went out and traded in that 1950 Plymouth and bought a new car. Del Wilber, the former catcher, was working as a salesman at McMahon Pontiac. Every ballplayer, or so it seemed, sold automobiles in the winter. He sold me a green and yellow Pontiac, the ugliest car I've ever seen. People used to say to me, "Who the hell sold you that thing?" The only car worse than that one was the beat-up Plymouth we traded in. There was no upholstery left in that five-year-old buggy because of all four kids.

Nobody at the time knew how well Garagiola was going to do in the broadcast booth. Today it's rather common for players to become announcers when their careers are over, but then it was a novelty to go directly from the field to the microphone. I'll say one thing about Joe, he walked right in and started doing it. It helped that Harry liked him, but I give Joe a lot of credit for working at it.

It was difficult for me, because Joe became Harry's right hand and I was the odd-man out. I was all set to go to spring training that year, 1955, and Joe bumped me out of the trip. He talked the brewery into sending him instead. He also became the full-time partner for Harry on the road, leaving me at home in the studio to do the commercials and scoring updates of other games. That's when I began to become involved in other sports, like bowling, soccer and wrestling, on the radio. I also made public appearances around town, speaking at banquets for various organizations.

At one of those appearances, I told an off-color story. Some kind soul pulled me aside afterward and said, "Your speech was very good, but I want to give you a little advice." The talk had lasted 30 minutes, and he said, "The only thing these people will remember when they leave this room is that you told a dirty story."

That was the truth. What prompted me to include the story in my talk, I don't know. If I had thought about it, I would have known not to do it, because that was the mistake that caused the Rochester broadcaster to be fired, and I got his job. That led to my position with the Cardinals. I remember that advice to this day, and it's still true for anybody who speaks in public. You can knock yourself out, give the best talk ever, but if you tell a dirty story, that's the only thing people will remember.

ə

One of the sports shows I did was on KTVI-TV. It was the start of deer season so we had an outdoors expert, George Carson, come in. He brought in a deer he had just killed and he was supposed to talk about how to dress the deer. It was 6 o'clock in the evening, dinner time. Everybody thought he was going to talk about it, but he decided to demonstrate.

While I was interviewing him, he took out a knife and slit the throat of the deer, then plunged the knife in and ripped it down the stomach. The guts spilled out on the floor.

The cameraman passed out, and the camera tipped up, providing a great picture of the ceiling. People started calling the station by the hundreds. I almost passed out myself.

While I was doing shows like that, Caray was helping make Garagiola the success he became, but they probably were too much alike to remain partners for long. Harry resented the fact that Joe became a national celebrity and never gave Harry credit. Now that Harry is in Chicago and doing games on WGN, broadcast across the country on cable, he became famous for singing "Take Me Out to the Ballgame" during the seventh-inning stretch. He's become one of the most famous announcers in the country.

An accident involving my daughter Christine had something to do with Garagiola being noticed by network executives in New York. The Giants and Dodgers had moved to California but there was still interest in those teams. A television station in Newark, N.J., arranged for some of their games to be broadcast back into New York when either the Giants or the Dodgers played in St. Louis or Pittsburgh. Anheuser Busch was the sponsor, and I did the on-the-air work by myself. The telecasts were receiving a lot of attention in New York and the people there seemed to like me, and I was beginning to think there was a chance it might lead to job possibilities there.

I was doing one of those telecasts from St. Louis one day when I received a startling telephone call. Christine and my oldest daughter Beverly had been riding a horse in our neighbor's backyard. The horse spooked and started running down Macklind Ave. Beverly fell off on the grass; Christine landed on the sidewalk and suffered a fractured skull. I raced to the hospital.

The telecast was about to begin, and Garagiola moved over from the radio booth. That was how the people in New York first heard Joe, and helped propel him into the national picture. He always could talk, tell funny stories, and when he got opportunities to be a guest on the "Tonight Show", he was terrific.

It bothered Caray that Joe was introduced as "Joe Garagiola, the Cardinals' broadcaster." Harry thought that was his title, and he also resented the fact that Joe was getting all of that attention and never mentioned Harry. A few years later, I missed two weeks of games to appear in a stage show at the Muny Opera in St. Louis, and Harry never mentioned me or said where I was or what I was doing. When you're dealing with egos, a broadcast booth can become quite cramped.

The relationship between Harry and Joe fell apart to the point that they're still not friends today. Joe gave him a pair of cufflinks inscribed, "Thanks Joe," for helping him start his broadcasting career. I'll bet Harry threw them away.

Another relationship that really soured over the years was between Garagiola and Stan Musial. They owned a bowling alley along with Stan's business partner, Biggie Garagnani. Garagiola thought that Musial's son, Dick, and Biggie's son, Jack, didn't operate the bowling alley properly. He sued Stan.

The headline in the newspaper, "Garagiola Sues Musial" made Cardinal fans wince. It was a dagger in Stan's heart. Who the hell could sue Stan Musial?

It was no coincidence that the only year Musial did not go to Cooperstown for the Hall of Fame ceremonies was the year Garagiola was inducted into the broadcaster's wing of the Hall.

If I want to get a rise out of Musial even today, I'll say, "Heard from Joe lately?" Stan will answer, "You mean DiMaggio?" Then I'll respond, "No, Garagiola," and he will become airborne. It's a shame, but they'll never patch it up. I know Joe feels badly about it and when Stan was ill a few years ago, Joe was really hoping they could get back together, but it never happened.

Musial and I have become the best of friends. I knew how great a player he was, and it was a treat to meet him. He's the sort of person that when you hear so much about him, you think to yourself, "He can't be that good." Then when you first meet him, you think it must be an act. After you get to know him, you realize it's not an act at all—he really is that sincere and that nice. He is kind to everyone he meets.

Stan does have a temper, however. One night we were in Toots Shor's restaurant in New York with Red Schoendienst. A group of five from Omaha brought a menu to Stan and asked him to autograph it. Stan obliged.

When he handed it back to one of the guys, he promptly ripped it right in half. Why would anybody do a thing like that? Stan flipped and started after the guy, but Toots' bartenders got there first. They jumped over the bar and had four of those people out on the street in a blink. They kept one guy inside to pay the bill, and then hustled him to the sidewalk. It was a good thing Stan never got to them. By the way, I asked Musial once what he would have done if he had not been a baseball player, and he said he thought he would have been a boxer.

One of my favorite stories about Musial was the day Stan was outside Sportsman's Park signing autographs surrounded by a group of people. His wife, Lil, was with him, and someone jostled her. She shoved him back—Lil is a feisty sort. Stan didn't say anything at the time, but when they were driving home, he said, "Lil, don't ever touch any of my fans."

Musial got the 3,000th hit of his career at Wrigley Field in Chicago in 1958, and I've always regretted that I wasn't there to see it. Harry was on the air, as he would have been had I been there. Garagiola was with him on the trip, and I was in the studio in St. Louis. There was a large crowd to greet Musial and the Cardinals that night at Union Station, but I didn't go. Even though I was an-nouncing the home games, I felt left out, like I wasn't part of the team or the broadcast crew.

One night, Harry and Joe were broadcasting a game from the Polo Grounds in New York and there was a rain delay. There was no protection for the announcers, so every time they came back on the air they just said, "It's still raining," and sent it back to me in the TV studio. I talked for two hours. I talked about making double plays, how a baseball, a bat and a glove were made, about fielding and catching a ball, about playing the positions, everything. The director kept saying, "keep talking, keep talking." They'd put in a commercial every once in a while, but I talked for two hours. Many people in St. Louis still remember that session.

Eddie Stanky was the manager of the Cardinals when I joined the team in 1954. The club had finished third three years in a row. Stanky was the sort who liked to test people when he met them. He found out what sort of person one was by challenging you, sticking you, gigging you, trying to trick you. He was the sort of person that if he got you down, and intimidated you, he would keep you down.

Stanky never let up. That was one of his problems; he was totally intense. Harry Caray was much the same, and they never got along. A broadcaster doesn't have to be best friends with the manager, but it helps if they are not enemies. There is more than one way to announce a game, and if the broadcaster likes the player or the manager involved, he is going to promote him during the broadcast. If they don't get along, the broadcaster can go the other way with negative comments. Some managers have been fired because they didn't get along with the broadcaster, and the broadcaster was able to swing public opinion against the skipper.

During the broadcasts I've done, I've tried to keep my personal feelings about managers and players to myself. There have been those I've liked, and those I was not friends of, but I really don't think there have been too many times people listening have been able to tell that I personally didn't care for someone. Some announcers are more open with their feelings. My job is simply to be the eyes and ears of the people listening. Let them form their own opinions about whether they like a performer or not.

Stanky was always feuding with players, umpires, or the press and he had a volatile temper. On a train trip from New York to Philadelphia, Stanky and I were playing liar's poker in the dining car, and he said, "A pair of aces." I challenged him, he let out a cussword and slammed the cards down on the table. A gentleman across the aisle who didn't know either of us said, "Oh, the little boy is angry."

"Little boy" was not what Stanky liked to be called. He flew out of his seat, and landed on the fellow and grabbed him by the throat. Stanky was trying to choke him and we had to pull him away and calm him down.

Cardinals owner Gussie Busch liked Stanky's aggressiveness, but when the team didn't respond to his leadership, Eddie was fired as manager in the middle of the 1955 season and replaced by Harry Walker.

Harry Walker and I had been together in the minors, when he was managing Columbus in 1951 and Rochester in 1953. He thought he was going to have the job for a long time and he started making a lot of decisions, like conducting morning workouts. Harry was a great baseball teacher. The trouble was, if you asked him what time it was, he'd tell you how to make a watch. He knew the game and would talk baseball 24 hours a day if anybody would listen. He and Bing Devine were very close.

Devine was being groomed to become the general manager of the team by Dick Meyer, who wanted to move his own principle duties back to the brewery. Busch probably would have gone along with that plan, which would have included bringing Walker back as manager in 1956, except for the pleadings of J.G. Taylor Spink, the publisher of *The Sporting News*. Spink talked Busch into hiring veteran baseball executive Frank Lane as general manager to succeed Meyer.

Lane wanted his own manager, and he brought in Fred Hutchinson. While nothing much happened on the field during those years, Lane made a lot of noise with his trade of Red Schoendienst to the Giants and two proposed trades, one of which would have sent Musial to Philadelphia for Robin Roberts and the other swapping Ken Boyer to Pittsburgh. Busch stepped in and blocked the moves.

Gussie was frustrated because he was learning it was a lot harder to develop a winning baseball team than it was to run a successful brewery. In his business, if somebody else had something he wanted, he went out and bought it. He thought he could apply the same principles to baseball, but he found out the Dodgers weren't willing to trade or sell Gil Hodges and the Cubs wouldn't part with Ernie Banks. You couldn't buy a pennant then—now you can.

Busch admired and wanted Willie Mays for his team. Horace Stoneham, the Giants owner, wasn't interested in the offer of a million dollars and that shocked Gussie.

There is no point in trying to separate the really great players, in any sport, but if anybody pinned me down and made me pick the best baseball player I ever saw, it would be Mays. He was as good or better than anybody in the game in every category—hitting for average, power, running the bases, fielding and throwing. He didn't get along with some people, but he and I always got along well, I think in part because of what I've said earlier about being polite and appreciative.

Once I wanted to do an interview with Mays at the ballpark. The night before I asked him if he would please do an interview with me the following evening, and he said yes. We did the interview, and after we were finished, a reporter came up and grabbed Mays by the shirtsleeve and said, "Hey Willie, over here now." Mays told the fellow to get his hands off him and walked away. That reporter probably goes around saying, "Willie Mays is a jerk." The reporter was the jerk, not Willie.

There is a right and a wrong way to conduct yourself as an announcer. Not everybody in my business acts as if they have a degree in human behavior. Somewhere along the line, you have to learn the way to do things properly. When an interview is over, I always say thank you. If I'm still closing out the interview and the guest leaves, I will find him later and thank him. It's not a common practice among announcers.

It's not just the broadcasters and writers who treat the players badly. I see kids and adults approach some of the players as if they really owe the fans an autograph. Once I was sitting with pitcher Jim Bunning, a Hall of Famer, and later a member of Congress, a very distinguished gentleman. We were sitting on the bench visiting, when a reporter walked up and said, "Hi Jim, how you chucking?"

Bunning looked at him and said, "Who are you?" The reporter identified himself, and Bunning said, "Why are you calling me Jim? You don't know me. Why don't you introduce yourself, tell me who you are, tell me what you want? And by the way, I don't chuck. I'm a pitcher. Would you please leave? I don't really care to talk to you." Bunning taught him a lesson.

I always make a point of introducing myself to new players, either with the Cardinals or another team. That way I won't be a stranger to them when I ask them for an interview later on. They will usually be cooperative.

It has never bothered me when someone refuses to be interviewed. George Hendrick played for the Cardinals in the 1980s and was well known for not speaking with reporters. Steve Carlton didn't talk for many years with the Phillies. That was their choice. It's no big deal. I tried to do an interview with Cleveland's Albert Belle before a spring training game in 1996, and he turned me down, saying he was done with his interviews for the year. It was only March. Fine, I wouldn't waste time asking him again.

There was a rookie pitcher for the Astros in 1996 who was from Festus, Missouri, Donnie Wall. He was going to pitch against the Cardinals at Busch Stadium the next night, and I asked him to go on the Dugout Show with me. This kid probably grew up listening to me. He said he wouldn't do the show because he didn't give interviews the night before he pitched. That was a new one on me, but so what? I simply found another player willing to go on the show and receive the gift certificate that came with the interview.

Being able to survive as a broadcaster, especially in baseball, is driven by one truism—you have to find a way to stick around long enough for people to get used to you.

Every broadcaster has his own style, some will like him and some will not. A broadcaster who has had success and is well liked in one market could go to another city and find the audience totally against him. If you can survive on the job for several years in the same city, people will learn to put up with you even if they don't like you.

Bob Prince had a very loyal following in Pittsburgh. The fans loved him and thought he was great. He had his own style and personality. He was in Pittsburgh so long that everybody thought he was the best. Audiences in St. Louis or Chicago would not have had the same reaction if he started doing games for the Cardinals or Cubs. When he became a national broadcaster, doing the game of the week on ABC-TV for a while, the results were not favorable.

My favorite story about Prince occurred at the old Chase Hotel in St. Louis, where most of the visiting teams stayed. Prince was a tall, skinny guy and a great swimmer. Each day when in St. Louis, he followed the same routine. He'd show up at the pool, order a Double Canadian Club and a Coke. Then he would dive into the pool, swim the length underwater, turn around and come back underwater. He would get out of the pool, fire down the Canadian Club, chase it with the Coke. His day had begun.

At the end of the pool the hotel windows are about a story and a half high. Some of the Pirate players were sitting around the pool, and their second baseman, Bill Mazeroski, said to Prince, "Do you think you could dive out of that window into the pool?" The window was about 15 feet from the water across the deck.

Prince said, "Hell yeah, I could do that." The players put up $100 and dared him to do it. Prince went into the hotel, appeared at the window, dove in and just made it. He almost wiped out on the deck. Harold Koplar, who owned the Chase, went crazy when he found out about it. He put cages in front of all the windows so nobody would try it again.

People listening to Prince broadcast a game never knew what Bob did on a hot summer day. The first thing he did when he got into the booth was take off his trousers. He sat there in his shorts, and then he'd take his shirt off also. He usually was eating an apple and reading a book at the same time he was announcing, but he never missed a pitch or failed to tell his listeners what was happening. That's tough to do —eat an apple, read a book and broadcast a game.

Once when I was in Houston to televise a bowling tournament, a group of bowlers were sitting around the Olympic-size pool at the old Shamrock Hotel. They had a 3-meter diving board, a 10-meter platform and a 30-meter platform. Carman Salvino was one of the best bowlers at that time. Some of the other bowlers made a bet with Carman that he would not dive off the 30-meter platform.

When you're looking at that platform from the ground, it's one thing. When you're standing up there looking down at the pool, it's another. And the bet was that he had to dive, not jump.

I had been to that pool with my kids before and my son Dan, who was a little daredevil, asked, "Dad, would it be all right if I went off the top?" Thinking he was going to jump, I said "sure." He didn't jump, he dove, and he looked like a pencil going through the air. Fortunately, he wasn't hurt.

Salvino wasn't lucky. He hit the water, and it sounded like a rifle shot. His chest was black and blue; the insteps of his feet were black and blue. He did the biggest belly flop I've ever seen and hurt himself so badly he couldn't bowl that weekend and it cost him a lot of money. He won the bet, $100, but I'm sure he would have made more that weekend if he hadn't taken the dare.

ૐ

I have met so many interesting people and seen many unusual things in my career. Hack Ullrich, the maitre de at the Chase Hotel, and I were playing golf at the Creve Coeur Country Club. We ran into a fellow who wanted to join us. He was introduced to me by his first name, Joe.

As the temperature warmed up, Joe took off his shirt. He had bullet holes in his back—I know bullet holes when I see them. We stopped after nine holes because of the heat, and went to the clubhouse to have a drink.

I asked Joe what sort of business he was in, and he told me he owned Ace Cab Co. His last name was Costello. Then I realized he had been a central figure in a major kidnapping and murder case in St. Louis involving a boy named Bobby Greenlease. About half of a $600,000 ransom disappeared after the two suspects were arrested, and the St. Louis police always believed that Costello had the money.

Bob Anthony, who worked at KMOX, sat down at the table as we were having a beer. When he was introduced to Costello, his eyes bulged. He looked Costello right in the eye and asked, "Do you mind if I ask you a question?" Without waiting for Costello to answer, he asked, "Do you have the Greenlease money?" I almost slid under the table.

Costello paused, then said, "No, but after all I've been through, I wish I did have."

I've always thought I could tell when people were lying or telling the truth, and I believed Costello that day. To this day, the St. Louis police still believe he had the money.

The next day, a car pulled up in front of my house. The driver took a go-cart out of the trunk and brought it to my door. Go-carts were expensive at the time, about $750. I asked what it was all about, and the driver said Joe Costello had sent it over. I told the driver to wait, called Costello and told him that in my line of work, I couldn't accept gifts. "Oh, OK," he said. "Just send it back."

Later, Costello was busted on a gun charge and sent to the penitentiary, and I arranged to leave tickets to a baseball game for his wife and son. The next day I received a call from an FBI agent, saying some guys in the office wanted tickets to a game. I asked what he was talking about and he said, "Well, you left tickets for Joe Costello's wife and kids, maybe you can do the same for us." They followed every move of Costello and his family, still looking for the ransom money.

Later, I was the emcee of the premiere of the motion picture "Hoodlum Priest." A man tapped me on the shoulder and said someone wanted to see me in the lobby. Costello was standing behind a pillar. He was out of the penitentiary, and wanted to thank me for being nice to his wife and kids.

About a year later, I ran into Costello again at his Tick Tock lounge. He bought me a drink then said, "Jack, do me a favor. Drink your drink, then leave." When someone with his reputation says to leave, I leave. Later that night Costello was shot and killed in the bar. He knew someone was coming after him that night, that's why he told me to clear out. Whether he indeed had the ransom money or not, no one will ever know. Like I said, I've met all kinds of people in this job.

&

In the 1950s, discrimination was still a big problem in baseball, not only against black players but against those from Latin America as well. As the game opened up for the black players, it also opened up for those from Cuba, Puerto Rico and the Dominican Republic. They were good players, the best of whom was Roberto Clemente, but they were still adapting to our customs and lifestyles, and there were a lot of American players and managers who resented them and didn't make them feel welcome.

One of the first Latin players I knew was pitcher Luis Arroyo, my first roommate in 1950 during spring training in Daytona Beach, when he was pitching for Columbus. He couldn't speak a word of English, and I was his English teacher. He picked up the language somewhat during his years in the minors, and when he joined the Cardinals he could express himself well enough.

We were playing in the Polo Grounds in New York and I was walking from the clubhouse to the field with Johnny Riddle, the pitching coach and Arroyo. Luis was supposed to pitch that day and he said, "John, I no feel pretty good today." Riddle exploded. "Well, go back to the clubhouse. You blank-blank Puerto Ricans are all alike. I'll tell Stanky you can't pitch." I knew then it was the end of Luis Arroyo with the Cardinals.

Later on the same trip, Arroyo came out of the bullpen to pitch against the Dodgers at Ebbets Field. He gave up a grand slam to Jackie Robinson and his Cardinals' career was over. He went to the Yankees, developed a screwball, and had a fine big league tenure.

Some other people in this country also had negative thoughts about Cubans, and most of them formed their opinions without knowing any Cuban people or visiting the country. If they had visited there, they might have had a different opinion.

Mike Gonzalez was Cuban, and was a coach with the Cardinals. He lived in Havana in the off-season, and I went to visit him at his home during the winter of 1957. Castro was just beginning his rise to power, and there was a policeman or a soldier, armed with a machine gun, in every establishment and standing on every street corner. Whenever I tried to talk politics with Mike, he'd silence me. It was really scary, like fearing the Gestapo in Nazi Germany.

While I was visiting Cuba, Mike took me to Veradaro Beach, where the sand was just like Daytona Beach once was, so white you couldn't look at it. The big hotel on the beach was closed, but Gonzalez, who owned the baseball team there, ran Havana. They opened the bar for us and we had a drink. They served some food. Mike made a phone call and arranged for a piano player. They moved the piano out to the patio by the beach. The next thing we knew, there was a trumpet player, a saxophone player and a guitar player showing up. A drummer walked in with a vocalist and a dancer. We had a party that lasted forever, and it was one of the most memorable days of my life.

The Cuban situation now is as bad as it was 40 years ago when I was there. Their current problems are creating problems in this country, especially in Florida. One of the dumbest things we ever did in this country was allow Castro to come into power. We were supporting Batista, which wasn't good either; he also was a dictator. What the people in this country failed to recognize was that one dictator was going to be worse than the other. The *New York Times* and others supported Castro, so did Clare Booth Luce with *Time* magazine. Castro nationalized all the international holdings in the country and he had thousands of people killed.

Castro's been in front of the United Nations and on the streets in Harlem to try to get support for his cause. The man was and is just as bad as Hitler was, only on a smaller scale. He still prevails. Castro loves baseball, though—isn't that wonderful.

I remember the way Cuba used to be. The people there are proud and honorable. They possess a certain type of elegance, with their style of music and manner of living. Castro disrupted that. He took the lower class and made it the upper class, and it just doesn't work that way. The lower class cannot sustain a country. The upper class is the upper class because it is industrious, intelligent and productive.

Castro is going to end up losing in the long run, but the Cuban people have already lost so much—40 years of living with freedom. Many of them wanted out so badly they did anything they could to get to Florida, and now there are college professors driving taxis in Miami and doctors who can't practice their profession here. It's very sad.

The Cardinals weren't doing very well during the late 1950s. Caray was getting critical of the team, and after the Phillies swept a doubleheader in Philadelphia—without three or four of their top players in the lineup—Caray said on the air, "How can you lose to a team like this?" Dick Meyer, president of the brewery, didn't like it and wanted to do something about it. Garagiola was criticizing the team as well, so Meyer called the three of us together for a meeting. Gussie Busch was there.

Meyer started out by saying, "I want to tell you guys something and I don't want anybody to say a word until I'm finished." He proceeded to lay into us, and in the middle of it, Harry jumped up and started defending himself.

Gussie was just sitting there, and he shook his head approvingly. He loved it, loved the Prussian attitude. Meyer made his point, but nothing happened—at least that time.

Gussie was friends with Ben Kerner, who owned the St. Louis Hawks. Buddy Blattner was the broadcaster for the Hawks, and he also was doing baseball games on CBS with Dizzy Dean, and the two were scheduled to work a playoff game between the Dodgers and Milwaukee. Dean said he was not going to do the game because one of the sponsors was Chesterfield cigarettes. Blattner said he would do the game, but Dean told him, "Partner, if I'm not doing it, you're not doing it either." Blattner went to Falstaff, the sponsor of the Game of the Week, and said, "It's either me or him." The Falstaff people said "It's him." Blattner was dropped from the telecasts.

Kerner was a big supporter of Blattner's and Falstaff also was sponsoring the Hawks. Kerner switched his allegiance to Anheuser-Busch, and he brought Blattner with him, to do the basketball games and the baseball broadcasts as well. That meant we had four announcers—Caray, Garagiola, Blattner and me. Someone had to go. Guess who?

I got the word that I was fired just before Christmas of 1959 from Buddy Reisinger, an executive at the brewery. He cried when he gave me the news. I should have been the one crying. I told him, "Don't worry about it. I'll have another job soon."

We had just built a six-bedroom house with a swimming pool and had bought all new furniture, on credit of course. I had to find a job quickly, or I'd have to sell the kids.

Al Fleishman, the public relations representative for the brewery, said the team wanted to keep me on to make speeches and public appearances and would pay me $250 a month. He also said he was going to call Bob Hyland at KMOX to see if he could give me some additional work. Hyland said yes.

8

Bob Hyland, KMOX and Talk Radio

In the spring of 1960, there were a couple of baseball broadcasting jobs open that I was interested in, one in Detroit and the other in Baltimore. Before I even applied for the jobs, Bob Hyland talked me into staying in St. Louis and going to work full-time for KMOX. He knew baseball was my first love, and told me he was certain things would work out. He also indicated that if I took one of those out-of-town jobs it would be the start of a ride on the merry-go-round a lot of announcers take. They hop on one place, work a couple of years, then hop off and take another job, stay a couple of years, and keep moving.

Hyland convinced me that he was right. I liked St. Louis, it was a good place to raise my family, and I liked the idea of having a base at KMOX. I had done broadcasts other than baseball, including   basketball, football, bowling and wrestling. Hyland told me there would be other opportunities that he would help send my way.

The other help I received was from Al Fleishman, who through the Fleishman-Hillard public relations agency had contacts with businessmen and civic organizations. He helped arrange speaking engagements for me. You talk about work! One year I made 385 appearances! Think about that—385 engagements—every time more than 10 people sat down to eat, I was there talking to them. I spoke to the Optimists, the pessimists, the optometrists, Lions, Kiwanis, church groups, boys' clubs, everybody. Looking back, I think that was a big help in developing a relationship with the folks in St. Louis.

I didn't get rich making those appearances. Some of them paid $10, others $25 or even $50 if it was a big event. I needed the money, and I appreciated every dollar.

Hyland was a big baseball fan. His father, Robert F. Hyland, had turned down a chance to play in the minor leagues and subsequently became a doctor and came to be known as the "surgeon general of baseball." He helped prolong a lot of baseball careers.

Young Bob was a good college player at St. Louis University and once hit a grand slam just as his father walked into the park. I think that was one of the proudest moments of Bob's life. Every once in a while he would play in our media fast-pitch softball league at Forest Park. He was a workaholic, but he did relax on occasion.

Hyland made certain I earned my money at KMOX. I did a record and interview show from Stan Musial and Biggie's Restaurant five nights a week, in addition to other broadcasts. Hyland's work hours were legendary, around 80 hours per week, and I think part of the reason he went to work in the middle of the night was to conjure up things for me to do.

Work was his passion. He was in the office by 2:30 a.m., took less than an hour for lunch, worked until 6 p.m. five days a week, went home, had dinner and was in bed by 9. He went to Mass every day at 6 a.m. at the Old Cathedral across the street from the radio station, and he was always in charge of or attending a meeting for one civic group or another. He did more than just direct KMOX, although his goal of making it the number one radio station in the country always was his first priority.

Among his hundreds of accomplishments was his leadership in building St. Anthony's Hospital in St. Louis, where the rehab center is named after him. He was persuasive enough to get Sid Salomon, the former owner of the St. Louis Blues, to underwrite the building of the chapel at the Catholic hospital, and Salomon was Jewish. Now that's salesmanship.

If I had a meeting with Hyland at 9 o'clock in the morning, he had already been at work for six hours. I would come into his office scratching and yawning and say, "OK, whatever you want me to do." I said yes to everything he asked me to do because I was still asleep.

There weren't many moments when Hyland wasn't listening to KMOX. I joked about the fact that he had an implant in his head and when his eyes opened, the radio went on. Actually, he did have a telephone hot line to the studio from his home, and if the red light on that phone lit up, you knew it was the chief, as he was called. He ran every department at the station.

Bob and I became close friends. More than once, he called me up to say that William Paley, the head of CBS, had asked him to become president of CBS Radio and move to New York. He coveted the job but never took it, it would have meant leaving St. Louis and his first love, KMOX Radio.

Since the 1960s, KMOX has frequently been the number one station in the country with the highest share of audience, number one in revenue and profit. The radio station made more money than KMOX-TV. That was unheard of—a radio station making more money than a television station. KMOX dominated the St. Louis scene and it was fun to be part of it.

Hyland spent a lot of CBS money but that was his way of making money. He had people on his payroll solely to keep them from working for another station. When he wanted them on the air, they were available. KMOX made so much money that no one at the network level ever interfered with Hyland. He operated autonomously, with the blessing of Bill Paley.

After I had been at the station for 25 years, I thought if I took my money out of the CBS pension plan and invested it elsewhere, it would grow at a faster rate. I checked to see what was in my pension account. Announcers at the station were paid in a certain way. If you earned $500 a week, $400 of that would be considered a talent fee and the other $100 was the base employee rate. What I learned was that I was only being vested for a small percentage of my income. After working at the station for all those years, making pretty good money, I had virtually nothing in my pension account.

I walked into Hyland's office and called him every name in the book. He was shocked. "You've been screwing me for 25 years," I told him. He said I didn't know what I was talking about, but he knew everything that went on at the station.

"I'm quitting, I'm leaving, I'm out of here," I said. He said, "Wait." We worked it out, and he increased my pension, but even then I had to work three more years to become vested at the new rate.

The most important contribution Hyland made to KMOX and the broadcasting industry was starting "At Your Service" (my title, by the way), which was the beginning of talk radio and talk television in this country.

Hyland decided to pitch the music programs and start doing interview and information shows. This changed the entire industry; it was revolutionary.

Hyland asked my opinion of what he had already decided to do and I told him he was nuts. "I don't think the audience is capable or interested in participating in talk radio." But Hyland said it was a go, and it would be my job to host two hours of the programming every weekday afternoon.

To be certain he wouldn't go back on his decision, Hyland gave the entire music library at KMOX to a Veterans Hospital. He didn't want to have an alternative. He was convinced it would work.

The station was owned and operated by CBS, so Hyland had to get permission from William Paley to make the format switch. I don't know if Paley thought it would work, but he trusted Hyland's opinion, and we started talk radio.

Roy McCarthy was an announcer at the station. He had done some talk radio on a very small station, but we were the first major broadcast entity to commit to this new genre. The programs started off rather mildly. There were times when people working at the station had to place calls and ask questions on the air to make it seem like listeners were calling. We had some shows that struggled. When we had an occasion to have an African-American as the guest, we received nasty calls saying, "Get that nigger off the air." The tone of those calls was very harsh and bitter.

I observed considerable change over the years, with callers showing more respect for the guests. Ultimately it didn't matter what race or sex a guest was. Our guests were experts and people listened and reacted.

The most popular shows were, "Ask the veterinarian," "Ask the gardener," "Ask the doctor" or "Ask the lawyer." The phones blew up; it was sensational. Hyland had been right. We learned quickly what sort of shows the audience would respond to and which ones brought less reaction.

One of the positive things that can be attributed to talk radio was to enhance better feelings between the races—up until the O.J. Simpson verdict. When Simpson was found not guilty, we saw the black students at Georgetown University on television punching their fists in the air in a victory salute, at the same time the white students at the University of Louisville were hanging their heads in dismay. Race relations had seemed to be getting more positive, and now they have stalled. I see things going the other way. I don't know what it's going to take to get things on a better track.

We hadn't been involved in the talk radio format very long when word spread about what we were doing and how successful it was. People from stations in other cities started to show up to check us out and learn how we did it. Soon they were coming from all over the United States, then Canada, Mexico, Australia and Europe. They used KMOX as a model, and eventually the radio talk format spread to television. It's amazing how many of those programs are on the air. Some should be taken off the air because they are dumb or dirty. Many of these programs don't entertain or educate people, yet people still listen or watch. I don't know why.

The worst shows on either radio or television are the ones where profanity is used and they talk about body parts and sexual situations. It's all right for the hosts of those shows to talk to *their* families that way, but I don't want them talking to *my* family in that fashion. The FCC should have better control over what is heard and seen. It's another example of how some of our "freedoms" are hurting this country.

The opportunity to conduct the "At Your Service" programs was educational. I learned more doing those shows than I learned in college. I enjoy meeting people who are smarter than I am, and you don't meet many Phi Beta Kappas in baseball.

I interviewed Eleanor Roosevelt during an "At Your Service" program. She was a lovely lady. I had my picture taken with her and it's on the wall at the radio station. Dr. Harold Urey appeared as a guest. He was the scientist who discovered heavy water, which led to the invention of the atom bomb. During the interview, I asked him if he believed in God, and he said. "No, but I think it's wonderful." I consider that the most intriguing response to a question I've ever heard.

Visiting with the guests helped improve my interviewing techniques and reminded me of the need to prepare before every program. The two programs that made the biggest impact over the years came on the day when the Cardinals traded Ken Boyer to the Mets, and when the Catholic nuns joined a black protest march in Selma, Alabama. Callers flooded our switchboard and caused problems at the telephone company. "At Your Service" was here to stay.

I have been lucky to meet many special people. I introduced Neil Armstrong in his first public appearance after he returned from the moon. He was in St. Louis to speak to the Boy Scouts, and I was the emcee. My wife Carole and I sat across from Armstrong during dinner before the program, and I couldn't take my eyes off him. This man had walked on the moon; he had moon dust all over him. I have a baseball autographed by Gene Cernan, signed "from the man on the moon." At this time, he was the last moon walker. When others look up at the moon and say, "Isn't that a pretty sight?" I look up and think, "I know some people who have been there." I always thought I would like to be one of those private citizens who would go to the moon if they ever opened it up to non-astronauts. That was before I watched the movie *Apollo 13*. Now I'm not so sure.

I once had the opportunity to broadcast the liftoff of a space capsule at Cape Kennedy. Officials at McDonnell-Douglas set it up, and I was as close to the launch pad as anybody could get, about 1,000 yards away. I was on the phone talking live back to KMOX, and I was going to describe the launch. When that rocket blasted off, there was so much noise, I couldn't even talk. The ground was shaking; it seemed as if the whole world was shaking. It was one of the most awesome sights I've ever seen.

The list of personalities I have met is endless. It includes thousands of people in sports, and entertainment people like Frank Sinatra, Tony Bennett, Bill Cosby, Sammy Davis, George Burns, Johnny Carson, Gordon McRae, John Forsythe, Gene Kelly, Pat O'Brien, Donald O'Connor, the Mills Brothers, Maureen O'Hara, and many others.

I've had the pleasure of meeting several presidents. I was in Rome on a trip and the president of Italy had a reception for President Eisenhower. I was standing in the receiving line as Eisenhower was walking past and our eyes met. He looked at me and said, "What outfit were you with?" Imagine that. He knew I was an American, and he knew I was just the right age to have been in the war. I said, "The ninth infantry, Mr. President." He said, "Good outfit." I was very proud.

Richard Nixon and his family were having dinner one night at Bookbinder's Restaurant in Philadelphia. The owner of the restaurant took me over to say hello. The president, David Eisenhower —his son-in-law—and I had a lot to talk about. I had met David's father, John, when he was a West Point cadet and came to Fort Eustis in 1943. In addition, David was writing a history of the 1st Army in Europe. I was there too long, and Nixon's wife Pat became irritated, but it was President Nixon who had kept the conversation going.

I had a shock one day when I was walking down the hallway at KMOX, and a gentleman I had never seen before walked out of Bob Hyland's office. He shook my hand and said, "I'm Jimmy Carter and I'm going to be your next president." This was early in his campaign, and I kept walking and thought to myself, "Who the hell was that?" But as you know, he turned out to be right.

I met George Bush when he was vice president, and later when he was president I had breakfast with him at the White House. I later discovered that I am related to him through Francis Cooke, who was the 17th signer of the Mayflower Charter. My mother's parents came from Dingle in County Kerry, Ireland. My father was English, and we have traced his genealogy back to King Arthur's Court. Issac Buck fought the Indians in Massachusetts in the 1600s.

Because I wasn't broadcasting the Cardinals games in 1960, other opportunities came about. ABC-TV decided to add a baseball game of the week, even though CBS and NBC were doing the same. I was hired, along with Carl Erskine, the former Dodger pitcher. Carl is a wonderful gentleman now living in Anderson, Indiana, one of the nicest men I've ever met in my life, and he and I became very good friends. We still visit on occasion.

The broadcasts didn't have great ratings because the other networks were already established, with Dizzy Dean and Buddy Blattner calling one game and Lindsey Nelson the other. We weren't able to beam our games into New York or Los Angeles because of rights conflicts, so the advertisers weren't very interested. ABC pulled the plug on those games after that year, but they gave me an opportunity to broadcast the Big 10 college basketball game of the week, and also gave me the chance to do one of the first games in the American Football League in 1960, the Los Angeles Chargers at Oakland. It was the first pro football game I ever broadcast, and those games were wild—all offense. I also made my first trip to Japan in 1960 when ABC sent me to Tokyo to do the Japanese All-Star Game.

I did a lot of bowling shows, including the College World Series of Bowling. It was an independent production, and Eddie Einhorn was in charge—he is now one of the owners of the White Sox. We made a deal for $750, and he told me he would send the check. I told him that when I got there on Saturday morning, if he didn't hand me the check, I wasn't doing the broadcast. Eddie was just starting out as a producer, and I figured if I didn't get the money up front, there was a good chance I'd never get it. I did some television work in St. Louis for a couple of people, and they still owe me $6,000. I don't think I'm going to be able to collect—they're both dead.

I started the Pro Bowlers Tour with Chris Schenkel on ABC. I had done a lot of work with the Budweiser Bowling team, even broadcasting some of their matches, from Chicago and Detroit, on the radio. That Budweiser team was the best bowling team ever with Don Carter, Dick Weber, Ray Bluth, Pat Patterson, Bill Lillard, Billy Welu, Whitey Harris and Tom Hennessey. They were remarkable, and a wonderful group of guys to be around.

I knew bowling. Schenkel was new to the sport, and he learned as we went along. To this day, he's still doing it every Saturday afternoon. It was a fun assignment, and because I knew a lot about it, it was easy. Soccer was another story.

A former St. Louis University soccer player, Kim Tucci, and I were broadcasting a playoff game between St. Louis University and Howard University in Brooklyn, N.Y. We were set up in the last row of the bleachers. A spectator seated directly in front of us turned around every time I said something that was wrong and gave me the bug eye. I'm sure he knew more about soccer than I did, but he was irritating.

During a commercial, I tapped him on the shoulder and said, "If you turn around one more time I'm going to pop you." He turned around again, and I drilled him in the forehead. I had a cigarette in my hand, and it landed in his hair. I knocked him halfway down the bleachers. I had been counting on Tucci coming to my rescue if things turned uglier, but I later found out that Kim can't fight a lick. Luckily, that was the end of it.

I broadcast three years of minor league hockey for the St. Louis Braves with the late Gus Kyle, a former NHL player. When the National Hockey League expanded into St. Louis in 1967, I broadcast their games the first year. The next season KMOX hired Dan Kelly. Kelly was the best hockey announcer the sport has ever known. He died from cancer at a very early age. His son, John, now carries the broadcasting torch.

I don't know much about the finer points of hockey. Dan Kelly, when he occasionally broadcast baseball with us, would ask, "How did you know that was a slider?" and I would ask in return,

"How did you know the shot hit the post?" He knew hockey the way I knew baseball.

For my first NHL game, I traveled to Minneapolis with Gus Kyle. Gus wanted to talk to me on the plane and explain some of the game's nuances to me.

"First of all," I told him, "I've got to get some sleep." I closed my eyes, and he told me later he had never seen anything like it. In seconds, I was gone, asleep, and didn't wake up until the plane landed. We got to the hotel, and talked for an hour, and I was a hockey expert.

Kyle's favorite phrase was, "agile, mobile, and hostile." He used to say, with me and later with Kelly, things such as "Toronto are at Montreal," and "Minnesota are a good team." That was Canadian grammar, and it used to make me shudder.

When the Blues were owned by Sidney Salomon, he hired ex-football player E.J. Holub as a color man on the broadcasts. Holub knew nothing about hockey, but he worked for the Salomons, taking care of their ranch, so they put him on the air.

My barber worked at a shop at a downtown department store, and he used to complain to me all the time about Holub being on the hockey broadcasts. He said, "He's the worst I've ever heard on the radio in my life." He said it every time I went to the barber shop.

One day I was at the station, and Holub was there. I asked if he had time to do me a favor and told Holub about the barber and sent him over there. Holub was huge, about 6-foot-5 and 260 pounds. He walked into the barber shop wearing a 10-gallon hat and cowboy boots. He looked like the state of Texas. As he walked into the shop, the barber was trimming a customer's hair and he looked up and saw Holub in the mirror and almost had a heart attack.

"I understand you have something you want to say to me," Holub said. I never heard the barber criticize another broadcaster.

❧

KMOX was and is a great station. In the 1960s 1970s, and 1980s, Bob Hardy and Rex Davis were doing morning drive, and Jack Carney, one of the best ever, was on from 9 a.m. until noon. Hardy was terrific, intelligent and easy to listen to. He had opportunities to go to New York and work for the network, but he wanted to stay in St. Louis. Unfortunately, he passed away a few years ago.

Carney was a hard worker. Hyland was always irritated any-time he heard music on KMOX because he didn't think it accomplished anything, a waste of time; one day was the same as the next. Carney's show was different, he used music, but always had a theme to his show. He was quite a joke-teller, had a vivid imagination, and developed assorted on-air characters. He took a cleaning lady at KMOX and put her on his program, and "Miss Blue" became one of the most loved citizens in St. Louis. Carney's radio shows made you laugh out loud; he had huge ratings, and KMOX never has had a comparable talent.

Carney made few public appearances, and that worked to his advantage, because it made him sort of a mystery character. He wasn't comfortable in crowds. His excuse for turning down speaking engagements was, "I'm not going to do that as long as Jack Buck's in town." It might have made my life a little easier if he had said yes once in a while.

Hyland was able to recognize talent, and when he heard a young broadcaster he thought was going to be good, he wanted him on his staff. When the Spirits of St. Louis were playing in the American Basketball Association and Hyland needed someone to do the games, he found a young man just out of Syracuse University—Bob Costas.

When Costas came in for an interview, Hyland hired him on the spot, and then sent him to see me. Bernie Fox, our sports program director, knew I was at a barber shop and brought Bob over there to meet me. He walked in and said, "Mr. Buck, I'm Bob Costas. I just visited with Bob Hyland and he told me to come over here and meet you."

Costas has always looked younger than he really is, and that day I thought he looked like he was 15. He said he was 23. "I've got neckties older than you," I told him, and that was true. I still have those neckties, and that was a long time ago.

The Spirits were a good team, with guys like Marvin Barnes and Fly Williams and others. I met Barnes one time, and he was wearing an earring. I said, "You've lost an earring." I thought he was going to punch me; I didn't know he had no sense of humor.

Costas was good on those basketball games, and even when he was just learning the business you could tell he was extremely talented. He did take some things for granted in the early days, like one time when he was scheduled to broadcast a game from Memphis.

The game was scheduled for 7:30, and I saw Costas walking down the hall of KMOX at about 4:30 in the afternoon. I said "Hey, I thought you were supposed to be in Memphis." He said, "I'm gonna be there."

I asked when he was leaving, and he said his flight was at 5:30, and he had plenty of time. "What time does it get in?" I asked, and he said 6:30. He said he would be at the arena by 7 p.m. and everything would be OK.

"What happens if the plane is delayed?" I asked. "Oh it won't be," he assured me, assuming the role of air traffic controller in addition to broadcaster.

Curious, I turned on the game at 7:30 and heard a voice I had never heard before, substituting for Bob Costas. He arrived later, but the next time I saw him I told him, "You ever miss one like that again, you'll be fired." He has many virtues, but punctuality is not one of them.

Early on, Costas had some problems in St. Louis, and the reason some people didn't like him was our fault at KMOX. He was only a baby in the business and we had put him on the talk shows where he offered his opinions freely; criticizing athletes without knowing any of the people and knowing very little about the issues he was dealing with. He irritated a lot of people, but we were to blame for putting him in that awkward position. Bob Costas is now one of the best of all time.

When he was hosting the Olympics in Barcelona in 1992, I was broadcasting a Cardinals game and I made a point of saying, "When we come back after the commercial, I have something I want to say about Bob Costas." I knew that would make people pay attention.

I then said I thought he was the best studio announcer I had ever heard. I talked about my admiration for Brent Musburger. I knew how difficult it was to do this sort of show because I had tried and failed. Costas was wonderful on the Olympics and the football wraparound shows and doing other things. During the Olympics, he never made a mistake, always was well informed and always appeared fresh.

He is a gifted person; blessed with intelligence, a good vocabulary, excellent speech habits and a nice appearance. I believe he's better on television than he is on radio. He's perfect for TV, and he's the best I've ever seen in the role of host.

Hyland was extremely proud of Costas' progress, and also the fact that when Costas went on to national prominence, he never forgot that Hyland and KMOX had given him his start. Hyland was a proud man, and it thrilled him when his on-air personalities became successful. He loved KMOX and St. Louis. The industry and the city lost one of its most important people when he died. I'm willing to bet a nickel that if Hyland had been alive when the NFL expanded, we would have had an expansion team in St. Louis instead of the Rams.

I was one of the pallbearers at Hyland's funeral, and I had the option of delivering a eulogy, but I declined. I preferred to keep my loving thoughts about Hyland to myself. After we put the casket in the hearse, I turned around and there was a television camera in my face and someone wanting an interview. I just shook my head. Those TV people never stop and they're getting worse.

Hyland wouldn't like a lot of things about our industry today. Some broadcasters have gone too far. When Hyland started talk radio, he had no idea it would create monsters. It would make him ill to think that "no-talent" people would get rich and famous through the use of shock radio. Of course it isn't just the radio business that has changed in the last 30 years. The sports world and the entire country have changed as well.

It turned out that Hyland was right with the advice he gave me about not leaving St. Louis. My situation changed again, and I found myself back in the booth, broadcasting for the Cardinals.

CHAPTER 9

Harry Caray and the 1960s

The broadcasting team of Harry Caray, Joe Garagiola and Buddy Blattner didn't last, as Hyland had predicted. Blattner took off for a job in California with the expansion Angels, and Garagiola moved on to the network level in New York. Staying in town, and remaining involved with the Cardinals and KMOX, had been the correct decision for me. I moved back into the booth with Harry.

Caray treated me better than he did the first time we worked together. I was older and more experienced, and he and Garagiola had become enemies. Caray didn't view me as a rival; I was content to just do a couple of innings and fill in when he needed a break.

I would have become frustrated if things had stayed that way forever. If a game went into extra innings, I might as well have gone home, because Caray was going to do all the play-by-play. It upset him if he was not on the air when something exciting happened. I liked the opportunity to make some exciting calls, but when I saw how much it bothered him, it took some of the enjoyment out of it for me.

The Cardinals had a lot of success in the 1960s, winning the World Series in 1964 and 1967 and losing in the seventh game in the 1968 series. It was fun to be a part of it, but those were really Harry's teams. He was the one shouting, "The Cardinals win the pennant!, The Cardinals win the pennant!" in 1964. Joe Schultz, the third base coach, was the one who coined the phrase "El Birdos" for the Orlando Cepeda-led team of 1967. Caray picked up on it and started using it all the time, even though the correct phrase in Spanish should have been "Los Birdos." Then he started singing during the games, "The Cardinals are coming, tra la tra la." It was catchy, and people liked it. It was Harry's show.

When the Cardinals clinched the pennant in 1967 in Philadelphia, I was on the air when Lou Brock pounded one off the scoreboard with the bases loaded. Caray cringed because he wasn't on the air at that time. I wish he had been. I was doing network football games on television and had my own identification. It didn't bother me that Harry dominated the broadcasts.

The victory celebration after winning the pennant the following year in Houston taught me a lesson—avoid the winning locker room when you clinch the pennant, or the series. Too much champagne. It's a silly tradition. People get hurt and that champagne really stings when you get it in your eyes. Then the players threw me in the shower with my clothes on. They haven't caught me since.

After Harry left the Cardinals, I shared the microphone whenever a dramatic moment came about. When there was a no-hitter in the making, I wanted Mike Shannon to make the call. I tried to let Bob Starr call Brock's record stolen base in San Diego, but Starr wouldn't go to the microphone. He wanted me to do it. When Brock was breaking Maury Wills' record for most steals in a season, I would have let Shannon do it, but he walked out of the booth so I had to stay on the air. It has meant a lot to me to share those highlight moments with my son Joe, and let him make some of the historic calls.

During his time in St. Louis, Harry was the equal of Russ Hodges, Red Barber and Mel Allen. In the Midwest, no announcer has been more revered or respected than Harry. He told it like he thought it was, and that's different from telling it like it is. He never hesitated to give his opinion, or to be critical of a player or chirp about a manager's decision, and I give him credit for that. He had the guts to do it; that was his style.

I can't be that critical. It's not my nature. Harry could live with that style, I couldn't. If someone resented his remarks, he became even more combative; he thrived on it. It's like Rush Limbaugh today. I have many of the same thoughts as Limbaugh, but I could never go on the air and express them as he does. I wouldn't have the guts to challenge people the way he does; I wouldn't be able to live with myself if I did. I took a lot of criticism when I introduced Bob Dole at a rally in St. Louis before the 1996 presidential election. When people told me I shouldn't be involved in politics, I said, why not? I should be able to express my opinion along with everybody else. I wouldn't do it in a forum like broadcasting a baseball game, but a political rally is another story.

Harry was successful with his style when he started his career, in the mid-1940s. The audiences didn't know how a broadcaster was supposed to report. He had free reign to broadcast in whatever style he chose.

I wonder if Harry would be able to get a job in today's marketplace. Today's announcers have become too vanilla and too commercialized. There is no room today for controversy created by the broadcaster. Teams will not hire an announcer who is going to be controversial and create problems.

There is a difference between being critical and being nasty. I talk about using common sense a lot with young broadcasters. If you were to see tomorrow's starting pitcher out drunk at midnight, would you talk about it on the air? Of course not. Announcers must think before they talk and be smart enough to know what to say and what to let go. Tongue-in-cheek humor is no longer acceptable in our business. There will always be someone unwilling to laugh it off and anxious to create an issue.

An announcer can criticize. People don't want to hear a syrupy company man who never has anything negative to say about the game. When I'm broadcasting for the Cardinals, who am I going to root for, San Diego? Most of the people listening to me—and the sponsors who are paying for the broadcasts—want the Cardinals to win. They don't want me rooting for the Padres. It might be different in larger cities, like New York, Chicago and Los Angeles, but I think it's OK in St. Louis to be a homer as long as you are fair and give credit to the other side.

Harry constantly criticized Ken Boyer, who did everything so gracefully that some people thought he was not giving 100 percent. It appeared he was loafing, but he wasn't; but Harry used to pick on him relentlessly.

The Cardinals were playing the Dodgers in Los Angeles at the Coliseum, before Dodger Stadium opened. The broadcast booth was behind the screen at field level. Boyer came off the field, after making a good play, and Caray called out to him. "Kenny, Kenny, here's Kenny Boyer. Let's talk for a minute."

Boyer said, "Harry, the ballgame's going on. I can't stop and talk to you on the radio."

That ticked Caray off, and thereafter when Harry got a chance to say something critical about Boyer, he blasted him. Harry was wrong for thinking Boyer should stop and talk to him during the game.

Things are a little different now with teams televising most of their games. An announcer must strive for accuracy and he had better know what he's talking about.

We were in Vero Beach, Florida, during spring training and Howard Cosell was there. Howard and I always got along well, and he's a person who changed sports broadcasting for the better. He was educated and opinionated, and when he talked, people listened. On this day I decided to have some fun with him and Caray.

I walked over to Harry and said, "You ought to hear what Cosell's saying about you. Aren't you friends? I thought the two of you got along."

Harry said, "Why, what did he say about me?" I made up something, then walked over to Cosell and said, "Harry's after you again." Cosell said, "What do you mean?" and I told him, "He's over there shooting you down."

Then I sat in the press box and watched the two of them navigate toward each other. In about a minute they were going at it like a dog and a cat. They loved it, and so did I.

When the Cardinals made it to the postseason, Harry got the assignments. The announcing setup was different than it is now, with one announcer from each team broadcasting the game on network television and radio. Harry did it in 1964, and I had to pay my own way to New York just so I could be there and see the games.

When I showed up at the press gate at Yankee Stadium, I didn't have a credential and couldn't get in the park. I didn't know the station had to apply for them. Bob Fishel worked for the Yankees at the time, and he found a seat for me in the stands, and that's where I watched the games.

Harry also did the World Series in 1967, and this time I stayed home. When the Cardinals won again in 1968, I went to Dick Meyer at the brewery and told him, "You can nominate two announcers for the World Series, one for radio and one for TV." I got the radio assignment to do the games with Pee Wee Reese. Harry was angry and snapped, "I won't do any of it," but he changed his mind and did the games on television.

An awkward moment with Harry came in 1965. The Cardinals were playing in Cincinnati, and I received a call from Chet Simmons at NBC-TV inviting me to broadcast the All-Star game in Minneapolis. I was thrilled, of course, but the first thing I thought of was, "How do I tell Harry?"

I saw him on the field before the game and said, "Harry, shake my hand. I'm going to do the All-Star game." He congratulated me, but I knew it hurt him. Later he got into an angry confrontation about it with Tracy Stallard, the pitcher who was famous for surrendering Roger Maris' 61st home run in 1961.

Stallard was with the Cardinals, and he and Harry were on the team bus. They were getting on each other and Harry said, "At least I didn't throw the home run ball to Maris, and I'm the best at my business and you're not." Stallard came back at him with, "Oh yeah, then why is Jack Buck up in Minneapolis to do the All-Star game and you're riding this bus?"

There is a rule I have lived by ever since I started traveling with a team on a bus or a plane. I never get into a conversation or discussion for everyone to hear. I just sit there and read or sleep and keep my mouth shut.

When Harry and I were doing the games together, we were as good a team as there ever was. His style and mine were so different, that it made for a balanced broadcast. The way we approached the job, with the interest and love both of us had for the game, made our work kind of special.

In Cardinal territory—Arkansas, Oklahoma, Kentucky, Tennessee, Louisiana—you name it—Harry is still extremely popular. The Cubs' telecasts on WGN would not do nearly as well as they do in the ratings if someone other that Harry was announcing. He's part of the show, and some people tune in just to hear him. After recovering from a stroke, he has had to cut back on his travel, and he has a few problems but he still has a great love for the game.

Harry and Gussie Busch were close friends. Gussie didn't mind it when Harry was critical of a player. They used to drink and play cards together at Busch's home at Grant's Farm and talk about the team. That was what Whitey Herzog did when he took over the team in the 1980s.

My stint as Harry's partner might have been shortlived if Branch Rickey had been able to talk Mr. Busch into having me change jobs.

ð

Busch brought Rickey back for a second tour of duty in the front office, and Rickey didn't care for Leo Ward, the Cardinals' traveling secretary. The traveling secretary arranges for planes, buses and hotels and makes certain the players and the equipment gets to the destination on time. It's one of those thankless jobs that nobody pays attention to until something goes wrong, then he catches all sorts of hell.

Rickey was trying to get rid of Ward and put someone else in the position, and he had me in mind. He wanted me to leave the broadcasts to become the traveling secretary. One of the directors of the ballclub, Mark Eagleton, Sen. Tom Eagleton's father, stepped in and blocked the attempt. I would have left before I changed jobs.

ð

Gussie Busch always told people who worked for him to let him know when something was going on. He wanted to hear about problems before anybody else did. That was what put Bing Devine in trouble and caused him to be fired, two months before he could celebrate the pennant win in 1964.

Devine and manager Johnny Keane used to see Gussie at the brewery on a routine visit every 10 days or so. Gussie always asked if there were any problems, and the answer was usually no. Keane had a problem he didn't tell Gussie about: the manager and shortstop Dick Groat were not getting along. They argued about whether Groat should have the privilege to hit-and-run when he desired. They had aired it out themselves and both Devine and Keane considered the matter resolved and saw no reason to tell Gussie about it.

Busch then heard about it from his daughter Elizabeth, who was dating Eddie Mathews of the Braves. Mathews told her about the Groat-Keane feud and she told her father. Gussie fired Devine to prove his point that he didn't want anything going on that he didn't know about. The incident harmed the relationship between Busch and Keane also, and that was a shame.

Johnny Keane was one of the nicest persons ever in sports. Keane had studied for the priesthood before going into baseball. He became a manager in the Cardinals' farm system at Columbus and Rochester and had the nickname of Father John. When he argued with umpires he would just stand there with his arms folded appearing to be very calm. Frequently he was kicked out of the game and the crowd went nuts. It didn't appear that he had been arguing in a combative manner. Later the umpires told me, that despite the fact he had studied to be a priest, Keane could use some of the dirtiest words the umpires had ever heard.

An important contribution Keane made to the Cardinals was in 1964, when he changed Lou Brock's hitting style. Devine had made the trade with the Cubs to acquire Brock for Ernie Broglio in June, and a lot of people criticized the deal, not knowing Brock would become a Hall of Famer. He had been a power hitter with the Cubs, one of the few who ever hit a ball into the centerfield seats at the Polo Grounds. Keane convinced Brock he could help the ballclub more by getting base hits and stealing bases, rather than trying to hit for power.

In 1964, Busch didn't think Keane was doing a good job and was planning to fire him and hire Leo Durocher, but the team came roaring from behind, won the pennant and World Series, and Busch had to ask Johnny to return. Keane told Busch to stick it. He knew they had planned to fire him and hire Durocher, and he didn't appreciate that.

A big surprise came just after the World Series when Keane was named to replace Yogi Berra as manager of the Yankees, the team the Cardinals had just defeated. Going to the Yankees virtually killed Johnny Keane. He believed in authority. If he had gone to the Pirates, who also were in need of a new manager, he might have had more success and would have been a lot happier. With the Yankees, he encountered the likes of Mickey Mantle, Billy Martin, Whitey Ford, Hank Bauer and other free spirits who wouldn't let anyone tell them what to do or how to do it. They weren't bad people, they just did things their way.

The Yankees fired Keane 20 games into the 1966 season, and he died not too long after that. He was fired because he "couldn't handle the players." He could handle the job, but not the players.

The firing caused him to die of a broken heart at his home in Houston at age 56.

Durocher didn't get the Cardinals job. In a move designed to put the best public relations face on Keane's departure, Busch promoted Red Schoendienst, who had been a coach. Red was perfect for the teams of the late 1960s. The players were so talented he didn't have much to do except run them out there everyday and let them play. He was a Hall of Fame player, and knew how to get the most out of their ability. He did that throughout his 12-year career, the longest anyone ever managed the Cardinals.

Schoendienst became one of my best friends as we spent so much time together on the road. The Redhead gave me ideas about protecting yourself in a hotel room—having the bellboy wait while you look in the bathroom, behind the shower curtain and under the bed, how to prop a chair underneath the doorknob when you go to sleep at night. Red never took any chances.

The Redhead played the outfield, shortstop and second base, was a terrific player for the Cardinals, Giants and Milwaukee. He was different than Musial, not only as a player but as an individual. He was more quiet and liked to stay out of the spotlight. He was that way as a manager too.

When a general manager puts a team together, he has to make the right decisions about the type of players he wants on his team. The truth is, you never know about a player until he wears your team's uniform. It's like getting married. People get along when they date and when they are engaged, but when they marry, something strange happens. It's the same with a player. You watch him perform on another team and you wish you had him. Then when you get him, you learn he's not anything like you thought he would be. Sometimes he's better, sometimes he's not. They say when you're in love to the point where you can't stand it, you get married. Then you can stand it.

Stan Musial was the general manager and Schoendienst the field manager in 1967. They never looked at the waiver wire to see which players were available. Their philosophy was simple: The reason that player was available was because somebody else didn't want him, so why should Stan and Red?

Managers aren't always at fault when they get fired. That was the case with Keane in New York, but sometimes it seems the same managers get recycled job after job. I like it better when a fresh choice is made.

My mother, Kathleen, a sweetheart who did a great job raising seven kids.

Corporal Buck, three years in the Army and one month in combat. One war is enough for any man's lifetime.

See any future major leaguers on this Army softball team that played throughout Germany following the war? No, but there is one future announcer, kneeling on the bottom row, far right.

Behind the microphone for the first time, at WOSU, the university station at Ohio State.

Reading the scores and sports news on WCOL, my first professional job.

Doing an interview with Olympic star Jesse Owens. I had gone to college with his daughter.

The staff of WBNS-TV in 1952. A couple of these people became famous. I'm in the far left, back row. In the back row, two over from me, is Jonathan Winters. Standing in front of Winters is Woody Hayes.

Little did I know when I had this photo signed that Gene Autry and I would later become good friends.

Ken Boyer, the MVP in 1964, receives an award following the World Series victory over the Yankees.

The thrill of "At Your Service" on KMOX was meeting famous people, such as former First Lady Eleanor Roosevelt.

I considered myself good friends with Jackie Robinson, the man who broke baseball's color barrier.

Learning baseball from two of the best, Red Schoendienst on the left and Howie Pollet on the right.

I probably didn't say a lot during this interview with Dizzy Dean, who was one of the best storytellers of all time.

Ross Randolph, former warden of the Menard Penitentiary in Chester, Illinois, promised he would get the key and let me out of jail to play softball against the inmates.

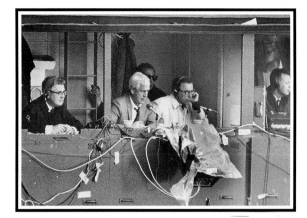

Doing the World Series for the first time, in 1968, on radio with former Dodger shortstop and Hall of Famer Pee Wee Reese.

Robert Hyland, on the right, was influential in both my career and Harry Caray's. This picture was taken in 1968.

With Arthur Godfrey, radio's best-ever salesman.

Before we met, Carole Lindsey (her stage name), was an actress on Broadway who appeared in "How To Succeed In Business Without Really Trying." After we met, Carole was still smiling. So was I.

Receiving an award from my former football broadcasting partner, Pat Summerall.

With Harry Caray, broadcasting a wonderful event: Stan Musial's induction into the Hall of Fame. Wearing the headphones is engineer Chris Sarros; sports producer Bernie Fox is on the telephone.

Some of the heavyweights from the St. Louis sports scene in the 1960s. Left to right, football Hall of Famer Larry Wilson; dinner chairman Hank Siesel, me, and Ben Kerner, former owner of the St. Louis Hawks.

My pick for the best baseball player I ever had the privilege to watch, Willie Mays.

The boss, Gussie Busch, probably checking the fine print of my contract to make sure he wasn't overpaying me.

Interviewing perhaps the best pitcher of all time, Sandy Koufax, while Stan Musial looks on.

Casey Stengel, American League manager for the 1966 All-Star game in St. Louis, where he said his impression of Busch Stadium was that "it holds the heat well." It was 130° on the field.

I'm glad this guy wasn't ever mad at me or he could have hurt me, glasses and all. St. Louis was proud of Heavyweight champ Michael Spinks.

Although this photo was staged, there probably were times when Harry Caray did want to choke me.

The smartest baseball man I ever met, Whitey Herzog, and he was a pretty good actor when we were filming commercials as well.

The stable of announcers at KMOX was deep, and three of us pay homage to our leader, Robert Hyland. On the left is Bob Costas, Hyland, me and Dan Dierdorf.

This looks like I was telling President Bush what to do, but I was just listening.

With two of the best baseball players of all time, Ted Williams and Joe DiMaggio, during a taping for CBS-TV in 1991.

Fredbird clowns around with two of my kids, Joe on the left and Julie on the right. Julie is now a radio personality in St. Louis. Joe does baseball, including the World Series, on the Fox network.

Watching daughter Julie at a debutante ball. From left, Joe Buck, Lil Lintzenich, Carole's mother; Carole, and me.

My three sons; Joe, Jack Jr. and Dan, with their proud father.

Some days it got pretty hot at the ballpark, and our booth is not air conditioned. You had to do what you could to cool off, including sticking your feet in ice water.

Other days were long, forcing you to get a little extra shuteye whenever you could.

Three of the four Buck boys. From left to right, me, my oldest brother Frank, and my older brother Earle. My younger brother Bob, also a sports announcer, wasn't with us on this day.

With my son, Joe Buck, who has made it fun to stay in the broadcast booth these past few years. Hey kid, it's not nice to be better than your old man.

One of the proudest days of my life, going into the broadcaster's wing of the Baseball Hall of Fame in Cooperstown in 1987. I was the eleventh announcer inducted.

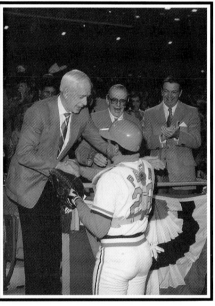

Shaking hands with catcher Tony Peña after throwing out the first pitch before the World Series in 1987. Gussie Busch and his son, August Busch III, look on.

A future Hall of Famer, Ozzie Smith, the greatest defensive shortstop of all time.

I've had a lot of reasons to smile, I've had a great life.

Leo Durocher got another chance to manage with the Cubs, and he was there when they collapsed and blew the pennant in 1969. One day I was walking on the field before a game, and a cameraman was walking beside me, taking Durocher's picture. Leo was leaning on a fungo bat. He flipped the bat at the cameraman, and it went whizzing past my ear. I said, "Was that meant for me?" He said, "No, it was for that SOB over there aiming his camera at me. I didn't give him permission to take my picture." Durocher was about 64, and still as feisty as ever.

A manager I always respected was Danny Murtaugh in Pittsburgh. Many thought because of the way he looked that he drank a lot. But he never took an alcoholic drink in his life. Irish people, including myself, have a bad reputation for being big drinkers. It's not true; but we do live in mortal fear of dehydration.

ᕱ

Those were exciting times in St. Louis. I did a broadcast from the top of the Gateway Arch the day it was topped of at 640 feet. The new stadium was built and the Cardinals were winning. Next to buying the ballclub in 1953, Gussie Busch's efforts to lead the campaign to build the new stadium was his finest hour. Even after spending $2.5 million to fix up old Sportsman's Park, Busch was able to persuade the brewery's directors to kickoff the stadium funding drive with a $5 million donation.

The new ballpark saved downtown St. Louis. Those who have moved to the area since it was built or just visit for a game have no idea what the downtown area was like previously. It featured run-down homes, buildings and factories. There were a lot of shacks that started on the shores of the Mississippi River and ran all the way west to Union Station. It was one of the worst looking downtowns in the United States.

When they built the stadium, they were forced to clean up the area. The Arch was built and new office buildings went up, and today downtown St. Louis is beautiful and clean. If you looked at a before-and-after picture you would be shocked.

The success of the team and the lure of the new ballpark produced good crowds, and enhanced the image of St. Louis as a good baseball town. It's the same everywhere; if the team wins, people will come out to support it. Even if they don't come to the games, people get more interested in the team when it is winning, sometimes even deciding to put a few dollars on the outcome of a game.

Gambling on baseball is financial suicide. The game is not as predictable as other sports. You can't convince some people of that.

I had a friend who worked as a bartender at the Las Vegas Lounge on DeBallivere Ave. He was a gambler and a funny guy. He had plans to get married, but always gambled his money away. Evidently his dog was married, because when the dog became pregnant, he and his fiance threw a shower for the dog. I was wacky enough to buy a present and go to the party.

Finally he was able to save enough money for the down payment on a house, which would be followed by the wedding. They found a house they wanted to buy, and his fiance insisted he make the down payment, because she wanted to know if she could trust him or whether he still had the gambling habit. He had the money, and was supposed to take it to the bank.

The Cardinals played the Pirates that night, and Dick Groat was playing shortstop for St. Louis. The Cardinals were leading by a run, Pittsburgh had two runners on with two outs in the ninth, when the batter hit a routine ground ball to Groat. It took a bad hop and went 10 feet over his head. Two runs scored and the Cardinals lost.

The gambler went back to his fiance, and she asked, "Did you do it?" He responded, "Sweetheart, your new house just took a bad bounce over Dick Groat's head." To this day, I can close my eyes and see the flying house.

People who bet on baseball go broke. I like to gamble, and occasionally I'll bet on football games. I can afford to lose a little money, and gambling adds to my enjoyment of the game. It's awful when people gamble when they can't afford it and risk their mortgage or food for their kids if they lose. I have never bet on a baseball game, and I joke about the fact that I once bet on a football game I was broadcasting. Minnesota scored a touchdown, and I said, "The Vikings now lead 13 1/2 to 7."

Even the experts in Las Vegas will tell you the most treacherous sport to bet on is baseball. Who would have thought Atlanta would lose to the Yankees in the 1996 World Series? I know someone who lost $50,000 betting on the Braves.

I voted against legalized gambling when it was on the ballot in Missouri. It tempts people to go out and lose money they can't afford to lose. If I was governor of a state that had legalized gambling, I would lobby for a law that anybody who was receiving welfare checks would not be allowed on any of the gambling boats or casinos. The boats and casinos would have to check the welfare lists, just like they have to check IDs to make sure people are old enough to be there. Anybody who was on the list couldn't gamble.

Once Harry Caray and I were in Chicago, leaving Wrigley Field, and we shared a cab downtown with Shecky Greene, the great comedian. Shecky got out of the cab at an intersection during rush hour, cars were coming at us in all directions, honking their horns, and he held up traffic by running back to the cab. "The double-header tomorrow, how should I bet?" he asked.

"Shecky, don't ask me," I said. "I don't know anything about how you should bet." He insisted, so I told him, "If it were me, I'd bet the Cardinals in the first game and the Cubs in the second."

You know what happened of course; the Cubs won the first game and the Cardinals the second. I tried to warn him.

I once saw Greene perform at the Chase Hotel and I was in the front row. He did a routine about coal miners trapped in a mine, which ordinarily might have been a funny routine. On this night, he kept going on and on, and he was getting no laughs from the audience. What he didn't know was at that moment there were several coal miners trapped in a mine in Illinois. It had been on the news that evening. Many in the audience knew it, but Shecky didn't. It was a dilemma for me, whether to interrupt him or not. I didn't say anything, and he laid a big egg and was really embarrassed.

Something similar happened in Houston, when I was in a nightclub watching Bob Newhart perform. Some in the crowd were making noise, and Newhart stopped his act and got into a shouting match with them. It was really awkward. I was surprised that Newhart couldn't handle it better than he did. Another entertainer, Sergio Franchi, adjusted better when I saw him perform in a nightclub in Los Angeles.

It was an overflow crowd at the Century Plaza Hotel, and some of the tables were inside the ropes surrounding the stage. An older couple was seated ringside, and the husband fell asleep and started to snore. Sergio was singing, but everyone in the room could hear the snoring. Franchi stopped the orchestra, walked to the table and I thought, "Man, here it comes."

Instead, he said to the woman, "Is this your husband?" She said that it was. Sergio then asked, "Does he always snore like that?" She nodded yes and looked like she wanted to disappear. Sergio said, "He must be very tired." Then he waved to the orchestra and started to sing "Brahams Lullaby" and the audience joined in. The snorer slept through the entire incident. Franchi had turned an awkward situation into a golden moment.

I used to make a lot of trips to Las Vegas. I was seated at the Sands one night and the four people around me were Frank Sinatra, Joey Bishop, Dean Martin and Sammy Davis Jr. That was a foursome.

Sammy Davis impressed me as the greatest entertainer I ever saw. Harry Caray and I were at his show at the Copa in New York until 3 o'clock in the morning. Elizabeth Taylor and Richard Burton also were in the crowd. They were a better looking couple than Harry and I. Davis was doing everything— tap dancing, telling jokes, demonstrating the quick draw, doing impersonations, singing, playing the drums. He was the best.

I've come to know Tony Bennett and Donald O'Conner and John Forsyth over the years, and Bill Cosby as well. Cosby is an acquaintance of Joe Torre's, the Yankee manager. Recently, when I was being honored by a charity, Torre asked Cosby to come to St. Louis and perform. He did so for no fee. He flew in on his private plane, delighted the audience for an hour and a half, and left town that night. How can you ever repay a favor of that sort?

☙

I enjoyed being around the great players for the Cardinals in the 1960s, like Bob Gibson, Lou Brock, Ken Boyer, Tim McCarver, Bill White, Mike Shannon, Nelson Briles, Ray Washburn, Dal Maxvill, Barney Schultz, Curt Flood, Carl Warwick, Dick Groat and Julian Javier, and the not-so-great, like Bob Uecker. Javier's nickname was "The Phantom" and a few years ago when Stan Javier, his son, named after Musial, was in town playing for the Giants, he asked me why his father was called the phantom. I told him to meet me at the Cardinals' offices the next afternoon and I'd explain.

I showed Stan Javier a picture of his dad making a double play. He had already thrown the ball, the runner was sliding into the base and Julian was about 15 feet toward third base. There was no way for the runner to get him and break up the double play. He was called the phantom because he got out of the way so quickly that no runner could slide into him. He just disappeared. I asked him one time who the last runner was who had slid into him on a twin killing, and he said Duke Snider. Snider had been retired for six years.

The word that best describes Bob Gibson is tough. He was one of those pitchers that if the other team was going to get him, they had to do it early in the game. If it was late in the ballgame and he had the lead, you weren't going to beat him. It was that simple. Opponents could run against Gibson because he seldom paid attention to the baserunners. He always figured he'd get the hitter out, which by the way is the essence of the game —get the batter out.

I've seen a lot of pitchers get themselves in trouble worrying about baserunners who weren't going anywhere. If there's a runner at second and two out, so what if he does steal third? Get the batter out, the inning's over. Pitchers stand on the mound and step off, and make pickoff throws to the point where they drive everyone crazy. Then they lose their concentration and make a bad pitch. The batter will get a hit, the run scores, and the trouble continues.

Gibson and I had one confrontation. He was injured and went home to Omaha. When he came back, a reporter interviewed him and asked if he had listened to the broadcasts of the games while he was at home. He said, "No, it put me to sleep." I went on the air that night and said, "I see where the broadcast put Bob Gibson to sleep when he was back in Omaha. I'll tell you one thing, when he pitches as he did two nights ago, it would be impossible to go to sleep because of the basehits flying all around the park."

I knew somebody would tell him what I said and we would have to talk it out, so I went to the clubhouse after the game. As expected, he jumped me. "What the hell was that all about?" he said. I told him I was reacting to what he said in the newspaper, and he said, "I wasn't talking about you. I was talking about Jim Woods (my broadcasting partner at that time)."

Many experts I know would pick Gibson to pitch if they had one game to win. His performance in 1968, setting a record with a 1.12 ERA, was the best many have ever seen. Taking nothing away from Bob, I think if I had to go with one pitcher for a must-win game, I would pick Sandy Koufax. At his best, he was unhittable.

Lou Brock was just as tough as Gibson, but happier. I never saw anyone who combined those two characteristics as well as

Brock. He was a Hall of Fame player who did everything with a smile.

Lou was the most arrogant player I ever saw, just as Maury Wills had been when he was in his prime. He was going to take that lead, he was going to steal the base, and there wasn't anything anyone could do about it. A pitcher could step off, could throw over, he wasn't going to stop Brock from stealing.

Lou is remembered for the stolen bases, but he also had 3,000 hits. It was fitting that his 3,000th hit was a line drive off the leg of pitcher Dennis Lamp of the Cubs. Lamp had knocked Brock down with a pitch at Lou's chin, and on the next delivery, Lou ripped one off Lamp's knee for number 3,000. Brock reminded me a lot of Dizzy Dean. They each had a different story for everyone and they were always entertaining.

Often times, people try to compare great players to someone who is playing today, but there is no need to do that. It is a futile exercise. Today's players are faster, but I think those of the 1960s were better overall performers because expansion has watered the game down. Today's players make more mistakes than they should, even in the big leagues. Youngsters today have too many choices and too many diversions that take away from going out and just playing baseball. That's why so many of today's players come from Latin America, where the only thing for kids to do is play sports.

If the stars from earlier generations, like Gibson, Brock, Mays, Mantle, Musial, Jackie Robinson, Hank Aaron, Ted Williams, Joe DiMaggio, Frank Robinson and others were playing today, they would be better than today's stars. They were complete players. One of the things people don't talk about enough in baseball is the strength of the players. Those players were strong. Now everybody hits home runs. The ballparks are smaller, the baseball is juiced and the pitchers aren't as good as they used to be.

The 1960s also was a golden era for broadcasting. I was quoted a few years ago as saying I thought the quality of baseball broadcasting had dropped a peg, but now I think it's down two or three pegs. Almost anything is acceptable now in the big leagues.

Some broadcasters have been successful in other sports and thought they could do baseball. But people who are just pretty good can't do baseball. There's a lot of time to fill that you don't have in other sports and you can't fake it.

The best baseball broadcaster in the business is Vin Scully. He probably is the best ever, better than Red Barber, Mel Allen, Russ

Hodges or anyone working today. He has a great appeal and knowledge of the game, and his voice, style and consistency are the best. His audience never gets tired of listening to Scully. I'll tell you what I think about Joe Buck later.

One thing about Scully is that he doesn't share the microphone. When he is doing the play-by-play on a Dodgers game, the announcers working with him are never on the air at the same time. There is no interplay, because that's the way Scully wants it. There are some broadcasters who have no sense of timing. They will talk and continue to tell a story when the ball is in play. That's irritating to the listeners who can hear the crowd reaction.

When broadcasting a baseball game, the announcer must tell the listeners, "The pitch is on the way." There are lots of ways to do it, but you have to let fans know that the pitch is being made.

As the decade of the 1960s came to an end, I knew I was reaching a point in my career where I would have to break up my partnership with Harry Caray. My salary level had stayed the same, $20,000, and I was under an exclusive contract and couldn't work for anyone else. I did a college football game in Illinois and was paid $750, but I had to turn the money over to the brewery's advertising agency. I was going to have to move elsewhere to become a lead announcer. Then Harry blew the job.

Harry was having problems in St. Louis, and Gussie Busch was aware of the situation. Mr. Busch told Harry he was leaving for a trip to Europe and for Harry to keep his mouth shut until he got back and he would take care of the problem. The Cardinals were playing in Wrigley Field, and the *Post-Dispatch* had reported that Caray was in danger of losing his job. Instead of saying nothing as Gussie had told him, Harry interviewed Neal Russo, the newspaper reporter, on the pre-game show and asked him about the story.

Gussie was on his way to the airport and heard the interview, and said, "That's it."

Don Hamel was in charge of marketing at the brewery, and he was the one who told Caray he was fired. Al Fleishman of the public relations firm called me into his office and said "We've just fired Harry. Do you want his contract?"

Harry had already been fired; I had nothing to do with it. So I said yes, and took the job with a clear conscience. People picketed outside the ballpark, upset about Harry's firing. Harry and I had been together for 16 years. It was time to turn another page.

10

Mr. Busch

August A. Busch Jr. was always "Mr. Busch" to me and he always called me "Buck." Considering what he called some others, I guess he liked me—at least he knew one of my names.

Mr. Busch and I never had social contact except at functions at the brewery or with the Cardinals. I never tried to force my way into his inner circle; he had his close friends and associates, and I wasn't one of them. He always treated me fairly, and I considered it a privilege to work for many years for Anheuser-Busch and the Cardinals.

Gussie liked to mix with the players during the early years when he owned the ballclub. He loved spring training—which is the favorite time of the year for everyone in baseball except the players. He put on a uniform and worked out and cavorted with Stan Musial and Red Schoendienst. Owning the Cardinals changed his life. He said he was recognized more and quoted more often in the newspaper for owning the Cardinals than for running Anheuser-Busch, a larger and much more important company.

He was in his 50s, but it was a simpler time in baseball and Mr. Busch could relate to the players more than an owner can today. There aren't many owners like Gussie Busch any more. He was like Horace Stoneham with the Giants, Walter O'Malley with the Dodgers and Tom Yawkey with the Red Sox. They were sportsmen, they were fans, they were adventurous—they didn't worry much about the bottom line.

Gussie liked to show off his Clydesdale horses and his home, at Grant's Farm, and each year he threw a party for the players and their families. He'd hand out toys and prizes for everyone, and there always was a drawing for a major prize. One year pitcher Gerry Staley won a pony and a cart. What he did with it, I don't know.

Because salaries weren't near the level they are today, players needed financial help from time to time. Mr. Busch would generously give them an advance on their pay, to help them buy a house or whatever.

On December 24 each year, he hosted an elaborate Christmas party at the brewery for executives and Cardinals' front office personnel, including the announcers. He walked into the room with his pockets stuffed with envelopes containing the Christmas bonus checks for everyone who was invited

Folks would sit and play cards, have a Budweiser or a Bloody Mary, then lunch was served. Everyone kept an eye on Gussie, waiting for him to stop what he was doing and hand out the checks. The size of the bonus depended on one's salary, plus the sort of year the brewery was enjoying. When I was earning $16,000, the bonus was $5,000 if the brewery had a good year, or $2,000 or $3,000 if sales had been slow.

The numbers then don't compare with today. Anheuser-Busch is the largest brewery in the world and sells more than 80 million barrels of beer a year. Back in the 1950s, it was a big moment when the 10 millionth barrel of beer was brewed in one year.

One year at the party, Busch get involved in a discussion with one of his top aides, and he decided not to give out the bonus checks. He stuffed them back in his pocket. Everyone had been counting on that money, and I already had spent mine. That took the financial joy out of Christmas that year.

Mr. Busch was a perfectionist, and always wanted the brewery's activities to be first-class. When he bought the Cardinals he was embarrassed about the condition of Sportsman's Park. The St. Louis Browns owned the stadium, and they didn't have the money to repair it, so Gussie spent an extra $1 million to buy it, then spent more to upgrade it.

Busch knew it wasn't the sort of stadium he wanted for his team. He led the drive to build a new stadium in downtown St. Louis. Even though the "new" stadium is now 31 years old, the efforts of Anheuser-Busch and the current owners make it one of the best stadiums in baseball.

Busch spent time at his winter home in St. Petersburg, where the Cardinals trained every spring. During each spring training, the St. Petersburg folks threw a big party for Gussie and some of the Cardinals' personnel.

One year the party was at a restaurant on Tierra Verde, a small island between St. Petersburg and St. Pete Beach. The St. Petersburg group called itself the "Bat Boys," and there probably were about 50 of us there to enjoy cocktails and dinner. Someone went to the bathroom, and a prankster poured water on his chair. When the guy came back, sat down and got wet, he soaked a napkin, and threw it at someone across the table. Another took a dinner roll, soaked it in water, and bopped someone at the other end of the table. It was a free-for-all.

The waiters had just served the food, 16-ounce strip steaks, and people started throwing anything and everything they could get their hands on. Bob Howsam was the general manager of the Cardinals, and he grabbed Musial and picked him up with one hand, pinned him against the wall. He almost took his feet off the ground, and he poured a beer over Musial's head. Then he grabbed another bottle and poured that on Stan. Musial couldn't get away, that's how strong Howsam was.

Someone else picked up a large bowl of cheese dip, chased Harry Caray into a corner and dumped the cheese dip on Harry's head. The chef was standing at the door to the kitchen, and he was crying. He had prepared a lovely meal, and it was completely wasted.

I was under a table and heard someone say, "Where's Buck? We've got to get Buck." They were looking for Schoendienst also, and they hadn't found him either. Dick Sisler, one of the coaches, was avoiding the mayhem as well.

I darted back into the kitchen, and ran into Schoendienst and Sisler. Sisler is a stutterer, and I can still hear him say, "We've gotttta tooo geeeettttt ooouuuuutttt offfff heeeerrrreeee." We went through the kitchen, opened a door and found ourselves in the middle of the Guy Lombardo orchestra, which was performing in the nightclub half of the restaurant. Sisler was the first one through and he walked right past Carmen Lombardo, who was singing, and stammered, "Parrrrrddddddooooonnnn ussssss."

Gussie Busch loved this sort of action, even when the bill came from the restaurant for the cleanup and damage. I don't know how much it cost to repair the carpet and drapes and pay for the dinner, but Gussie and the Bat Boys didn't care. They even decided to hold the party again at the same place the next year.

At the party the following spring, the same people were there and everyone was seated as the meal was being served. The only one missing was Gussie. He had missed the cocktail party, and hadn't told anybody he was going to be late, and some were starting to worry. Suddenly the door opened, and there he stood—wearing boots and a bright yellow rain slicker and a hat. He bellowed, "Let the party begin!"

On another occasion in St. Petersburg, I was invited to dinner with the Cardinal boss. There were 18 of us, and Mr. Busch said to the waiter, "I want plenty of Budweiser and Michelob up and down the table." The waiter left, then came back and said that they didn't have either beer on hand.

Gussie was in a good mood that evening, so he didn't get upset about the absence of his product. He told the waiter to have the manager send out for some Budweiser, the group had plenty of time to wait. The waiter left and again returned, this time informing Gussie that the manager said they were short-handed and didn't have anybody available to go pick up the beer.

Once again Gussie was nice. He gave the waiter the name and phone number of the local beer distributor, and said to call him; that he would see to it that the beer was delivered.

When the waiter returned this time, he was accompanied by the manager, who made the mistake of saying to Gussie, "What's the difference? It all tastes the same."

He had barely finished saying that when Gussie got up and headed for the door. Seventeen others followed him, and nobody said a word. To this day, that poor manager probably has no idea what he said that irritated Mr. Busch. And he was wrong; all beer does not taste the same.

The ballclub's success when it won in 1964, 1967 and 1968 brought a lot of joy to Mr. Busch. He was seated next to the dugout in 1964 and Harry Caray was down there next to him broadcasting the final inning of the pennant-clinching game. When the final out was secured, they both started whooping and hollering and I don't know which one was happier. It was great to see them both have that moment.

In 1967 after clinching the pennant in Philadelphia, Busch reserved the entire Old Original Bookbinder's Restaurant for a party for all the Cardinals personnel. He always did things that way. He could afford it, he had a glamorous and generous approach to life and always wanted to share his happiness with those who had made it possible.

Gussie ran the brewery with an iron fist. One of his decisions that affected both his baseball team and the brewery involved Roger Maris, who should be in the Hall of Fame. The Cardinals had acquired Maris before the 1967 season, after he said he wouldn't play in New York any longer. The media attention and pressure in the Big Apple ever since he broke Babe Ruth's home run record had nearly destroyed him. He said later the two years he spent in St. Louis were his happiest years in baseball. After the Cardinals beat the Red Sox in the World Series, Maris decided to call it a career.

Mr. Busch talked him out of retirement and promised to give him a beer distributorship if he played in 1968. He did, and the Cardinals again made it to the World Series, only to lose to Detroit. Again Maris wanted to quit, and again Busch tried to talk him into playing one more year.

"BS," Maris said, in a language Busch could understand. "You told me if I played in 1968 I'd get a distributorship."

Busch knew Maris was right and he backed off. He took part of Art Pepin's sales territory in Florida, which included Tampa and Gainesville, split it up and gave the Gainesville area to Roger Maris and his family.

The same thing happened with Frank Sinatra. Sinatra had been hired to perform at an Anheuser-Busch convention. He and Busch started talking about distributorships, and Sinatra said, "How about giving me one of those things?" Busch simply said, "OK partner, you've got it." Sinatra got the outlet in Long Beach, California. That's how autocratic Busch was; he ran the entire company, which had not yet gone public. If he made a decision, no one questioned him— at least at that point in his life. Those distributorships were automatic gold mines at that time. Now it takes a sizeable investment, and a long time, before it becomes a profitable venture but they are still very valuable.

After a few years of owning the Cardinals, Busch's thoughts about baseball started to change. Players were demanding more money and more freedom. The player's union was stronger than ever, and the entire atmosphere around the game wasn't the same.

Two players on his team who most affected Busch's attitude were Curt Flood and Steve Carlton. Both got involved in ugly contract disputes, and Busch said at the time about baseball, "Instead of being a sport it has become a headache."

He was fed up, and thought most of the fans were also. The players were talking about a strike, and their attitude toward the fans and owners bothered Gussie. He probably did more for his players then most owners, and Joe Torre was quoted after the strike in 1972 that if all of the owners had been like Busch, the players probably would not have gone on strike.

In an interview at that time, Busch said he was not totally disenchanted with baseball, but was worried about its future. It bothered him that Torre and shortstop Dal Maxvill, the player representatives on the team, had rallied the players against the owners. It was ironic years later that both came back to the Cardinals, Maxvill as general manager and Torre as field manager.

Winning another pennant might have cured Busch's blues, and the Cardinals did come close in 1974. If the Cubs had beaten the Pirates on the final day of the season, it would have forced a one-game playoff between the Cardinals and Pirates for the pennant.

Busch and some of his friends, including Ben Kerner, former owner of the St. Louis Hawks basketball team, had a party as they watched the game. The Cubs led by a run going into the ninth, but a passed ball by catcher Steve Swisher allowed the tying run to score and the Pirates went on to win the game and clinch the pennant.

Busch was 75 years old, and the sadness on his face was quite visible. He turned to Kerner, and quietly said, "Take me home, Hawk." Kerner said later that Busch didn't say another word all the way to Grant's Farm.

His days of being actively involved in the Cardinals were over by then, and his son, August Busch III, had taken control of the brewery's operations. The Cardinals fell into a slump, keeping Busch depressed for years—until the decision was made to bring in a new manager in 1980—Whitey Herzog.

Herzog spoke the same language as Busch, could match him swear word-for-swear word and beer-for-beer, and the two quickly developed a strong bond. Herzog tore the ballclub apart, put it back together again and gave Busch another World Series champion in 1982 and two more pennant winners, 1985 and 1987.

I became closer to Mr. Busch in his waning years because of my friendship with Art Pepin, the Anheuser-Busch distributor in Tampa. When Gussie wasn't feeling well, he would call Art and ask him to fly to St. Louis to be with him, and Pepin always came. My wife, Carole, also became close to Gussie. She was an entertainer, and in his own way, so was Busch. At all of the World Series parties, and other gatherings, Carole would get him up on stage and they would sing "LeRoy Brown" together. Those were happy days.

Once during spring training, Gussie almost fired me. I spoke to a class at Webster University in St. Louis and I was relating a story Herzog had told me about how he and Busch were able to get along so well. According to Whitey, Busch would say, "Don't you think we ought to trade so-and-so?" Whitey said he would jokingly respond, "Drink your beer, you senile old son of a gun." Whitey was the only one who could talk to him in that fashion.

I told this story to illustrate the freedom that Whitey had to run the ballclub. He could do anything he wanted, just as long as Busch knew about it in advance. They were great friends. They drank beer together, played gin together, and developed an unusual relationship. I didn't know there was a reporter from a small newspaper in the classroom.

He wrote in his column in the newspaper that Jack Buck had told his audience Whitey Herzog said Gussie Busch was senile. The newspaper came out during spring training, and caused things to boil at the brewery.

I received a message that Busch wanted to see me. "Buck!" he yelled. "What did you say about me?"

I pleaded my case, and I knew my job was in jeopardy. It became a big deal. Lou Susman, Busch's attorney, was involved. August the 3rd was involved. Fleishman-Hillard, the public relations agency, was in the middle of it. The only person attempting to help me was Tommy Ryan, an executive at the brewery.

Busch was really upset. "Jack, why did you say that? Why did you say I was senile?" "Mr. Busch, I didn't say it." I tried to explain I had used the word senile in a different context, but I could tell I was getting nowhere.

Carole recognized the gravity of the situation. She took it upon herself to go see Mr. Busch and his wife Margaret. She went to their house on the beach and explained the whole story. Gussie believed her. Carole saved my job.

It truly was the end of an era when Mr. Busch died in September, 1989, at age 90. The brewery took over the full operation of the Cardinals, and August III didn't really care much about baseball. It was just another division of the brewery, and as long as it didn't lose money, it was OK with him. He showed up for a few innings on opening day, but seldom came to the ballpark thereafter.

Continuing labor problems and mounting costs led to baseball strikes and fewer fans in St. Louis. The ballclub's bottom line became an irritant for the folks at Anheuser-Busch. August III couldn't balance paying baseball players more money than his top officials were earning. When he decided to sell the Cardinals, he did the right thing.

August III had worked at every job at the brewery, that's how his father wanted him to learn the business. He worked on the railroad, in the ice plant, on the packaging line, in the hops house and the brew house. Anheuser-Busch has thrived under his leadership.

Busch III handpicked a group of young sportsmen he knew were dedicated to keeping the ballclub in St. Louis and making it competitive. He sold the team, stadium and downtown parking garages for $150 million to a group headed by Fred Hanser, Drew Baur and Bill DeWitt Jr. before the 1996 season, and also spent $8 million on stadium improvements before turning the team and stadium over to the new owners.

The new owners have a lot in common with Gussie Busch— they are sportsmen, they have fun, and they enjoy watching the Cardinals win. All of St. Louis was happy for them when the team was able to be so successful in their first season and miss going to the World Series by only one game.

Gussie would have been happy for them, and would have enjoyed sharing a Bud or two with the new owners. Everybody loved the Big Eagle.

11

Pro Football:
Monday Nights and Super Bowls

During the summer of 1960, when I was doing the baseball Game of the Week for ABC-TV, I received a telephone call from Tom Kelly, an announcer in Peoria. He wanted to know if I knew of anybody who was looking for a football announcer.

I told Tom to call Ed Scherek, an executive with ABC Sports. The network had been awarded the contract to televise the games of the newly formed American Football League.

It was only a few minutes later when Kelly called back with a message for me from Scherek. "He said you were kidding me; you're going to do the AFL games."

Surprised by that news, I called Scherek and explained to him that I already had made a commitment for the football season. I was going to broadcast on KMOX the games of the Chicago Cardinals, who were moving to St. Louis.

Scherek told me that if I wasn't going to do football for him, then I had done my last baseball game for ABC. I didn't know what to do. I had already told Bob Hyland I would do the Cardinals' football games. I was looking for work since I had just been fired in December from the Cardinals baseball broadcasts.

The football Cardinals' sponsor was Falstaff, and I had already talked to the Falstaff people. I was switching my allegiance from Anheuser-Busch to another beer. I decided I had to stick with ABC, and when I told Hyland, he fired me.

I had built that house, had a mortgage and now had six kids; Dan and Betsy had come along. I needed the salary I was drawing from KMOX to pay the bills. Working the games for ABC wasn't going to bring in enough money.

If I had done the football Cardinals' broadcasts for Falstaff, I would not have been able to go back to the baseball broadcasts when a spot opened up in 1961. Hyland didn't stay angry with me for long, and a week later I was back working at KMOX. He also gave me the weekends off to do the football games for ABC.

During my year away from Cardinals baseball, I did the St. Louis Hawks' basketball games with Don Cunningham, who had moved to St. Louis from Buffalo. Don and his wife Millie had three little boys. He and I toured with the Hawks and the Philadelphia 76ers. We opened the Forum in Los Angeles and the arena in Las Vegas. We were traveling with some high-powered players, including Bob Pettit, and Wilt Chamberlain.

When it was determined that Buddy Blattner would continue to broadcast the Hawks' games, Cunningham lost his basketball job. Subsequently, he was going to take over the record and interview show I was doing at Stan Musial and Biggie's Restaurant. Don got contact lenses one day, and developed a headache. He stopped at Busch's Grove restaurant for a drink. His wife, Millie, was a nurse, and she gave him a pain pill when he got home. He fell asleep on the living room floor. She took the kids out to get dinner, and when they came back, he was dead. He was only 35. Millie worked at KMOX and was my part-time secretary. She later married Bo Schembechler, the football coach at Michigan.

As mentioned earlier, I also had done the Big 10 basketball game of the week for ABC. The brewery told me in the fall of 1959 that I couldn't do those games anymore because some of the sponsor conflicts. I had to call Dick Bailey at ABC and tell him that I couldn't do the games anymore because Anheuser-Busch wouldn't allow it. Just after the brewery told me I couldn't do the basketball, they fired me from the baseball.

The first thing I did was call Dick Bailey to tell him I was available again. He had just given the job that morning to Bill Fleming in Detroit. He said, "I can't take it away from him."

In the span of six months, I lost the college basketball, was fired from baseball, was threatened to be fired by ABC and was fired by KMOX. The winter of 1959 and summer of 1960 was tumultuous. My head was still spinning when the AFL season began.

Those early AFL games were wild. It was like most startup companies, some knew what they were doing, others didn't. A few of the owners had a lot of money, others operated on a shoestring. Some players were in the league because they received more money than they were offered in the NFL, others because they weren't good enough for the already-established league.

Many of the original owners are still around, like Lamar Hunt, Ralph Wilson and Bud Adams. They had paid $25,000 for their franchises. When the AFL merged into the NFL in 1970, the value of those franchises had skyrocketed. Talk about a wise investment. I didn't have $25,000 in 1960, but if I had known what the future value of those teams was going to be, I would have gotten it somewhere.

The New York Titans were one of the teams in the league and were coached by Sammy Baugh. A scene I will never forget was when I walked into their lockerroom before a game and saw the players passing around shoulder pads trying to find the right size. It was a spartan beginning for the AFL. The teams were throwing a lot of money at college players to sign with them, but they had little money to spend for equipment.

The signing war that broke out between the AFL and NFL for college players was incredible. The AFL teams knew they had to have players with star appeal to attract fans and TV viewers, so they went after the quarterbacks, those coming out of college and those already in the NFL. Some owners practically kidnapped some of those players and put thousands of dollars in cash in front of them. Sometimes they kept the players hidden in hotel rooms until they signed. Some of the new graduates agreed to terms with teams in both leagues and took the money from both, and spent it. They didn't go to college for nothing.

When the New York Jets signed Joe Namath it was the key to the success for the AFL. By the way, Namath had been drafted by the Cardinals in the NFL, and I often wonder what would have happened had he played in St. Louis.

When the AFL teams improved to the point they were closer to the NFL teams in talent, and were a legitimate threat to signing players, all of the pro football team owners got together and agreed to a merger. The recently deceased Pete Rozelle was the central figure in the negotiations.

I televised AFL games for three years, through 1962, with George Ratterman. One of the other announcing teams was Curt Gowdy who worked with Paul Christman. Gowdy was a very good announcer, and had a better name than I had. He was connected with the right people in New York. He and Christman soon took over as the number one announcing team. That helped me make the decision to move to CBS to televise the Bears games.

The networks handled assignments differently than they do now, where announcers go from one team to another and don't know much more than a week in advance what game they will be doing next. In those early days, an announcing team stayed with one team the entire season, and I was hired with former Notre Dame star and Hall of Famer George Connor to do the Bears, succeeding Irv Kupcinet and Red Grange.

George Halas was the coach and owner of the Bears. He remains one of the legendary figures in the history of the NFL. Halas was tough, and known to use a great deal of profanity. He probably couldn't get away today with the way he treated some of his players.

Johnny Morris was a receiver for the Bears, and was playing in Wrigley Field one very cold afternoon. He dropped a pass in the end zone, and when he came off the field he sat down on the bench as far away from Halas as he could get. Halas always wore a hat, and walked with a limp. Halas walked all the way down the bench to where Morris was sitting. Morris thought he was going to get a pat on the shoulder and a little pep talk. Instead, Halas called him a four-letter word, then kicked him in the shins. I guess in a way that is a pep talk.

Rosie Taylor was a Bears' cornerback, and during practice on a Saturday morning, Halas took him to a position on the field and said, "You stay here on the kickoff." The game Sunday was against Green Bay, and Travis Williams had been running kickoffs back for touchdowns for the Packers. Halas told Taylor, "I don't care if he runs 105 yards on the other side of the field. You stay here." Taylor later said the last thing he remembered were two blockers wiping him out, and seeing Williams blazing past him on his way to the end zone. Taylor went and sat on the edge of the bench also. Halas limped down to him, called him the same four-letter word, pulled his hat down even tighter over his ears and kicked Taylor in the shins. Another pep talk.

Jerry Waldman was a businessman who owned the Philadelphia Eagles. He was building the Hancock Building in Chicago, and ran into construction problems that eventually forced him into bankruptcy. The NFL owners called a meeting to decide how to dispose of the team.

One owner stood up at the meeting and said, "There was a time in this league when we would talk about how we were going to help this person retain his franchise, not how we're going to help him get rid of it. Here's my million dollars. If the rest of you will do the same, Jerry Waldman will keep the Philadelphia Eagles." That owner was George Halas.

Not enough owners came through, and Waldman lost the franchise. I was in Philadelphia later to televise an Eagles game, and ran into Waldman the night before the game at Bookbinder's Restaurant. He had gone back into business, and I asked if he was going to the game. He said, "I can't get a ticket." I handed him a press pass. "Here, you're my spotter." It was one of the few times I've seen a millionaire cry.

I was working a full schedule of NFL games for CBS, and Lindsey Nelson was doing both college and pro games. Bill MacPhail, my boss at CBS, called and said they wanted me to take a week off so Lindsey could work a Bears game. I said OK, and we agreed on which game I would miss. That turned out to be the contest where Gale Sayers scored six touchdowns in the rain against San Francisco at Wrigley Field. I missed one of the games of the century.

Hall of Famer Sid Luckman had been the Bears quarterback for a long time, and he and Halas remained close friends. After his football career, Luckman became a well-to-do stockbroker in Chicago, and every Saturday morning when the Bears were working out at Wrigley Field, Luckman would pull up in his limo, come out on the field and talk to the quarterbacks. He'd watch them, give a little demonstration, get back in his limo and leave.

I was broadcasting a Cardinals baseball game in Pittsburgh one night, and went back to the Hilton hotel after the game and went to the bar. The bartender's name was George. He said, "Jack, do you know Sid Luckman?" I said I did, and George said "Well he's over there in the other room, why don't you go say hello?" I said I didn't want to bother him, and stayed at the bar.

George must have thought I didn't know Luckman and he kept bugging me to go over and say hello. Finally we walked over to the other room, and I looked around and said, "Where is he?" George pointed, and I said, "That's not Luckman."

George said it was Luckman; he was wearing a Bears ring. "He's been here for three days, and has had some of the damnedst parties the hotel has ever seen."

I told George he would be doing the manager of his hotel a big favor if he told him the man who was claiming to be Sid Luckman was an imposter.

On a later trip to Pittsburgh, I got off the airplane and bought a newspaper, and there was a story about the phony Sid Luckman. He had just been sent off to a mental hospital after posing as Luckman for a week, and running up a massive bill at the Hilton Hotel.

Along these same lines, I once walked into a bar in Gaslight Square in St. Louis and the bartender told me, "Jack, there's Clyde Lovellette, the basketball star." I looked down the bar and said, "Where?" "There, the big guy," the bartender said. "That's not Clyde Lovellette," I said.

"The hell it isn't," he said. "Go down there and say hello." Just for fun, I walked down to the end of the bar and looked directly at the fellow and said, "Hi Clyde, Jack Buck." He looked at me, and he knew that I knew he wasn't really Lovellette. "How ya' doing Jack," he said and shook my hand. I didn't blow his cover.

It's amazing how people do that. I was at the office at KMOX one day and received a phone call from a Salvation Army officer in Michigan. The man on the phone said, "Mr. Buck, we have a problem here. We have John David Crow at our unit of the Salvation Army. He is destitute and homeless."

"How do you know it's him?" I asked, and was told he was wearing his Texas A & M ring. I told the officer I knew it wasn't him, but I took his number and promised to call back.

I called Northwest Louisiana State University, where John David Crow was the athletic director at the time. I said, "Do you know you're supposed to be in Michigan?" He said, "What?" I told him the story, and we got things squared away. The John David Crow in Michigan was an imposter. I don't know how people get those rings and pull off stunts of that sort.

I also don't know why people get a thrill out of running onto the field during an athletic event. It used to be the television cameras would follow them until they were caught by security, but now they don't show the idiots on TV anymore.

I was involved in a couple of incidents when I was in California to televise a game between the Bears and the Rams that prove sometimes you can get into trouble without even trying.

The teams were to play in the Los Angeles Coliseum on a Saturday night. The schedule worked out great for me. The baseball Cardinals were also in Los Angeles, playing the Dodgers, so all I was going to miss was the Saturday night game. I could do the baseball game Sunday and then fly with the team to San Francisco. This was in 1965, and it happened to be the weekend when the Watts riots broke out. The football game was postponed until Sunday, messing up my perfect travel plans.

During the game, the Bears were driving down the field and had a first and goal. They were really clicking, until a kid delayed the game by running onto the field. He was tall and skinny, about 16 years old, and could really run. He was running away from his pursuers, and the security guards and police officers were running into each other. It looked like the Keystone Cops. The crowd in the Coliseum started to root for the kid, but then he made a mistake.

He got too close to the Bears' huddle, and they were angry because this youngster had interrupted their drive to a touchdown. Mike Ditka was the tight end for the Bears, and POW, he hit the kid with a forearm under the chin. He flew in the air and pancaked to the ground. The crowd started to boo, and I thought another riot was going to break out. They hauled the youngster off, and luckily he wasn't seriously hurt. The next day I read in the newspaper that when they took the kid to court, the judge asked him, "You won't do that again, will you?" The answer was no. The judge said, "You've suffered enough. Case dismissed."

I kidded Ditka about it later, asking him how he could have done what he did, and he said, "Jack, what would you do if you were a businessman and somebody came in and stood on your desk? You'd do the same thing. That football field was my desk. I got him off."

When the game was over, I went back to Gene Autry's Continental Hotel on Sunset Blvd. I went into the bar, but it was too busy and noisy, so I turned around, went to my room and ordered room service. The next day I went to San Francisco and rejoined the baseball team.

The following spring training, I was in Florida and received a summons from the federal court in Chicago to report immediately. I called the prosecutor's office to ask what it was about, and they said they couldn't tell me but I was needed there to testify at some future date. I explained I was broadcasting baseball, and they said they wanted to know where I would be every day, so I could come to Chicago when I was needed.

About a month later, FBI agents came to see me. They showed me a picture of a man, and asked if I knew him. I said no. "Study that picture," the agent said. "We want to know if you've ever seen him before." My answer was still no, which prompted the agent to say, "Then you never will, because he's gone." They still wouldn't tell me what the case was all about.

That summer I was in Los Angeles doing baseball when I received a call to report to the federal court in Chicago. I flew to Chicago and checked into a hotel, then rented another room under a fictitious name and stayed there. I didn't know what I was in the middle of, but I knew it wasn't good.

At court the next day, the FBI was there again, and they had me look through a window into the courtroom to see if there was anybody in the room I recognized. There were perhaps 100 people or so in the courtroom, none of them familiar to me.

I took the stand, and the prosecutor asked me to look around the room and see if I recognized anybody in the courtroom. I said, "Other than the FBI agents whom I just met this morning, there isn't anybody in the room that I know." Then the defense attorney took over.

He asked if I was in Los Angeles one particular weekend. I was. What were you doing there? A football game between the Bears and the Rams on Sunday afternoon. Isn't it true that that game was played on Saturday night? No sir, the Watts riots broke out and the game was postponed until Sunday, I said. He asked, what were the dates of the Watts riots?

"I don't know," I said. "I could go to the library and look them up for you."

The judge slammed his gavel down on the bench. His name was Moscowitz. He said, "You will save your wise remarks for the airwaves."

At the end of the day, the FBI agent finally told me what was going on. If I had recognized a lady sitting at the defense table, they would have made their case. He told me when I went into the bar at the hotel after the football game, she was in there. They had wanted me to say I had seen her in the bar. She had been there to deliver some stolen negotiable securities to a go-between from Chicago. The go-between was the man whose picture had been shown to me by the FBI. He had told the FBI that he could prove he was in the bar because he offered Jack Buck a drink, but I had refused and gone to my room. Those stolen securities were taken to New York and the culprits constructed a building there. In the end, the prosecution obtained a conviction. As I said, you can get into a lot of trouble without even trying.

*

The most feared player on the Bears in the early '60s was linebacker Dick Butkus, another Hall of Famer. He was ferocious and enjoyed tackling and hurting people. I did a game between the Bears and the Browns in Cleveland. Mike Phipps was the Browns' quarterback, but he was out with an injury and Frank Ryan was playing. He got hurt, so Bill Nelson had to come in with his two bad knees. He could hardly walk out to the huddle.

Butkus was eyeballing him like a dog looking at a T-bone steak. They snapped the ball, and Nelson dropped back to pass, and Butkus roared up to him untouched. He grabbed Nelson, picked him up in the air, and then gently put him to the ground and tapped him on the shoulder. I talked to Butkus about it later and he said, "Yeah, I knew he had those bad knees. I knew I was going to get him. I could have killed him." That was the only time I ever saw Butkus let up. Butkus was the best football player I ever saw. Heck, when he intercepted a pass, he might have been the best running back in the game.

*

Mugsy Halas, George Halas' son, was not enamored with my work and wanted CBS-TV to assign Lindsey Nelson to the games. So Bill MacPhail, one of my best friends, had to call me and tell me I was fired.

A few days later, Frank Glieber, the Cowboys' announcer, switched over to the Cleveland Browns. The job in Dallas was open, but MacPhail told Bill Creasy, a CBS producer, that he didn't have the nerve to call me after just tying a can to me. Creasy said, "I'll call him." He did, and I became the Dallas Cowboys' announcer in 1966.

The Cowboys were a talented team featuring Don Meredith, Bob Hayes, Bob Lilly and Mel Renfro and coached by Tom Landry.

Landry's coaching record speaks for itself. He was like Don Shula, Vince Lombardi or Paul Brown. He could take *his* team and beat you, or he could take *your* team and beat you.

A few years ago, Bob Hyland arranged for Landry to speak to a Boy Scout gathering in the dead of winter. The day Tom was to fly up from Dallas, it was snowing heavily. I called him and said the weather was bad and didn't know if he should try to make it. Most people, scheduled for a free speaking engagement and given an out like that, would probably have taken it. Not Landry.

"Are the planes still landing there?" he asked. I said they were, but that everything was backed up. Landry had every excuse in the world not to come.

"I'm coming," he said, "I'm coming." I told him I would meet him at the airport, and he said, "You don't need to meet me, I'll take a cab." I told him, "You won't be able to get a cab. I'll meet you."

I had a heck of a time getting to the airport, then to the hotel where he freshened up and then to the auditorium for his appearance. I learned all I ever needed to know about Tom Landry that night.

My trips to Dallas to broadcast Cowboys games usually ended with an ambulance ride, but not for the usual reason. The games there began at 1 p.m., which meant they ended around 4 p.m. There was a flight back to St. Louis at 5 p.m., but with all of the traffic leaving the stadium, it normally would have been impossible to make that flight. That's where the ambulance trips came in.

I made a deal with the ambulance driver that if he wasn't busy at the end of the game, I would pay them the equivalent of the cab fare to take me from the stadium to the airport. I would get into the ambulance, put my luggage under the bunk, lie down and we would take off for the airport. I had to lie down on the bunk, just in case the police stopped us.

Part of the deal was that the ambulance driver didn't just drive to the airport, he took me directly to the plane. We would pull up at the gate, I would hop out and board the plane, usually with only minutes to spare. Until the stewardesses got used to the procedure, they would see me get out of the ambulance and say, "Oh my, are you OK?" I'd say, "I'm good. Please give me a VO and water." There were a few times when we wouldn't have made the flight without driving down the median or the sidewalk with the siren blaring.

On one trip, my first father-in-law, Paul Larson, was with me. We got into the ambulance after the game, and all he could say during the entire trip to the airport was, "Oh my God, Oh my God."

The Cowboys' tight end those days was Pettis Norman, and I constantly referred to him as Norman Pettis. Blackie Sherrod, the excellent sportswriter in Dallas, wrote one Sunday morning that Dallas fans were tired of Pettis Norman constantly being referred to as Norman Pettis by broadcaster Buck Jack. That's what the folks at CBS call me, Buck Jack.

During those Cowboys games, Landry was always in control on the sidelines. He was impeccably dressed and always wore a hat; he moved slowly and talked softly. He was quite a contrast to other coaches who rant and rave. I've seen both approaches be successful and both kinds fail.

Every football coach is compared with Vince Lombardi, the mastermind of the Packers during their glory years. Lombardi came off as a strange character to a lot of people. He was so intense while preparing for a game that if you tried to talk to him, he would ignore you.

Lombardi was an actor. I've seen a lot of others behave like him, in football and other sports. Walter Alston, Whitey Herzog, and Tony LaRussa were like that. So it was with George Allen, Paul Brown and others, all actors.

Every week the Packers had a happy hour on Saturday evening. Lombardi was always there with his wife, and they were always pleasant. "Hi Jack, come on in. Have a drink. Have something to eat." His preparation for the game was over, and the actor was off-stage. The next morning he was back at work. I never would have thought about walking up to him to say hello on a Sunday afternoon.

George Allen, the long-time coach of the Redskins, was also like that. On Sunday, if he saw me on the field, he would give me a signal to stay away. "Don't come talk to me. I'm in a mood, I'm on stage, the play has begun, don't interrupt me." I understood that. Most of the great coaches in the NFL are the same way. They are all actors to some extent.

A coach I felt sorry for when he was in the NFL was Lou Holtz, who resigned as coach at Notre Dame at the end of the 1996 season. He left the job at the University of Arkansas to become the coach of the New York Jets. Hank Stram and I would visit with him the night before a game, and he was always a miserable wreck. He was so distraught trying to coach the Jets that it reminded me of the Johnny Keane episode when he was trying to manage the Yankees. He wasn't the type of coach one has to be to succeed in New York or with the pros.

Holtz was an outstanding college coach, but he encountered the pro attitude, the New York attitude and the New York press all at once. "They all go together," he confided to us. "These guys are killing me. I'll die if I stay here. I've got to get out." He bounced nicely to Notre Dame, which is not exactly an easy job, but was a better fit for him. Every time I hear someone bring up his name as a possible coach for a pro team, I laugh. I know he'd never coach again before he would go back to New York, or go back to the pros.

Another coach who had a tough time making the adjustment from college to the pros was Dan Devine, who left a successful program at the University of Missouri to take the job with the Packers. At least he wasn't the guy who had to directly follow Lombardi in Green Bay, but it was still soon enough after Lombardi left that everyone compared him to Vince.

Despite some success with the Packers, Devine was always under fire in Green Bay. The fans wanted former quarterback Bart Starr to be the coach, and he wanted the job. Bart was my broadcasting partner at that time, and we were frequently assigned to the Green Bay games. It was awkward for both of us; neither one of us wanted to be critical of Devine, but sometimes it was impossible not to be.

We worked one Green Bay game at Philadelphia, and the Packers trailed the Eagles by nine points. They had a fourth and goal from the 5, and instead of kicking a field goal they went for the end zone, didn't make it and lost the game. Both Starr and I had no choice but to say that it was a dumb decision.

The night before the Packers played a game in Atlanta, Devine and I went to dinner. He told me he was taking the best college coaching job in the country. I said, "You're going to Ohio State?" No. "You're going to Southern Cal?" No. "Michigan?" He was starting to get irritated with my kidding. Then he confided to me that he was going to Notre Dame.

I was the first media person to know, but I couldn't use the information. He told me I couldn't tell anybody, and of course I didn't. I had the scoop, but someone else broke the story.

Most people don't realize the pressure that coaches are under. When I was doing the television show "Grandstand", Ohio State was getting ready for a trip to the Rose Bowl and we set up a camera to follow Woody Hayes from dawn to dusk. We had a camera set up outside his home before daybreak, and one tiny light went on in the house, then it was turned off. Down the driveway came a pickup truck with no lights on. Hayes was leaving for work. We had camped outside waiting to get pictures of him leaving for the stadium, and it was 4 o'clock in the morning. All we got on film was one light going on in the house.

Some coaches spend the night sleeping in their offices because they work so late and want to get back at it again early the next morning. Joe Gibbs did that frequently with the Redskins and Don Coryell did it with the Cardinals, then the Chargers. Dick Vermeil was like that with the Eagles. Obsessed with getting the edge on the other guy, they believe that's what it takes. Other coaches say when they have to start sleeping in the office to get their work done, it's time to look for another job.

Football playoff games are wonderful assignments. I was selected for the NFL championship game in 1967 in Green Bay between the Packers and Dallas. Ray Scott—perhaps the best football announcer ever—and I split the play-by-play and Frank Gifford was the analyst. Tom Brookshire had the best job, working the pre- and post-game, which meant he could stay indoors during the game.

The night before the game I went to a party hosted by the Packers at a country club. The snow was frozen, the moon was full, it was about 30 degrees; a lovely winter night. We knew it was going to be cold for the game the next afternoon, December 31, and I thought I was prepared. The next morning, the hotel operator woke me with the startling news that it was 17 degrees below zero.

I was staying at the Northland Hotel, and some of the Packer players were there as well. I went down to breakfast and sat next to Willie Davis, the Green Bay defensive end. "I'll leave if you'll leave," I told him, but he had no idea what I was talking about.

"Do you know how cold it is outside?" I asked Davis. "How cold?" he said. "17 below," I answered. "Bullshit," he said. He couldn't believe it. He hadn't been outside, and he hadn't turned on the radio or television. He hadn't talked to anybody but me. I was going to have a hard enough time trying to broadcast the game, but he had to play.

We went to the stadium, and Gifford and I were standing on the field preparing to open the broadcast. I had borrowed a stocking cap from Elijah Pitts, one of the Packers' running backs, and had it pulled down over my ears. Gifford stood there without a hat with his hair combed perfectly, and I said, "Frank, aren't you going to put something on your head?" He said he didn't have anything to wear. I told him I could get a cap for him, but he said he didn't want one. I said to myself, "You're a better man than I am."

I stood there shivering, and a Packer fan walked by about 15 yards away, wearing only a T-shirt. He was a Green Bay native, wearing formal attire. He yelled, "Hey Buck you stink." I tried to cry, but my tears froze.

We had an open broadcast booth, and I was trying to stay warm drinking coffee laced with VO, but even that mixture froze like a popsicle. Gifford said, "Give me a bite of your coffee." That was the funniest thing he has ever said. CBS had brought six electric blankets, not for the announcers, but to keep the cameras warm. The game is famous for Green Bay's touchdown in the final seconds, on a quarterback sneak by Bart Starr behind Jerry Kramer, that gave the Packers a 21-17 victory. I was so cold when it ended, I didn't care who had won, just as long as the game was over.

Little did we know that the most harrowing part of our day was just beginning. Gifford, Brookshire and I had arranged to fly to Chicago in a private twin-engine plane. We became airborne and had just started to thaw out, when the door popped open about eight inches. Gifford was in the front seat, and said he was going to unlock the door totally and slam it shut. I advised him to leave the door alone. He took hold of the door handle and the armrest, tried to slam the door shut, and pulled the armrest right out of the door. Now the door was flapping with the wind. I was in the backseat with my arms around Gifford. Brookshire, also in the back, was shooting scotch into Gifford's mouth from a rubber flask. The pilot had his parka hood pulled over his head and was trying to read a map while keeping the windshield defrosted.

The pilot managed to land on an icy airport strip in New Holstein, Wisconsin, and we stopped about 50 yards from the woods. When we came to a stop, we closed the door, turned around and flew to Chicago. That was one New Year's Eve where I really celebrated.

I have broadcast many Super Bowl games on CBS Radio, but the only one I ever did on television was Super Bowl IV in New Orleans with Pat Summerall. The Chiefs, coached by Hank Stram, beat the Vikings, coached by Bud Grant.

When Bill MacPhail called and asked me to do the game, I never asked how much I was going to be paid and I didn't have an agent. CBS paid me $1,250. The head linesman made more than I did that day, but I was so pleased to get the assignment I didn't care. If I had turned it down, CBS would have given it to Lindsey Nelson or Ray Scott and they would have been glad to do it.

That Super Bowl weekend was crazy. In the rehearsal of the pre-game activities the day before the game, a declawed tiger broke loose from its keeper, let out a roar and pounced on our producer, Bill Fitts, who was hung over from the night before. The tiger's roar scared the hell out of all of us, and you can imagine how Fitts felt. Luckily he wasn't injured, but he tossed the tiger and the trainer out of the Super Bowl show.

On the day of the game, a hot-air balloon broke loose and drifted dangerously close to the stands before it fell to the ground. At halftime, during a re-creation of the 1815 Battle of New Orleans, a cannon misfired early and one of the workers lost his hand. I was glad to get out of that game unscathed.

That was the first Super Bowl after the merger of the AFL and NFL, and if I had made a different decision a few months earlier, I would not have done the game. I would have been announcing the Monday night football telecasts on ABC instead of working for CBS.

ABC started the Monday night package the year the leagues merged, in 1970. Chuck Howard was an executive in the sports division, and called and left a message that he wanted to talk to me. He was going to offer me the play-by-play job for Monday Night Football.

I had done the AFL games on ABC and had been their top announcer until I was bumped by Curt Gowdy. That was the reason I left to go to CBS.

In a fit of pique I decided I didn't want to talk to ABC. I had an appointment scheduled with Howard, and I said to myself, "Screw them. They dumped me, I'm not interested in what they have to offer." I never kept the appointment, and Keith Jackson ended up getting the play-by-play job for the first year. He was replaced by Gifford, and the team of Gifford, Don Meredith and Howard Cosell became famous.

In retrospect, I don't believe I would have become a star, as those people did. No one had any idea how popular Monday Night Football would become. It became the biggest sports show in the history of television, largely because of Cosell. Cosell was bigger than the game. I never tried to be bigger than the game; I never had a gimmick. Meredith had one with his "turn out the lights, the party's over" song.

As I've said, I always admired Howard Cosell. Some people didn't like him, and he always gave people reasons for not liking him. He was a pioneer. Cleverly, he accomplished just what he wanted to do. I liked Howard.

When CBS Radio was awarded the rights to the Monday night package, Hank Stram and I were hired to do the games by Dick Brescia. We had done some games on television together, and with the exception of one year when NBC owned the rights, Hank and I were together on radio from 1978 to 1996, and had a wonderful time. We did 16 Super Bowls, giving me a total of 17 play-by-play assignments for the Super Bowl, more than any other announcer.

Stram was a great partner, and of all the analysts I've worked with—more than 30—he and Paul Christman were the only two who predicted a play before it happened. Hank and I clicked. We both prepared well for the game, never rehearsed what we were going to say. I trusted him. He trusted me. Our work was all spontaneous.

During the AFL days, I worked a few games with Christman. Like Stram, Paul was able to anticipate the next play. Most of the analysts you listen to say, "As you can see, he dropped the ball." Well yeah, I saw it, so why are you telling me? There is constant chatter on TV now, particularly when there are three announcers in the booth. Stram and Christman were different because they said, "This would be a perfect spot for this play or that play," and frequently they were correct.

NFL teams are obligated to give time to the broadcasters, producers and directors the day before a game. The head coach has to meet with them, and the announcers can select a couple of players the team makes available for interviews. Frequently the players give out good information, but not the coaches. They're not going to give any secrets to anybody, so a visit with the coach is usually a waste of time. In fact, some of the coaches deliberately tried to give Stram and I some wrong information.

The advice I received in the baseball minor leagues about whether to criticize a player applies also in football. If I could have caught the pass myself and they didn't, lay it on them. If I couldn't have caught it either, keep my mouth shut. It's also true that a former player has much more license to criticize than I do.

Tom Brookshire and I were working a Packers game one time when MacArthur Lane was playing for Green Bay. He ran out of bounds, somebody hit him and he landed head first between the tarp and the grandstand. His feet were straight up in the air. I gasped and said I hoped he wasn't hurt. Brookshire was howling with laughter until they extricated Lane from the situation. He had license to laugh because he had played the game. It was not my place to laugh.

I mentioned I worked with more than 35 different partners, and the list is impressive: Elmer Angsman, Brookshire, George Connor, Christman, Randy Cross, Irv Cross, Len Dawson, Dan Dierdorf, John Dockerty, Dan Fouts, Gifford, Roman Gabriel, Pat Haden, Mike Hafner, Alex Hawkins, Dan Jiggetts, Sonny Jurgensen, Jim Kekeris, Nighttrain Lane, Floyd Little, Eddie LeBaron, Will McDonough, Paul Maguire, Matt Millen, John Madden, Jim Otto, Jim Otis, Dan Perkins, George Ratterman, Scott, Stram, Summerall, Bob Starr, Johnny Unitas, Joe Theismann, Harmon Wages, Wayne Walker and Larry Wilson. You could make a very good team out of those people.

With these partners, and producers and directors such as Tony Verna, Hal Uplinger, Bob Dailey, Bob Fishman and others, we had a lot of fun televising NFL games.

Those people stand out, for different reasons. I did a couple of games with Madden, who has worked with Summerall for years, and they are a good team because Pat is subservient to John. Part of my problem with television—and it was true in baseball as well as football—is that the TV producers and directors want the color man, or analyst, to be the star. That's OK with me, but there had to be one or two of the analysts I worked with that I had to be better than. I knew almost as much about football as they did, even though I never played it.

When I worked with Madden, I tried to do little things to set him up for comments, and the producer was barking in my ear, "John doesn't need that." Fine. From then on I said nothing more than third down and three, second and 10. Madden is a nice guy, a good friend and a terrific public speaker, by the way. He knows what he is doing and he's riding his act straight to the bank.

The only football partner with whom I didn't jell was Len Dawson, the former Kansas City quarterback and a Hall of Famer. We seemed to disagree about everything; I would say something, and he would say no, that's wrong. We got along well off the air, but once the game began he tried to be dominating. I never fought back, because you can't do that on the air. We had some awkward Sunday afternoons.

I tried to help the partners I worked with, especially the ex-players who didn't have experience on the air. Nobody tries to help these people. They are thrown into the job, and if they aren't good right away, the critics blast them and they get fired. Seldom does anybody try to help them with grammar, diction or the approach to the job.

I worked with Floyd Little, the former Bronco running back and one of the most popular players Denver ever had. We were doing a game in Kansas City on a cool October afternoon. I made a comment I knew Little would respond to, and I waited for him to talk. He didn't say a word. When I looked to my right, I learned why —he was asleep. We were broadcasting the game, and I had put him to sleep. I chalked it up to my soothing voice.

I've always considered Ted Husing, an announcer a long time ago, one of the best football broadcasters ever and I would put Ray Scott, Ken Coleman and Dick Enberg in that class. They are the best as far as I'm concerned.

It's true in football and in baseball that choosing announcers is very subjective. Someone may like an announcer that others think is the worst they've heard, and vice versa. That's why an announcer can't get too excited when someone says they like him or her, and not get too low when they are criticized.

It always helps if the boss likes you. I ran into a problem at CBS-TV when Bob Wussler was in charge. He didn't like me, and I didn't like him. I was in the upper echelon of announcers with regard to playoff assignments and thought I was doing a good job, but he didn't think so. We sat down for lunch one day in New York to clear the air.

He was from Chicago and was a big fan of Harry Caray's. He told me he didn't think I had a sense of humor. Well, that told me that if he didn't think I had a sense of humor, he didn't know me. At that time, the "Grandstand" show came along, and I took the offer and went to NBC.

I was in Houston when Wussler called me and said, "You can't go to NBC. You have a contract." I told him I didn't have a contract with CBS, and he threatened to fire the guy who was supposed to have me under contract. I told him, "You don't like me, you don't give me good assignments, you don't think I have a sense of humor, what do you care if I leave and go to NBC?" He didn't answer.

It's interesting to see how people react when a new boss comes on the scene. You see how the rats leave the ship and how everybody tries to cuddle up. Survival is an instinct, but why does it always go hand in hand with brown-nosing?

The broadcasting business is about as subjective as any; it's all personal, network executives either like you or they don't; fans either like you or they don't, and sometimes talent and ability aren't enough to get a job or keep a job.

As I said, the most enjoyable thing about my profession is to have met interesting people along the way. I did the radio play-by-play for the football Cardinals for a couple of seasons, and was fortunate to become friends with three Hall of Famers from the Cardinals: Larry Wilson, Dan Dierdorf and Jackie Smith.

Wilson was terrific. He was as tough as anyone who ever played the game. He played one game with casts on both hands. Losing a game killed him, and except for a few years when Don Coryell was the coach, all the Cardinals seemed to do was lose.

In St. Louis one year, the Elks Club named Wilson its Sportsman of the Year. I knew how much it would mean for Wilson if his father could be there to see him accept the award. I arranged for his dad, Whitey Wilson, to make the trip from Utah, and we were able to keep it a secret from Larry.

As Larry received the award, he said, "I'm only sorry that my dad is not here to share this with me." At that moment, Whitey Wilson came forward from the back of the room and the audience broke up. I was happy to have done that for Wilson. We are still the best of friends.

I also had a lot of admiration for Dierdorf and Smith, and was thrilled when both finally were selected to the Hall of Fame.

I have been on the football Hall of Fame selection committee for a few years, and it's rewarding when a player I've been representing makes the grade, as was the case with Dierdorf. Some seemed to resent Dierdorf because of his work on Monday night football. Others simply don't know how great a player he was because an offensive lineman seldom gets much attention.

Dierdorf paid his dues in the industry before he became a broadcasting star. He accepted every assignment offered him. He worked hard at getting better, and he's had wonderful success.

Only a few tight ends are in the Hall of Fame, and Jackie Smith had to sweat it out longer than he should have because of the pass he dropped in the end zone while playing for Dallas in a Super Bowl game. All is well now.

If the Cardinals had had more players like Wilson, Dierdorf, Smith, and two others who belong in the Hall of Fame—Jim Hart and Roger Wehrli, they would have had more success, but that success would have been limited because of the problems in the front office.

Ever since brothers Stormy and Bill Bidwill split up the family businesses, with Stormy getting Sportsman's Park race track in Chicago and Bill the Cardinals football team, there have been problems. Bill did some wonderful things for the community while he was in St. Louis that nobody knows about. He can be a charming man in private, but doesn't respond well to criticism or being in the public eye. He also has a problem delegating authority and picked some people for jobs they were not able to handle. The Cardinals picked some good head coaches, but their success was hampered by bad player decisions, especially in the college draft.

Jim Hanifan is the best offensive line coach in the history of the game. If I was ever a head coach he would be the first assistant I would hire. He was limited as a head coach in St. Louis because of poor personnel decisions, the same problem that affected Gene Stallings when he coached the team, both in St. Louis and Phoenix. I'm glad Stallings went on to better things at the University of Alabama.

Once I broadcast a Senior Bowl game in Mobile, Alabama, and as little as I know about it, there were at least eight players in that game who I thought were going to be good pro players, including Keith Van Horn, the tackle who played at Chicago all those years, and Tommy Kramer, the quarterback who went to Minnesota. That was the year the Cardinals drafted Steve Pizarkiewicz, the quarterback from Missouri as their number one pick. I'm surprised the coaches didn't stage a mutiny in the war room on draft day.

One year when Stallings was coaching he was desperate for a cornerback and the team drafted a safety. A coach can be the best in the business, but if he doesn't have those good players, and a lot of help from the front office, he's not going to win.

In the summer of 1996, I was honored to accept the Pete Rozelle Award from the Hall of Fame in Canton, Ohio. It was a kick to go there and rub shoulders with Ray Nitschke, Willie Lanier, Lou Groza, Bob Lilly, Deacon Jones and others, and then be part of the induction ceremony for the new Hall of Famers. I was only half-joking when I said, "This is the first award I ever won where I didn't have to buy a table."

Once I was at a Hall of Fame function and encountered Bronko Nagurski, the Hall of Famer from the Bears. He had been a team-mate of Joe Lintzenich, my wife Carole's father. Carole's dad played football at St. Louis University and later played in the Bears backfield with Nagurski and Red Grange. I was talking to my father-in-law on the phone when I saw Nagurski. Joe said he would like to talk with him.

"Hold on, let me see if I can get him," I told Joe. When I told Nagurski that Joe Lintzenich was on the phone, he jumped up, got on his two walkers and lunged across the room to get to the telephone to talk to his old friend. Moments like that to me are special.

So was the time I listened to Nitschke speak at the Hall of Fame luncheon. Nitschke, the linebacker from the Packers, was at the induction ceremonies in 1996 and stood up to talk at a luncheon. He directed his words primarily to the new Hall of Famers, the people in Dierdorf's class, but many Hall of Famers were also in the room.

"I shouldn't be here," Nitschke said. "My wife is very ill, but I came here to tell you guys what you owe to the Hall of Fame and what you owe to football. Don't forget to come back here. You should come back here every year, you belong here, and it's an honor few people receive." His talk was terrific, and moved everyone who heard him. A few days after he returned home, his wife died. The Hall of Fame in Canton, Ohio is a special place.

I don't know how many in the game of football today have the passion for the sport that Nitschke and some of those other Hall of Famers had. With all the problems in the game now, I see the same signs of trouble developing that have affected baseball for the last 25 years.

When Art Modell had to move the Browns from Cleveland to Baltimore for financial considerations, despite drawing 80,000 people a game, something's wrong. They can't find a team to move to Los Angeles, and soon the people there won't care any more. They already have other interests. Al Davis moved the Raiders back to Oakland, and he is raping that city financially. Bud Adams is moving the Oilers to Nashville, but the people in Nashville have to support the team for another year in Houston before they can move.

The city of St. Louis was knocked around, first in its efforts to get an expansion team, and then to give all that was required to have the Rams move from Los Angeles. Someday the football bubble is going to burst.

How much money is needed to sustain a pro football team? It doesn't help when you see deals like the one Emmitt Smith has in Dallas. It was great for him, an eight-year contract. The fact is he can't play for eight more years. Running backs, with a few exceptions, are unable to take that pounding for more than five or six years.

When pro football teams start guaranteeing contracts as they guarantee them in baseball, football will find itself in the financial mess that baseball is wallowing in. Guaranteed contracts, and arbitration, are the two biggest reasons baseball is in the financial mess that it is in.

The whole sports world lost some of his innocence and began to change in the late 1960s and early 1970s, a time when the entire country was undergoing a change. Television and money were the biggest influences that changed everything, especially in baseball. Financial success in sports is no longer automatic.

12

A Changing World

When I took over for Harry Caray in 1970, I needed a new partner for the baseball broadcasts. The Cardinals and Anheuser-Busch asked for my input, and I suggested Red Barber, the longtime Dodger announcer who had retired. The offer intrigued Barber, but he turned it down. He was living in Florida, and told me, "I'd love to do it Jack, but my wife would kill me if I got back in it."

I was trying to find someone with whom I would be compatible, who would be entertaining and educational for the fans. When I had been doing a lot of football, and some of the people I enjoyed working with the most were Wayne Walker, Eddie LeBaron, Pat Summerall and Hank Stram. We got along well and had fun doing our work. I wanted to have the same arrangement in the baseball booth.

I didn't know Barber that well personally, but had heard him broadcast all those years from back East. He would have been a good name for the broadcast. He probably would have overshadowed me, but that was OK. I didn't mind the competition and it would have been fun and I'd have learned a lot.

The next announcer I thought of was George Kell, the Hall of Famer who recently retired in Detroit. He's a wonderful gentleman, and lives in Arkansas. It would be more convenient for him to work in St. Louis rather than Detroit, but he said while he appreciated the interest, he wanted to stay with the Tigers.

We eventually hired Jim Woods, who had worked with Bob Prince in Pittsburgh for many years. That didn't work out too well. Woods became ill with a gallbladder attack shortly after he was hired, and later didn't do the things he was expected to do by our bosses.

There's more to a broadcasting job than most people know. Fans hear you during the games and think you show up a couple of hours before gametime, talk to some people, do the game and go home. If that's all there was to it, it would be a breeze, but that's not the way it is. That's where Woods got himself into trouble.

He thought Anheuser-Busch demanded too much of the broadcasters and didn't show at appearances they wanted him to make in the community, and didn't attend luncheons and banquets. He and Prince did pretty much what they wanted in Pittsburgh. Woods didn't like someone telling him he had to be here or there at a certain time, although he knew that was part of the job. He left as soon as he could, taking a job with the Oakland ballclub before the 1972 season. That's when Mike Shannon was hired, two years after he had been forced to retire because of a kidney ailment. He had worked in the Cardinals front office in the interim. Shannon has now been on the broadcasts for more than 25 years.

It's a challenge trying to make a bad team sound interesting. After the 1968 pennant year, the Cardinals were not a good ballclub. The world was changing because of drugs, civil rights actions and the anti-war movement, and baseball players were caught up in all those activities just like everybody else from their age group.

There were times when I didn't enjoy being around that group of players. Once at O'Hare Airport in Chicago, we got off the plane and walked through the terminal. The players were carrying music boxes, wearing sandals and T-shirts. One of the players was wearing Levis without undershorts and had a hole in the seat of his pants. I remember thinking, "These are the Cardinals?" Almost all of them had long hair, some wore earrings. Other ballclubs were just as motley looking, depending on their leadership and the control the manager and owner had over the players.

They were at the age to be rebellious, and they wanted to join in the activities going on around them. They wanted more freedom, and that's when Marvin Miller entered the picture with the player's union and started putting pressure on the owners. This led to the first strike and the start of the labor problems that still existed until the players and owners recently signed a five-year work contract.

I wasn't a baby boomer. I was in the boom—World War II. Those in my generation witnessed the happenings in this country in the early 1970s and thought they were aberrations. We couldn't believe that there would be protests against this country from within, or that so many people would start using drugs and have children out of wedlock. That became commonplace, no matter how much people of my generation couldn't understand it.

Television played a major role in the growth of this culture. When there is a group of eight or 10 people, television can make it look like a mob. Those people were crying for freedoms. What they didn't realize then and some people don't want to accept today, is that sometimes freedoms can destroy a society. World War II changed so much in this country. It brought women out of the house and into the workforce. Prices went up, forcing almost every family to work two jobs to exist. Families needed two cars. With both parents working, kids grew up by themselves; no one had time for them. One picture still in my mind is of a young girl I saw hitchhiking in the Haight-Ashbury section of San Francisco. She had a baby in a knapsack on her back. She was one of the flower children. I wonder whatever happened to her. When I saw her hitchhiking on the street corner, I thought it epitomized that era.

Drugs became a way of life for many. Nobody knew much about the subject, so drugs got a foothold in this country and crept into the sports picture before we knew it. Now there seems to be no way to stop it.

I was as stubborn about the war in Vietnam as most veterans of World War II. We believed if this country was going to be at war, let it be a war and let's get to it. Some protested the war, others protested against the protesters, and to this day the discussions go on about our actions in Southeast Asia.

One of my kids, Jack Jr., was at an age where he could have gone to Vietnam, but he enrolled in the reserves and didn't have to go. I didn't approve of the way we were fighting the war. We were so frightened of the Russians that we lost to the Vietnamese. We should have told the North Vietnamese, "You have 30 days to get your ships out of the harbor because we're going to bomb it. If you want your ships there, leave them there," and we should have followed through. That way civilians wouldn't have been hurt and we could have crippled their war effort. We should have told the Russians, "If you want to be a part of it, you stay there too, because we're going to be there at noon." That's the way it should have been fought.

ᶾ⬥

Marvin Miller and the union were good for the players. Miller was excellent at his job. He used to head up the steelworkers union, and he did a hell of a job of stripping the Pittsburgh area of almost every steel mill that ever existed there. He caused steel prices to rise and soon forced companies to import steel from Japan. He did a wonderful job of putting people out of work in Pittsburgh. He did to baseball what he did to the steel industry in this country.

When the courts threw out the reserve clause and granted players free agency, the owners were too stubborn to come up with a workable system. Bowie Kuhn was the commissioner during that first strike, and he ordered spring training camps opened to end the work stoppage.

Not only did forcing the teams to open spring training facilities cost Kuhn his job, it led to the system of arbitration, despite the protests of many, including Gussie Busch and Charlie Finley, both of whom had extensive background in dealing with unions. Busch and Finley reportedly were the only two owners who voted against arbitration.

If Kuhn had not given in to the players and the owners had stayed together back in 1972, the players would have had to eventually cooperate. The union was not as strong then as it is now. The owners and players could have arrived at a long-lasting, workable compromise. Until then, the owners were making most of the money, and they should have been more flexible with the players and worked out an agreement that would have benefitted both sides.

Originally, the owners screwed the players; now the players enjoy getting even. Every time they went to court, the ruling was in favor of the players. The owners never had the leadership necessary to prevent them from collapsing during every strike threat by the players. The biggest mistake the owners made was to agree to arbitration. Twenty-five years later, we are still dealing with the same problems.

Having to put up with the labor unrest, some undesirable players, and bad baseball, made coming to the park on some nights a real chore. Those are the times you earn your money. I've often said my favorite sport to broadcast is winning baseball, but losing and boring baseball is dreadful. During that time, I was able to look forward to the football season to get away from our national pasttime.

࣭

One of the great joys of baseball is that something wonderful can happen when you least expect it. That was the case on August 14, 1971, when the Cardinals played the Pirates at Three Rivers Stadium in Pittsburgh.

I was a total admirer of Bob Gibson as a pitcher. It didn't come easy for him; it took him many years to learn how to pitch. He was also someone I admired as a person. He was kind of cruising to the end of his career, and he had a lot of World Series success and his season in 1968 ranks as the best ever, when he set a record with an unbelievable ERA of 1.12. He had done everything there was to do, except pitch a no-hitter.

The tough-hitting Pirates' lineup included Willie Stargell and a player I always thought never got as much attention as he deserved, Al Oliver. As we played baseball in Pittsburgh, there was a Cardinals pre-season football game being played in St. Louis. People told me later they were listening to the baseball game on the radio while they were watching the football game. As Gibson continued to hold the Pirates without a hit, the cheers began to mount at the football game. Those who weren't listening to the game didn't know what was happening until the word began to go around the stadium—Gibson had a no-hitter going.

When he got the final out—the score was 11-0—on a called third strike to Willie Stargell, I cried. I still have a letter from John Toler, my engineer at that game. He said there were some things he wanted to tell me, and one concerned Gibson's no-hitter. He said when I cried, he cried. Calling the no-hitter was a real thrill, and it also is one of the highlights of Gibson's career.

There were many other nights when I was disappointed at the ballpark, and one was in Philadelphia when Tim McCarver and Lou Brock got into a fight. It tore my heart out.

McCarver, the former Cardinal catcher, didn't throw well any longer and every time the Cardinals got a runner on base the players on the bench were yelling, "There he goes." Sometimes they yelled that when the bases were empty. McCarver was getting ticked off. The reason he was still playing was because Steve Carlton wanted him as his catcher. All Carlton needed was a catcher, he didn't need a hitter or someone to throw out basestealers.

Brock was a fun-loving guy, and as he came to the plate, he said something that pulled McCarver's trigger. McCarver threw a punch, and in a blink he was on the ground with Brock on top of him. Lou put two fingers in each side of McCarver's mouth. McCarver was looking up at the heavens and Brock appeared ready to rip McCarver's mouth open. They were then separated, but I was miserable the rest of the night. The fight itself didn't bother me, I've seen fights before. What upset me was the sight of those two guys who had been through so much together and had been good friends going at each other like that. It really hurt.

Most of the players during that time with the Cardinals were just going through the motions. They were happy to be in the big leagues, making good money, but they weren't very good and the team had little chance of winning. There was not much enthusiasm or excitement. That's kind of the approach the brewery took at that time as well. The best word I can use to describe ownership in the 1970s was stagnant. The baseball team was a stepchild of the brewery and the only time it came to the forefront was when it got into the World Series. The brewery was expanding into a lot of different areas—diversifying—as were a lot of major companies, and they had little time to worry about baseball.

The Cardinals did have a chance to win in 1973, when the Mets slipped in with only 82 victories, and in 1974, when Mike Jorgensen's home run off Gibson in Montreal and the Pirates' win over the Cubs on the last day of the season gave Pittsburgh the division championship. The Cardinals might have been able to win if they had made some moves to improve the club down the stretch, but they didn't do it, leading to an argument between me and general manager Bing Devine that almost prompted me to quit.

The Cardinals needed a shortstop, and so did the Pirates. Dal Maxvill, the former Cardinal, was with Oakland and available. He wouldn't hit much, but he would be a big help defensively for either team. He ended up going to the Pirates, and we were in New York when the deal was made. On the bus going back to the hotel from the ballpark, I said to Devine, "I thought you and Charlie Finley were good friends." Devine said they were, and wanted to know why I was asking. "Why would he send Maxvill to Pittsburgh? Why didn't we get him? They're going to win the pennant now," I told Devine.

Apparently it didn't register immediately with Bing what I was talking about, but he did a slow burn overnight. We had an afternoon game the next day, and when I got on the bus to the ballpark, Harry Walker, one of the coaches, was sitting in the front seat. He jumped up and told me to sit down. I thought, "Oh oh, here it comes," as Devine got on the bus and sat down next to me.

"What did you mean by what you said last night?" Devine asked. I answered I meant exactly what I had said, that if Finley was such a good friend of Bing's, why would he send a player like Maxvill to the Pirates when we were in a pennant race with them and also looking for a shortstop? Devine was hot. He thought I was insulting his ability as a general manager, but I wasn't doing that at all. I didn't mean anything more than what I had said.

Everybody on the bus was watching us argue. Devine started chewing on me again, with his reasons about not making the deal, stopped, and a couple of minutes later started up once more.

To this day, every time the bus going to Shea Stadium passes a certain building, I remember the argument because I said to myself that day, "If he says one more word, I'm going to tap the driver on the shoulder, tell him to pull over and I'm going to stand up and say to Bing Devine that he can take this job and shove it and I'm going to get off the bus." Fortunately, Devine never said another word all the way to the ballpark. We have never talked about it again. If he had said another word, I swear I was going to quit.

ॐ

I got into an argument one time with George Plimpton, the writer, at the Beverly Hills Hotel in Los Angeles. He had just written the book *Paper Lion*, and he was with a group talking about how he had got a hit off Whitey Ford of the Yankees and how he had run the football against Roger Brown and Alex Karras of the Detroit Lions. I had a couple of manhattans in me, and I should never have more than one. He was belittling the abilities of some people whom I admired and I told him he was full of shit.

"If Bob Gibson was pitching and you were batting, and I told him you didn't like black guys and I gave him $100 he'd hit you in the neck. You wouldn't get in there for a million dollars," I told Plimpton. "If I told Alex Karras to break both your legs, you wouldn't run the ball against the Lions."

He said, "I don't believe this conversation is relevant." I said, "It may not be relevant, but you're still full of shit."

He couldn't hit Whitey Ford if Ford didn't want him too. Later when I told the story to Gibson, he said, "You wouldn't have had to pay me the hundred."

♨

About the time of Gibson's no-hitter, Lou Brock's pursuit of Maury Wills' stolen base record and the marathon 25-inning game in New York—I wondered later how many of those innings Harry Caray would have broadcast—I took a shot at the horse racing business.

My late friend, Bob Victor, owned a horse by the name of PlayFellow, which won the Bluegrass and the Travers Stakes. When he was going to the Bluegrass, I gave Victor $200 to bet on his horse for me. Listening to the sports scores on the car radio later that day, I heard that Playfellow had won and paid $45. I pulled the car over to call his kids to make certain they knew the horse had won. Victor answered the phone.

"What are you doing there?" I asked. He said he had missed his flight, and the second plane he took was unable to land because of bad weather, so he had returned to St. Louis. "So you didn't put my $200 down?" I asked. "I didn't get anything down for myself or for you," he said. That's horse racing for you.

Together we bought a two-year-old colt and named him Almighty Buck. He trained in Illinois, and he was a good horse so we sent him to run at Arlington Park in Chicago. He won his first time out, and we came home with a pocket full of money. We left him with a trainer in Chicago and he put the horse right back in another race and the horse broke down. That's also horse racing for you.

These things happen when you are in the racing business on a minor level. You need to be either in the business or not; you can't just have a horse or two and be successful.

All we did was pay bills. A bill from the veterinarian, the blacksmith, the guy who transported the horse to the track, for the exercise people, and the bill for the food. It's like you have another family. In addition, I was always busy or too far away to watch our horse run.

I enjoy horse racing and betting. But it's true that when you go to the track and bet 10 races, you're going to lose. Even if you win two or three times, you're still going to end up on the losing end. It's the same as going to Las Vegas or onto gambling boats. You either walk away right after you get ahead, or you're going to be stung. That's how they build those big casinos and float those boats.

ȥ

I had been broadcasting baseball for about 25 years, and when I received a phone call in 1975 from Chet Simmons at NBC-TV, I was in the mood to listen.

I was broadcasting NFL games for CBS-TV with Pat Summerall, and I was doing the billboards before and after the games, listing the sponsors. One of them was Schlitz, and I had to repeat their slogan, "The beer that made Milwaukee famous." That wasn't going over very well with some people at Anheuser-Busch.

Simmons had hired me to broadcast the All-Star game in 1965. The NBC executives had decided to create a show to wrap around their football programming on Sunday. They were going to call it "Grandstand" and model it after a show in England. They didn't have a pregame show for the NFL at the time and CBS did, with Brent Musburger the host. NBC decided it had to compete with CBS. Simmons was calling to offer me the job as host of the show.

Competing with Musburger without any other obstacles would have been hard enough for me. The only one I ever thought was as good as Musburger in that role was Bob Costas, one is as good as the other.

The money was great, $175,000 a year with a three-year contract. I could keep my job at KMOX during the week and commute to the Rotten Apple for the show on the weekends, but it meant I had to give up baseball. That wasn't a tough decision because the Cardinals weren't very good at the time and the players were not attractive. I was ashamed of the ballclub; the way they played, the way they dressed, and the way they acted on the planes, buses and in hotels. It seemed to be a good idea to take a shot at "Grandstand."

I never aspired to be a star on a national level. I did aspire for the big hit, and I always thought there were things I could have done, like "The Tonight Show," but I never had the opportunity. "Grandstand" was a chance to do interviews and use my other talents and get away from doing play-by-play.

From the start, the show was filled with problems too big to overcome. It would have turned out better if we had a different producer and director, or if they had a better announcer. It's a team effort and you have to make it work. The executives at NBC took a chance on me, trying to match what CBS was doing, but it never was a fair fight.

The idea was to have the host sitting in the grandstand, as though he was watching events, and then tie them all together as the afternoon went on. It was not a comfortable setting, and I couldn't relax. I was doing the show by myself, and the mechanics of it turned out to be more difficult than anybody believed. I needed someone to converse with. I hated being by myself even when I was on "At Your Service" on KMOX, because I thought it gave people the impression that I thought I was the expert and would tell them anything they wanted to know. Maybe some people are good at that, but I'm not one of them.

One problem was that the only sport NBC was able to acquire the rights to before the football games was tennis. NBC was and is big on tennis, but I don't think it's attractive as far as ratings are concerned, except for Wimbledon. It was difficult to believe a weekly tournament was a big story.

The hardest part of anchoring that show was waiting for all the football games to reach halftime. When one game reached that point, the announcers sent it back to me to update the scores of all the other games until their second half started. Those games reached the half at different times, and I had to repeat all of the information and come up with something to talk about to fill a couple of minutes before sending it back to the game announcers. I never knew exactly how long I had to talk. The producer would say two minutes and when I started talking he immediately was telling me to wrap it up in 15 seconds. It was mind-boggling.

They had built the set poorly, and I had problems reading the scores off the teleprompter. The production was bad. As I was talking about one game, they showed the highlights of another. When I came back to St. Louis on Sunday night, I'd ask Carole how the show went and she would say, "Fair." She knew me, knew what worked well and what didn't. She also knew what I could do and what I couldn't do. Every week it got worse. It was bad and I wasn't enjoying it, but didn't know what to do to make it better.

I had the idea then that because the people in charge were from New York, they were smarter than anybody else, that they were the best people with the best equipment, and so forth. I have since learned that St. Louis or Chicago or Detroit and many other cities have producers, directors and cameramen just as good as the ones in New York. Just because someone is working in New York at a network doesn't make him or her better or smarter than anybody else, even if they think they are.

We invited Joe Garagiola to be a guest on the show one Sunday, and he had a lot more television experience than I did. Garagiola and I were supposed to talk about something that was on the teleprompter. "What the hell's going on here?" Garagiola shouted. He told them to take the teleprompter out of there. Don Ellis, the producer, had worked with Garagiola before and he said. "Joe, we've got to do this." But Garagiola took charge and refused to do it their way. The red light came on, we talked and it went well.

That's the way I should have been. Garagiola had taken charge, but I'm not a take-charge sort of guy. I should have stood up and said, "You're killing me the way this show is being run. I can't perform this way." But I couldn't do it, couldn't tell the producer and director they didn't know what they were doing, so I suffered.

Each weekend I stayed at the Park Lane Hotel near Central Park, and would walk down to Rockefeller Center on Sunday morning. NBC had a makeup artist, but nobody else worked on Sunday morning. I had to take care of my own hair. Nobody told me how to dress. I was winging it, using my own wardrobe. If I was doing that show again, I'd have a hair dresser, a makeup artist, someone to select my clothes, a set consultant, and a different producer. It would be much different.

A few years earlier I did a pilot for a show that *Sports Illustrated* was considering. The producer was Bill Creasy, who knew me very well. If he had been the producer on "Grandstand," the show would have worked. He knew what I could do and what sort of a setting made me comfortable. I did an interview with football Hall of Famer Jim Brown for that pilot. To illustrate how long ago that was, the executive producer of that pilot was the father of Ed Goren, now in charge of Fox Sports and the one who hired my son, Joe Buck, to do football and baseball telecasts.

During the interview with Brown, on a movie set, he was holding a Thompson submachine gun. During a break, Brown said, "I wonder if you could do this." I replied, "I used to do it for real."

NBC knew the show wasn't working, so they added a co-host. They selected Bryant Gumbel, at that time unknown except in Los Angeles. I welcomed him, because I also was looking for anything that would improve the program.

We had started the show in September and went through the winter, and I thought we were getting better until one Sunday, when an NBC executive, Carl Lindeman, showed up before the broadcast and asked me to have a cocktail with him at 6 p.m. when the show ended. There was a flight from Laguardia to St. Louis at 7 p.m. and I told him I didn't really have time to have a drink because I had to get back to St. Louis. He insisted, and I thought, "Ought–oh." When the program was over, we sat down by the ice skating rink outside Rockefeller Center. I ordered a VO and water, and he said, "We've decided to make a change." That's what bosses say when they fire you.

"So do you want me to miss my flight?" I asked. They brought the drink, but I got up and left without taking a sip and made it to the airport in time to catch the flight home. I was meeting Carole and Joe Sullivan, the former executive of the football Cardinals, and his wife Joan for dinner at the Chase Hotel. I didn't want to tell Carole the bad news and spoil the evening. Abruptly, after we had finished the meal, I said it was time to leave. All the way home Carole gave me heck for being impolite. I didn't want to tell her until the next morning, but she kept harping at me and asking what the problem was. Arriving home, I went to the bathroom and while shutting the door I said, "Well if you really must know, they tied a can to us today." "What?" she said, knowing then why I had been acting so peculiarly. Fired again.

Because of my contract, I had not expected such a quick change. The executives figured out after I was gone the problem wasn't just with me, it was everything. Soon the producer was fired, then the director, then the fellow who replaced me, Lee Leonard, until it was a different show completely with Gumbel as the host and it worked out well.

I was committed to NBC for two more years, and they put me on their football telecasts. Mike Roarty was in charge of the Cardinals broadcasts for the brewery and he allowed me to come back into the booth. He said he had an idea the NBC show wasn't going to work, so he had kind of saved my job for me, even though they had hired Bob Starr to join the crew.

Roarty is one of my best friends, not only because we have worked so closely together over the years, but because he is a wonderful guy. He started working for Anheuser-Busch in Detroit and made other stops for the brewery, working in Denver and other places, before moving to St. Louis and advancing to the job as director of marketing. He was in charge during a period of time when the brewery had remarkable growth.

Roarty was born to be an executive. Some people know how to be a boss and others don't. Those who don't know, never will know. It isn't something you can learn at a university. It has to be innate, the ability to be able to tell other people what to do and how to do it and still be a nice person. Roarty was able to do that.

People liked to work for him, and I was fortunate that he was a friend of mine in addition to being the boss, or else It would have been impossible for me to return to the Cardinals broadcasts.

Mike was a baseball fan, and he would have liked to have been more involved in the team's operations, but he was never asked. The brewery tapped other executives, like Fred Kuhlmann and Stuart Meyer, to run the baseball team and they struggled in that role, whereas I think Roarty would have been successful. After Roarty retired from the brewery, Mark Lamping, who had worked for Roarty, became the Cardinals' president.

As had been the case when I left the Cardinals a year earlier, they were still struggling. Bing Devine decided to make a change in managers and replaced Red Schoendienst with Vern Rapp.

What Rapp brought to the team was chaos. On one of the early days of spring training in his first year, 1977, outfielder Bake McBride was there early to work out on his own. He put on the uniform, picked up his glove and was heading out the door of the locker room when Rapp stopped him. "Hey you, where are you going?" Rapp yelled, not even bothering to call McBride by name.

McBride explained that he was going on the field to work out. "Not like that you're not," Rapp shot back. McBride asked him what he meant, and Rapp pointed to McBride's beard and mustache. "That's not the way we're going to do it here," Rapp said. My antenna went up.

Rapp had a celebrated feud with reliever Al Hrabosky over his long hair and Fu Manchu mustache. Somehow the team made it through the year with an 83-79 record. Only days into the next season, the trouble intensified.

Rapp and catcher Ted Simmons got into an argument after a game the Cardinals lost. Simmons had gone into the locker room and turned on the stereo. Rapp forgot to shut his office door while he was yelling at Simmons, and everybody heard the manager call Simmons a "loser".

Simmons told me this about a week later when he invited me to lunch. Simmons asked, "Do you to know what's going on here?" I said I didn't want to know, but Simmons told me anyhow. Simmons thought Rapp was making decisions just to show that he was the boss and the moves or non-moves were hurting the team's chances of winning. He also told me the players were ready to rebel against Rapp.

We were in Montreal, and Rapp was scheduled to do an interview show with me on KMOX. I waited for him in the lobby, and a few minutes before we were supposed to go on the air, he showed up and told me he had decided he wasn't going to do the program that night. He said, "I know this doesn't show you much guts, but I'm not going to do the show." I did the program by myself, and one of the callers asked a question about the performance of the team.

I answered, "Doesn't anybody back there understand what's going on with this club? We have a rebellion going on." I proceeded to say what I had been told by Simmons. I had just hung up at the end of the show when the phone rang. Mr. Busch was calling. He was the last person I wanted to hear from.

"Buck, what the hell's going on up there?" he barked at me. I said, "Mr. Busch, I don't want to get into it. Please ask someone else." He said a few more cusswords and added, "Buck, I'm asking you!" What he meant was, "I'm telling you I want an answer about what's going on or you're fired." I told him the manager had lost control of the team.

"What would you do?" he asked. Again I tried not to answer him, which prompted another string of obscenities. "Tell me, Buck, what you would do." I said I'd fire Rapp. Then he wanted to know who he should hire, and I answered Ken Boyer, who was managing in the minors for the Cardinals.

After my conversation with Mr. Busch, the telephone rang again. I said "Hello, Bing," because I knew the call was going to be from Bing Devine. He also was all over me about what was going on, yelling at me because he had hired Rapp.

I felt badly for Rapp, but I knew I had said what I honestly believed. After the conversation with Bing, I went up to Vern's room and knocked on the door. When he came to the door, I didn't know if he was going to punch me in the nose or what. "I'm sorry this happened," I told him. "You didn't go on the program, and I said I thought the ballclub was falling apart. Mr. Busch called, and I told him what I thought and I'm sorry this has happened." He nodded his head, said "OK," and shut the door.

Bing arrived in Montreal the next day and fired Rapp. He named Jack Krol the interim manager until Boyer arrived. Ken was a calming influence on the team, but couldn't get the players to perform much better. Devine himself was fired and was replaced by John Claiborne, a move I never could understand. Everything related to the team was totally disorganized, but that was about to change—Whitey Herzog was coming to town.

C H A P T E R
13

Whitey and the 1980s

The problems with the Cardinals ran deep. John Claiborne, chosen by Lou Susman to be the general manager, was in way over his head. Susman was the attorney for Mr. Busch, and as Gussie got older, Lou became more involved in making baseball decisions. Margaret Busch, Gussie's wife, also was in the circle of decision makers, which meant there were three people running the show who knew nothing about baseball. Adding Claiborne to that group made it a quartet that couldn't sing.

They were all smart enough, however, to realize that they needed someone to run the team who was a take-charge guy, one who could evaluate players and wasn't afraid to speak his mind or make decisions. They found their man in Kansas City, where Whitey Herzog was playing golf and fishing after being fired by the Royals in the fall of 1979.

No one ever questioned Whitey's abilities as a manager. His Kansas City teams had won three consecutive American League West division titles, but he had a falling out with owner Ewing Kauffman, and when the Royals finished second in 1979, Whitey was gone. He was playing golf at the Lake of the Ozarks on that June day in 1980 when he was called to the telephone, and he said later he knew it was either bad news or a job offer. Luckily for him and the Cardinals it was the latter.

Boyer was fired in between games of a doubleheader, in Montreal, and Herzog was introduced as the new manager at a news conference at Grant's Farm. He soon learned about the mess the Cardinals were in.

What Whitey determined very quickly was that to rebuild the team, he would have to trade a lot of players. The way to do that was to get Gussie Busch on his side. He developed a close relationship with Gussie, playing cards and drinking beer with him at Grant's Farm. He spoke honestly and directly about what was wrong with Busch's team. Gussie gave him the authority to do what he had to do to clean up the ballclub, as long as Gussie knew about every move in advance. To make sure nothing got in Whitey's way, Claiborne was fired as general manager and Whitey was given that job as well.

Herzog decided the best way to determine what needed to be done was to step away from the field, so he named Red Schoendienst manager for the rest of the season. That allowed Whitey to see the minor league players and to check out those on other teams who might be available in trades, and then he went to work.

I was immediately impressed with Whitey and the way he went about his business. He is the smartest person I've ever met in baseball. I've said before how much I enjoy being around people who are smarter than I am, and Whitey definitely fell into that group. Baseball is a rather non-intellectual game; it's a do-it game. Whitey went into baseball directly out of high school and never went to college, but earned a master's degree in baseball from Casey Stengel and others he was associated with during his career.

Herzog was never tentative about making a decision. He wasn't always right, but he was right a lot more often than not. He was never afraid. He had the guts to trade Ted Simmons, and a lot of people wouldn't have done that. He traded Leon Durham and Ken Reitz for Bruce Sutter. He recognized what had to be done and went out and did it.

Whitey was a great evaluator of talent because he touched all the bases in his baseball career—as a player, coach, scout, farm director, manager, general manager and fan. He looked for more than just playing ability, he looked for the intangibles that made the difference between a winning player and a good player.

Herzog has a great sense of humor and really enjoyed his work. He has extensive energy; even his hair had energy. He has a great memory, and was not afraid of work. He respects the game, and always respected people like George Kissell and Bing Devine.

He recognized talent in other people, and had the confidence in his own abilities so he never found other people challenging to his position.

Some people shy away from Herzog because he never backs down, and he is quite dominating. Whatever group he walks into, he takes charge. If he is one of the speakers at a banquet, he'd be the one you'd remember from the evening. If he did a radio or television commercial, he did it with bravado. He is a drum major, not a piccolo player.

Whitey, Shannon and I frequently played cut-throat pinochle. When we were down to the last few cards in our hand, Whitey would know exactly what cards each person was holding. He laughs a lot, and when we did commercials for Busch beer we had a ball. The commercial with the shark chasing the boat and the one talking about umpires at a barbeque were hilarious. Herzog is a ham.

One of the best of Whitey's moves was the trade that sent Garry Templeton to the Padres for Ozzie Smith. It took him about three months to work the deal, and how he talked the Padres into it, I'll never know. Smith's agent had upset the Padres with some of his statements and actions, and the Padres thought a change of scenery would help Templeton become the player that everybody thought he should be. Luckily for the Cardinals, Smith was on a team owned by Ray Kroc, the founder of McDonald's, who knew how to make hamburgers and millions of dollars, but didn't know a lot about baseball.

Whitey's moves resulted in a pennant in 1982, and a win over Simmons and the Milwaukee Brewers in the World Series. That Cardinals' team wasn't great, and I don't think a lot of managers would have won with that personnel, but Herzog was a master of getting the most out of his players. He was able to figure out the best way to make use of players and seldom put them in a situation where they would not succeed. He was able to predict several innings in advance what was going to happen in a game, and he told players how they were going to be used and when, so if the situation developed, the player was ready to pitch, pinch-hit or pinch-run. The player didn't find himself trying to hurriedly get ready because the manager had a sudden brainstorm.

When Herzog pulled off the Templeton-for-Smith trade, I wonder if he knew he was getting a Hall of Fame player and the greatest defensive shortstop of all time. He was looking at the trade as more of addition by subtraction because he wanted to get rid of Templeton.

Of the thousands of players I've seen come and go, two who stand out are Templeton and Dave Parker. I thought both could have been among the greatest players of all time and certainly should have been Hall of Famers, but they didn't make it.

It upsets me when I see players with outstanding ability fail to make the most of it. That happened with both Templeton and Parker. Templeton had more tools than Ozzie Smith, but Smith made himself a great player by working hard at it, and Templeton let his skills diminish because he didn't work hard enough. There are many people who aspire to a major league career and don't have the necessary skills. When you see a player who does have the ability and then fails to make the most of it, it's sad.

Ellis Valentine is another who should have been a great player but wasn't, because of drugs. He was playing in St. Louis one night and got hit on the cheekbone by a fastball. It looked like it took him 10 seconds to go down to one knee. I think he was so out of it, he didn't know he had been hit by a pitch.

I resent people like Steve Howe and Darryl Strawberry. Strawberry shouldn't have been in the World Series in 1996 for the Yankees, that should have been somebody else. They say people deserve a second chance, but how many chances did Howe get? Too many. Compare those individuals with people in everyday jobs who run into the same kinds of problems. Nobody does favors for them or opens any doors. These players continue to get in trouble and still get more chances. Sometime it's going to have to stop if baseball is ever going to get serious about getting rid of drugs and cleaning up the game.

The drug problem in baseball started in the 1960s with Dexadrine, which was given to players by trainers and doctors because it increased their energy level. I've seen players take Dexadrine in the afternoon and then another pill just before the game that night. One pitcher would get to the ballpark at 2 o'clock if he was scheduled to pitch that night and start popping greenies, the slang name for Dexadrine. He'd have two or three by the time the game started, and thought he was going to pitch a shutout because those pills make you think you're doing better than you actually are.

One player on the Phillies ruined a great career because of greenies he got from the trainer. The team doctor told me the player started out taking one, then two, then three and the problem continued to escalate until he couldn't perform any longer. We were all ignorant about the harmful effects of drugs back then.

I took a Dexadrine once in my life. I had to go from a baseball broadcast in Philadelphia on Saturday night to a football game in Dallas the next afternoon. I knew I was going to be tired, and Bob Bauman, the Cardinal trainer, gave me a greenie and told me to take it about the time my plane was landing in Dallas.

I took it, and when that football game ended, I was on the ceiling. I was looking for another game to broadcast. Flying back to St. Louis, I had a cocktail, and I think I could have flown home without the plane.

Even though drug use in baseball is not as prevalent as it used to be, the game is still not 100 percent pure. No doubt there are still players in the major leagues using drugs who haven't been caught. They will continue to get away with it until they make a mistake or play their way out of a job. The union will not allow the players to be tested for drugs and I strongly disagree.

Players in the minor leagues are tested, but they'll never be tested in the major leagues if the union continues to stonewall the issue. I admire the umpires' stance; they have agreed to random drug testing. All NFL officials are tested for drugs, and they can test the players in football for cause. It's reassuring to know these people are clean. I wish major league baseball would do the same.

I heard a quote recently: "Somebody has kidnapped justice and hidden it within the law." That applies to many things. Justice does not prevail in this country; the laws prevail. Our constitution is constipated; and drug use is a perfect example. People cite their civil and individual rights and can not be tested.

If I'm a passenger on an airplane, I want that pilot tested for drugs. I'm not against drug testing in schools, either. I'd give my permission as a parent, as I think most parents would. Baseball has been stupid in not acquiescing to what should be the norm. The norm now is abnormal. If a player is caught using drugs, he shouldn't be given chance after chance to come back and play again. Players shouldn't be allowed to have it both ways.

Some of the players' leaders have done a disservice to the game, to my game, to our game. It's not *their* game. If you want to play professional baseball, you should have to remain drug free. It should be that simple. Wouldn't that be great?

The drug problem in baseball in general and on the Cardinals in particular was a lot more serious than I knew. Hank Stram and I were in Cleveland in the early 1980s to broadcast a Browns game. In preparing for the game we went to meet Browns' coach Sam

Rutigliano. Sam said, "Jack, how's your drug problem over there?" meaning the Cardinals. I told him I didn't know, but that I thought it probably was about the same as everywhere else.

"Baloney," he said. "You know. You know who they are, too." I said, "I do? Tell me who they are." He said, "One of them is Keith Hernandez, and if I know about it, you know about it."

I said, "Sam, I don't know anything about it. I can't recognize those problems and nobody has told me about it. I'm not being coy with you. There might be a problem, but I don't know anything about it."

It was proven later that there was a serious drug problem on the Cardinals in those years. Looking back it explains some of the things that didn't make sense at the time. I never saw players taking drugs or any evidence of it at the time, even when all of the activity was supposedly going on in the clubhouse in Pittsburgh.

Stram and I went to talk to another NFL coach before a game and started asking the usual questions, about the game plan, injuries, matchups, and so forth. The coach was not interested in talking about any of it.

"You guys don't know what's going on, do you?" the coach said. Hank and I didn't know what he was talking about.

"Do you know what these people are doing to the game and doing to me? And doing to themselves?" the coach asked. Without waiting for an answer, be continued. "On my team, I just got rid of seven players who were using drugs. We are treating seven more, and there are seven others that I haven't caught yet. That's 21 players off the roster. My wife is driving these people to the hospital or to an institution in the middle of the night. I'm trying to save lives and trying to win football games. Why do you think these players drop the opening kickoff? And can't catch an end-over-end kick? Why do you think they drop an easy pass and jump offsides? They fall asleep at halftime, when I'm talking to them trying to correct the mistakes of the first half. This is the biggest mess the game has ever known."

Hank and I were stunned. Neither of us had any idea the problem was that bad, and I know it was not limited to that one team. That team later played a Monday night game and it was one of the worst games ever played. Neither side could do anything right. There were missed field goals, fumbles, interceptions, dropped passes. The problem I had was that I knew too much from what the coach had told us and couldn't use the information in the broadcasts. "Stop telling me these things," I had told the coach. "I don't want to know." He told me, "Well you ought to know. Just don't blame me when they drop a pass or a punt or jump offsides. Don't blame me. Drugs are the reason."

The coach later tapped the telephone lines of those other seven players, and they were caught. That whole episode shocked me. The drug problem was that widespread.

The Cardinals were playing in New York when the drug trial against several players was going on in Pittsburgh. Ed Bradley of "60 Minutes" came to the ballpark and wanted to interview Herzog. Whitey turned him down, and Bradley asked me to intercede. Whitey said he would do the interview as a favor to me, but the one thing he wasn't going to talk about was the drug trial. He told Bradley "Don't talk about Pittsburgh."

The camera started rolling, and Bradley's first question began, "Keith Hernandez is on trial in Pittsburgh..." Whitey just stared at him before exploding, "Why do you do things like that? What's the matter with you? Are you that dumb? I just told you .. ." and then he got up and walked away. Bradley had tried to trick Herzog. It didn't work.

That non-interview reminded me of one many years ago involving Howard Cosell and Fred Haney, then the manager of the Milwaukee Braves. The Braves were in St. Louis, and Eddie Mathews had a fight and threw someone through a glass door at the Chase Hotel. The Braves went to New York the next day, and Cosell showed up at the Polo Grounds. Haney agreed to do an interview, but told Cosell, "Don't ask me anything about last night. These players were arrested, we have to deal with that." Cosell said OK. The camera started rolling, and Cosell's first question started out, "Fred, last night at the Chase Hotel in St. Louis ..." Haney looked right at Cosell and said "Go screw yourself, Howard. Try that on your blank-blank camera," and he turned and walked away. Some broadcasters give others a bad name.

I was doing the morning show on KMOX and the subject of drugs came up. I said I would like for someone to call me who was taking cocaine and would be willing to talk about it. The lines lit up. One caller told me all about what he was doing, and how much his drug habit was costing him. It was difficult to comprehend.

Dr. David Ohlms was a psychiatrist at St. Anthony's Hospital in St. Louis who did some work for the Cardinals. He was dealing with drug abusers, so he himself took cocaine to try to understand the ramifications. He told me it was the greatest feeling he ever had in his life. It was understandable to him how people got hooked. It did not become a habit for him, but he knew what it was all about.

We had a player on the Cardinals, David Green, whose problem was alcohol. He was from Nicaragua, and was another player with tremendous ability that just went to waste. The Cardinals tried to help him. Anheuser-Busch went to great efforts to get his mother out of war-torn Nicaragua and into the United States. I don't know if Green's drinking problem was caused by worrying about his family or some other reason. Joe McDonald, the general manager at the time, tried to get Green to check into a rehab center. Green finally was persuaded to go when the Cardinals were at the airport leaving on a trip.

Green went to the rehab center, but McDonald made the mistake of not informing Mr. Busch before the story was in the news. Busch had made it clear he did not want to be surprised by anything he heard about his team. He wanted the information first, and that was one of the reasons McDonald was fired as general manager.

Whitey had given up the title of general manager to concentrate on his work on the field. Whitey was freed from having to spend time in the office, especially during the winter when he wanted to be skiing and hunting, and it meant he didn't have to spend all day on the phone talking with agents, something he didn't like to do.

McDonald's departure meant the Cardinals had to find a new general manager, and I was surprised one day when Bob Hyland called me one day and said Lou Susman wanted to meet with me. Susman wanted my opinion on who the Cardinals should hire. I repeated my often stated desire of not wanting to get involved. I didn't feel comfortable recommending people for that job or badmouthing others.

Susman said he understood, but he had a list of candidates he was considering. He said, "how about if I give you the name, and then you give me a thumbs up if you think the person is qualified." I said that sounded OK, so he read the list. I don't remember all the names, but one was Dal Maxvill, and I commented that he probably would be the right choice since he was a smart guy, a college graduate, had played the game and was involved as a coach, at that time with Joe Torre in Atlanta.

I thought that was the end of it—until my phone rang early the next morning. Hyland was calling again.

"Get down here, we've got a problem," Hyland told me.

I got to Hyland's office at 9 a.m. and he greeted me with some startling news. "Lou Susman is going to be here shortly. He wants you to be the general manager of the Cardinals."

I wonder what I looked like when that statement registered. I thought Hyland was playing a joke, but he was serious.

"I'm not going to be the general manager of the Cardinals," I told Hyland. "In the first place I don't know enough about it. Secondly, I'm quite content broadcasting, and thirdly, that's the sort of job you get fired from very easily. I'm not at all interested." That made Hyland happy.

I left before Susman got there, and Hyland took care of the matter. I never talked to Susman about it again, and before long Maxvill was named to the job.

In talking with Maxvill later about the pressures he was under, I knew I had made the right decision. The baseball general manager's job is the toughest job in sports, and to do it the right way you have to have total access to the boss. Maxvill couldn't ever get in to see August Busch III.

Dal is a polished person and he's not going to burn any bridges, but I know he was frustrated that he was so limited in what he could do and decisions he could make. One year when the team was desperate for a reliever for the stretch run, the best he could find was Todd Burns—Maxvill couldn't get the approval from the brewery to spend the necessary money for a better pitcher.

Whitey was such a good manager and judge of talent that he and Maxvill were able to put together two more pennant winners, 1985 and 1987, despite the constraints the brewery placed on them. Both teams probably should have won the World Series. The call by umpire Don Denkinger at first base in the sixth game of the 1985 series against the Royals cost the Cardinals the chance to win that one. An injury that kept Jack Clark out of the lineup in 1987 probably cost the Cardinals any chance they had of beating the Twins.

Sometime during that stretch of three pennant winners in six years is when I came up with the call, "That's a winner!" which I say at the end of each Cardinal victory. It was something that developed and caught on. I eased into it by saying one night, "There's a ground ball to short, throw to first, that's a winner." I did this before giving the score.

I stopped saying it for a while, and people wrote or called and said they missed it and wanted me to continue using the phrase. It was easy to do, and the listeners enjoyed it because it emphasized the Cardinals' victory. I guess if I have any sort of trademark, saying, "That's a winner!" has turned out to be it.

ช

The 1980s were fun. We had just come off a decade of bad baseball. Whitey had taken charge and was getting rid of the problem players. When we won again in the 1980s, most of the players were a lot more professional in their approach to the game and in their personal lives. Whitey had two rules at the ballpark, be on time and give 100 percent. He had a lot of unwritten rules, however, and behaving like a professional on and off the field was one of them.

The player whom people will remember most from that era is Ozzie Smith. A home run he hit in the 1985 playoffs against the Dodgers stands out. It's the call that has been replayed the most often over the years, with me imploring the Cardinals fans to "Go crazy, folks!" after Smith's home run just cleared the right field wall.

I don't know why I said it. When Smith had apparently been trying to hit a home run on two previous pitches, I said to myself, "Who does he think he is, Babe Ruth?" I said his approach should merely be to get on base, not try for a home run. There was one out, there was nobody on base, and the score was tied 2-2 in the ninth inning. For Smith to hit a home run was the furthest thing from my mind. It wasn't a predetermined call. He hit it, and the words just came out as the ball sailed into right field.

"Smith corks one into deep right field, down the line. It may go... Go crazy folks! Go crazy! It's a home run, and the Cardinals have won the game 3-2, on a home run by the Wizard!"

As the crowd roared, I turned to engineer Colin Jarrette and motioned for him to turn up the crowd mike as we stood and listened to the ovation. Honestly, I thought I had blown the call. Why did I say that? It wasn't until everyone started talking about the call that I relaxed and knew it had been appropriate.

One of the reasons the call gained popularity, even though it was broadcast only on KMOX and the Cardinals network, was that the game was played on Monday afternoon, and many weren't able to leave work or watch the game on television. Thousands were in their cars headed home when Smith hit the homer, and I was told later that those stuck in traffic were honking their horns and punching their fists in the air in triumph. It was a great moment for the entire city.

The call of the Smith home run compares with my call of the home run hit by Kirk Gibson of the Dodgers off Dennis Eckersley of the A's in the 1988 World Series. I was calling that game on CBS Radio with Bill White, and Gibson was hurt and not expected to play when he limped off the bench to pinch hit for the Dodgers in the bottom of the ninth.

When Gibson hit the ball, with a man on base, and it disappeared into the right field bleachers, it was as unexpected a moment as Smith's homer had been three years earlier.

"Unbelievable! The Dodgers have won the game on a home run by Kirk Gibson! I don't believe what I just saw!"

That call had more impact because it was on the national network during the World Series. It was another time where I said what came to my mind, and thought about it later. An announcer can be much more dramatic on radio than he can be on television. These are the moments you live for as a broadcaster.

During my career, I have never said anything on the air that insulted a player. There isn't an athlete in any sport who would be justified walking up to me and punching me in the nose for something I said about him on the air. The last to say something to me at all was Milt Thompson, an outfielder who was with the Cardinals for a few years. He was playing left field one day, and couldn't make a throw and a run scored. I said, "If he can't throw a guy out from where Thompson was, he'll never throw anybody out."

Somebody told him about it, and he approached me the next day and said, "We're only human, Jack. I'm only human." I don't think I helped the situation when I told him, "You're human, but you can't throw."

There is a right way and a wrong way to criticize during a game. If an outfielder makes a bad play, I could climb all over him by saying, "How long has he been playing the game? How long do you have to play the game before you stop making stupid plays like that?" If you throw in a comment about the guy hitting .240 and making $5 million a year, you can have the crowd sizzling when he comes to bat. That's inflammatory. A better way to handle the situation is just to describe the play, and let the listeners form their own opinions about whether the player should have been able to make the play or not. The crowd reaction that the listeners hear helps to tell the story.

Some probably would have been critical on the air about George Hendrick, because he didn't talk to the media. That didn't bother me, in fact I had fun with it. I tried three or four times to make a polite approach and ask him to do an interview, but he wouldn't do it. So I started calling him "Silent George." The listeners knew what it was all about. I think even Hendrick enjoyed the nickname.

I never had to make any negative comments about Ozzie Smith. He made some of the most unbelievable plays anybody has ever seen. He also had a style and a grace about him that was unique. When Smith was on the Cardinals, the team won. During his 15 years in St. Louis, the team won its division and went to the playoffs four times with one World Series victory. That's a percentage any player would be proud of.

There have been a lot of discussions about whether Smith was the greatest shortstop of all time. If I had to choose between Smith and Ernie Banks, I'd take Banks. After all, Ernie hit 511 home runs. Lou Boudreau also would be a plausible choice. He had hitting ability, plus he was a pretty good fielder. Luis Aparicio was another shortstop who did many of the same things Smith did, so Smith is not without competition as the best shortstop ever. The most outstanding thing about Ozzie is the Cardinals did win while he was here. He played in three World Series; Banks never made it with the Cubs.

There probably were times in his career when Smith could have signed with another team, but realized his future would be better in St. Louis. Some other players who were on those good Cardinal teams, like Jack Clark and Vince Coleman, weren't as astute. They signed for more money as free agents—Clark with the Yankees and Coleman with the Mets—and neither was the same player they had been. Both should have stayed on the Cardinals. They belonged in St. Louis.

Of all those great Cardinal players during the 1980s, the only one certain to get elected to the Hall of Fame is Smith. Bruce Sutter might make it, and I hope Whitey gets elected, they certainly deserve it. Whitey won with teams that were not loaded with great players.

The baseball Hall of Fame is the best in all sports, and that's why it was such an honor when I received the Ford Frick award and was inducted into the broadcasters wing of the Hall of Fame in 1987. It's the highest honor I've ever received, and there won't be anything that can match it.

I knew the award was out there, and I wanted it. I knew the people on the committee who made the selection, but I never wrote to anybody or talked to them or had any of my friends politic to get the award. If I was going to receive the award, I wanted those people to decide on their own.

Mike Roarty and I were having lunch one day at Charlie Gitto's in downtown St. Louis, and Dolan Walsh was seated at the bar. I was told I had a telephone call in the offices upstairs. The only people who knew I was there were at KMOX, and I thought someone from the station was calling me. It turned out to be Chub Feeney, the president of the National League. I still didn't figure it out; I thought he was calling to talk about the St. Louis Baseball Writers dinner the following week, which he was scheduled to attend.

"You know why I'm calling," Feeney said. "You're going to receive the Ford Frick award."

The hair stood up on the back of my neck. Even though I had thought about the award, the news that I had been selected hit me like a rock. There were many other qualified announcers to chose from, including Harry Caray, and others who had been broadcasting longer.

I came downstairs and told Roarty and called Walsh over to the table. It was appropriate he was there that day, because he had played a big role in bringing me in St. Louis in the first place. I went home and called all my kids and told them I wanted to see them for dinner; I had something I wanted to tell them. We reserved a table at Cunetto's and I think there were about 15 of us there, counting spouses.

Some of the kids were frantic. Each had their own guess about the news I was going to announce—I was ill, I was moving, I was dying, I was getting a divorce, I was quitting. None of them were right, and we had a great evening when I told them they were all going to Cooperstown with me.

They all did go to Cooperstown, along with two of my brothers, and it was terrific. We had a dynamite time. Many folks came from St. Louis, including executives of Anheuser-Busch and Bob Hyland, who was afraid of flying. It made it more of a special tribute that all those people were there.

I had been to the Hall of Fame induction ceremonies on three previous occasions, when Musial and Gibson were inducted, and one year when I was the master of ceremonies. Having been there helped prepare me, and I knew what a hectic and emotional scene it would be.

The morning of the ceremony, I had breakfast with Jack Lang, a writer from New York who was receiving the writer's award. He told me, "I know I'm going to cry." I said, "If you're telling me that at breakfast, I believe you. I'm not." I was happy I had written my speech, otherwise it might have been overwhelming, but I just breezed right through it.

ॐ

By the mid 1980s, I had been broadcasting sports for more than 35 years, and I had never missed an assignment. Frequently I had the flu or other excuses where I could have stayed home, but I never did. The only time I ever messed up and forgot an appearance was when I was scheduled to speak at a dinner in the St. Louis suburb of Florissant. The Cardinals were in New York, and I stayed over an extra day to go to the theater. I was walking down Fifth Avenue when I remembered "I'm supposed to speak in St. Louis tonight." I was able to reach Al Fleishmann, and he made the appearance for me.

I thought my job was to do all the games and I never would have thought of taking a vacation in the middle of the baseball season, until Mike Roarty told me I was going with him and other Anheuser-Busch executives to Ireland for the Irish Darby.

Anheuser-Busch had acquired the rights to be the sponsor of the horse race as a means of introducing Budweiser to Ireland. They wanted to make a big splash, and spent a lot of money upgrading and fixing up the racetrack. Roarty told me, "You're going with us." I told him I couldn't go, because the Cardinals were playing. "You're going with us," he repeated. Carole and I not only made that trip, but for several years thereafter we went to the Darby and always had a sensational time.

Previously I had gone to Ireland with Carole on our own vacation in February. It was the only month of the year I could go, because of baseball and football assignments, and we learned that February is not the time to tour Ireland. It was cold, and the rain was coming down sideways. We rented a car and drove around trying to see what we could, but Ireland was closed for the winter. We finally found a motel, but it had no heat. I think suffering is a way of life for those folks. Carole wore socks and my cashmere sweater to bed.

During our tour, we were going past Shannon Airport. I already had looked at the flight guide, and I knew there was a plane leaving for New York in 45 minutes. I said to Carole, "Have you had enough?" She shook her head yes. I drove into the airport, stopped in a no parking zone, threw the keys and the rental agreement on the front seat of the car and we ran in and boarded the flight. I still don't know what happened to that car. We flew back to St. Louis and checked into a hotel in Clayton and spent three days hiding from our kids before we went home.

The brewery trips to Ireland were a lot more enjoyable. Anheuser-Busch always does everything first-class, with limousines and all the amenities. Some years we stayed in a giant castle in Luttrellstown. It had 17 huge bedrooms. When we pulled up in front, all the employees were standing there with their arms folded waiting for us. There were as many of them as there were of us.

At first, some of the Irish people resented the way Anheuser-Busch took over in an overwhelming fashion. Later they realized the company was not a hit-and-run outfit. They did it right, and now have built the Darby up to where it's the richest payoff in European racing. The effort also has given Budweiser a foothold for sales in England and throughout Europe.

One of the neat things about those trips was Mike Roarty always brought along several celebrities, including John Forsyth, Stephanie Powers, Donald O'Connor, Lou Rawls, Norm Crosby, and Tony Bennett. I call Forsyth the Stan Musial of the motion picture world, because he is so nice to everyone.

Gene and Jackie Autry always traveled with us. The people in Ireland loved Autry because they were familiar with his old cowboy movies, which still play over there on television. They don't know Autry as the owner of the California Angels. Gene and Jackie became close friends of ours, and we have visited their home in Los Angeles. The last time we saw Gene was for a surprise 88th birthday party.

I wrote a poem about Gene Autry that I recited that night at the party. I called it, "The Last Cowboy."

As America grew and headed west
Gene Autry was there, and he was the best.
He tapped telegraph keys,
then starred on the screen,
the greatest Saturday star
young eyes had seen.

He wore a white hat and the
kids always knew
he'd do the right thing,
they wanted him to.

He could shoot at a target
and invariably hit it
while jumping a river
and he sang as he did it.

He crooned "South of the Border"
and sang on Christmas morn
the most glamorous cowboy ever born.

His ride through life is
matched by no other
a business tycoon
yet everyone's brother.

He has enjoyed life to the
fullest and made our lives richer,
but he'd have traded it all for a
World Series pitcher.

We salute him today
and we'll love him tomorrow,
the last cowboy's life was
ours to borrow.

Little did he know when
he named his horse,
he was describing himself—
Champion, of course!

Many people would like to have seen Autry's Angels make it to the World Series. Gene hired Whitey Herzog after Whitey left the Cardinals to try to build a team to win it for him as he had done for Gussie Busch. Whitey was the general manager and not the manager, however, and this time he wasn't able to pull it off.

ᴥ

I have had the pleasure of doing the World Series for CBS Radio for many years, including the 1989 Bay Bridge series between Oakland and San Francisco. San Francisco has always been one of my favorite cities, and I was looking forward to spending the time there. The A's won the first two games at home, and the series shifted to Candlestick Park.

I was on the field before the game when Neal Pilson and Ted Shaker of CBS Sports approached me and began talking about the new television contract they had signed with major league baseball. They had hired Brent Musburger as the number-one announcer, and wanted me to be the number-two guy. I said that would be wonderful, and if I could get permission from the brewery, I would love to do it.

That had me pumped up when I went to the booth to prepare for the game, which I was broadcasting with Johnny Bench. We were in a commercial during the pre-game show when the earthquake hit.

We still had the feed, and we had the network send it back to us out of the commercial and we broadcast after the earthquake. The quake lasted for 22 seconds, which doesn't sound like a long time until you're in the middle of it. The worst thing about an earthquake is the uncertainty—you don't know when it's going to end.

Bench's wife was at the game, and she was pregnant. He tore out of the booth to look for her. He ran right under the edge of the upper deck, never thinking it might collapse. I knew Carole was there with a friend of ours, Joe Kordsmier, and I knew she would be OK. My first thought was that the press box would collapse, and I was ready to stand on the counter and ride it on my hands and knees down to the seats, about 60 feet below. I said to myself, "You may break both legs, but you're not going to get killed." As it turned out, nothing collapsed. I told Bench later that if he had run like that when he played he never would have hit into a double play.

We lost our broadcast lines after about 10 minutes and Bench, his wife and I tore out for the parking lot and got into our rental car. He was the driver, I was the navigator. Using a couple of illegal turns, we got out of there ahead of the crowd and made it downtown, where we were staying at the Clift Hotel. There was no electricity or telephone service. I had to hike 14 flights of stairs to get to my room. The next day I climbed down the 14 flights of stairs and finally was able to talk to Carole, who had driven out with our friend to a hotel he owned in Saratoga, about an hour from San Francisco.

They were coming to pick me up, so I had to hike back upstairs to pack the bags. A bellman went with me, and he had to carry the luggage down 14 flights. It was the first time I ever tipped a bellman $50. He deserved it.

I had been in an another earthquake a few years earlier when the Cardinals were playing in Los Angeles. I was in my hotel room on the 33rd floor on the phone with Bob Hyland back in St. Louis. We were about to conclude the conversation when it hit. I told Hyland, "We're having an earthquake." He said, "Really? Hold on and I'll put you on the air." I said , "Screw you, I'm getting out of here." He wanted me to go on the radio and do a play-by-play of an earthquake. No thanks.

The excitement of the San Francisco earthquake almost made me forget to tell Carole my big news—I was going back into network television with CBS, doing baseball.

14

The 1990s

I hoped that what I learned from the mistakes on "Grand-stand" would prepare me for another shot at national television. At that point in my career, I was very comfortable, but thought it would be fun to do the network games. It would be an easy way to make some extra money.

Brent Musburger was the fair-haired boy at CBS, but some had doubts about the quality of his baseball broadcasts, I was pleased to be working with Jim Kaat on the secondary games. I was going to earn $250,000, and I had a two-year contract, with an option for a third year when I left for spring training in 1990.

Late in March, I was in Bradenton, Florida, with the Cardinals when someone from KMOX called Carole in St. Petersburg and told her Musburger had been fired. She called me, and I was shocked. It turned out that his brother, acting as Brent's agent, had angered some of the big shots at CBS and they decided to let Brent go.

What it meant for me was a sudden jump to the number-one team, working with Tim McCarver. CBS wanted me to do the games for the same amount of money, but I didn't think that was right. They finally kicked the salary up to $700,000 a year, less than McCarver was making, but a nice sum for me.

CBS had not broadcast baseball for a long time. NBC had the Game of the Week for more than 30 years, but Neal Pilson and CBS had overpaid—more than $1 billion for a four-year deal—and NBC wouldn't match the offer.

We quickly ran into a problem with the television critics, who compared our broadcasts to those NBC had done. No matter how good the crew is, when people are working together for the first time, it is going to take a while before the broadcasts become top notch.

My biggest problem was understanding my role. As happened earlier in football when I was paired with John Madden, I learned the CBS people wanted McCarver to be the star. They wanted him to dominate the broadcast and have me be the mechanic and stay out of the way.

I didn't want to broadcast that way. I guess I should have accepted it more readily, but relying on my experience on "Grandstand," when I had not challenged anyone, I couldn't let others make all the decisions which put me in a position where I couldn't perform at all. I didn't want the same thing to happen again.

I intended to assert myself, but quickly learned this was not the time or place to do it. Ted Shaker told me he wanted McCarver to be the number-one guy, just as they wanted Madden to be number one in football and Billy Packer number one in college basketball. I wanted a 50-50 proposition, not in terms of money, but in terms of broadcast balance.

The people in charge knew nothing about baseball. McCarver was their man. Anytime they needed guidance, they turned to Tim. He pretty much ran the show, on and off the air.

McCarver and I knew each other well. I was hoping we would develop a good relationship on the air, but it never happened. I wanted it to be a broadcast where we laughed and had fun.

Tim and I went to dinner a couple of times and tried to arrive at a plateau that would be comfortable for him and acceptable for me. I didn't want to be number two on the broadcasts to McCarver. I guess I should have just accepted it, but I couldn't.

We did have some fun. We were doing a Mets game in New York, and the subject of outfielder Kevin McReynolds' sour disposition came up. I said he never smiled, and you could never tell what sort of day he was having by looking at him. I got carried away, and said on the air that I would pay $1,000 to any cameraperson who could get a picture of McReynolds smiling.

A couple of innings later, up came that picture on the monitor in front of me. One of the lady camera operators near the Mets dugout had told McReynolds she would get $1,000 if he smiled as she took his picture. I wrote out the check and gave it to her after the game.

Our broadcasts were good. The ratings were rather low, but when compared to those for the Fox broadcasts in 1996, ours had been a lot higher.

The executives in New York rely too much on ratings, and frequently never give a program a chance to grow. They also listen too much to the critics, like Rudy Martzke in *USA Today*. The viewing audience would be amazed at how much impact Martzke has on the TV executives. It's ridiculous. I think the presidents of the sports divisions of all the major networks read Martzke's column before they brush their teeth in the morning.

Some of his comments about our broadcasts were wrong, but that didn't matter to the network executives. Martzke should have been going after Pilson because of the effect his actions had on all the networks and the sports world. Pilson overpaid greatly to get the baseball contract, and it elevated the price for the NFL rights. That helped the Fox network get the NFC games away from CBS, and also escalated salaries in both football and baseball. Pilson's hand grenade blew the industry apart.

Martzke had worked in St. Louis for the Spirits basketball team, and seemed to have it in for me right from the start. Every time he mentioned my name in his column, he indicated my age, as in Buck, 65. He didn't do that with other people and I thought he was implying that age was affecting my performance. It was a cheap shot, and I didn't appreciate it.

Another thing that bothered me about Rudy's criticisms was that I knew he had to be receiving inside information from someone. There were comments about camera angles and technical details that he wouldn't have known anything about unless someone whispered it in his ear.

We received favorable reviews from people around the country, including Los Angeles, Chicago and elsewhere, but not from Martzke or the critics in New York. Unfortunately, it seemed those were the only opinions the executives in the Big Apple considered.

Pilson, who eventually was fired along with Shaker, demonstrated how little he knew about baseball and sports when he was talking to me about Vin Scully. Scully had done golf for the network and was starting to broadcast football games. "You know what Vin Scully is doing?" Pilson asked me. "He's taking lessons from some of the Rams assistant coaches with film and everything. Isn't that wonderful?" I looked at Pilson and said, "Yeah, that's terrific. I've been doing football games since 1950, isn't that terrific?"

ﬆ

I did an interview with Ted Williams and Joe DiMaggio before the 1991 All-Star game in Toronto. CBS prevailed upon the commissioner at that time, Fay Vincent, to get Williams and DiMaggio to do an interview to be used as part of the pre-game show before the All-Star game. We taped the interview at the studios of the CBS affiliate in Washington, D.C. We were supposed to talk for 20 minutes.

The interview lasted 45 minutes, and it was outstanding because Williams and DiMaggio offered critical comments and opinions about other players and raved about each other's ability. The bright people at CBS thought so much of it they aired two minutes of the interview during the All-Star pre-game show. The rest of that interview is still in their archives, gathering dust.

After the interview, a group of us, including my wife Carole, invited DiMaggio to join us for a late dinner. I had brought a dozen baseballs that I was hoping DiMaggio would sign that I could use for charity events. Carole had the baseballs, and I kept nudging her to bring them out and give them to Joe. Finally after the meal, she took them out of her bag.

"Goddammit," DiMaggio exploded. "Can't I go anyplace, can't I do anything, without people pulling out baseballs?"

He hates to sign autographs. He took a deep breath, held up four fingers and said, "I'll sign four." That's what he did, and I gave one to each of the other people who were with us at the table. Neither Carole nor I got one.

I was at an old-timers game in Atlanta once with Joe D. There was a huge crowd, and DiMaggio got a big ovation as he was introduced and came up to bat against Bob Feller. Feller threw him three big curve balls and struck him out. I was in the dugout with Musial, and DiMaggio came back to the bench and said, "I'm not mad, I'm not angry, but I'll never do that again. I'll never bat again in an old-timers game. I'll attend; I'll do the things I'm supposed to do, but I didn't come here to be struck out by that damn Feller on curve balls in an old-timers game."

I don't like old-timers games. I enjoy seeing the old players invited back, where they are introduced and wave to the crowd, but I hate to see them try to play. I don't like watching Lou Brock when he can't go back on a fly ball and catch it, or Catfish Hunter when he can't throw a strike, or Richie Allen when he can't hit the ball. It tugs at my heart.

The Cardinals had a home run-hitting contest at an old-timers game one year, and as a gimmick they brought in Satchel Paige to pitch. He must have been about 75 years old. It was a brutally hot day, and he couldn't get the ball over the plate. It was excruciating as he stayed out there for about 20 minutes. I want to remember great players from their playing days and not see them embarrassed.

CBS-TV did not pick up my option after the second year of broadcasts in 1991. I knew the night of the seventh game of the World Series in Minnesota that I wouldn't be back, even though nothing was said. We went to a restaurant for a midnight snack and I sat next to Pilson and he never said a word to me. Hey, if they don't like you, they don't like you.

ટੇ

Because of a CBS assignment I missed one of the biggest sports stories in St. Louis in years, when Whitey Herzog resigned as the Cardinals manager in 1990.

The Cardinals had played poorly during a series in San Francisco, and Whitey was frustrated. Some of his players were laughing and clowning on the bench and didn't seem to care whether the team won or lost. Whitey knows some players have more talent than others, but he wants everybody on his team to do his share and not be satisfied with less than their best effort.

We played cards on the flight from San Francisco to San Diego, and there was no indication Whitey was thinking about quitting. I got to San Diego and turned around and went to Los Angeles for a CBS telecast. The next day KMOX called and said Whitey was resigning from the Cardinals.

It surprised me, but the terrible games in San Francisco bothered Whitey. He also was having trouble with the front office, and his relationship there wasn't the same after Gussie Busch died the previous fall. The team had a lot of free agents, and Whitey wanted decisions made about whether they would be re-signed and if not, he wanted them traded. None of that was happening.

Whitey and I have never talked about why he left, but a few years later after Dal Maxvill was fired as general manager, I called and asked Herzog if he would consider coming back to the Cardinals if he was asked. He said he would think about it. I had the impression he would have taken the job if it was offered to him.

That never happened. There was a perception at the Anheuser-Busch offices that Whitey had taken advantage of Gussie Busch during their relationship in the last years of Busch's life. That's as far from the truth as anything could be. He helped make the last years of Gussie's life some of his happiest years. Seeing the Cardinals win again kept Gussie alive and vibrant.

It was just as well that Herzog didn't come back. The Cardinals hired Walt Jocketty as general manager and he's done a fine job. Jocketty used his Oakland connections to hire Tony LaRussa as the manager before the 1996 season after Joe Torre had been fired in the summer of 1995. Whitey doesn't need any more aggravation.

When Maxvill hired Torre to replace Herzog, I thought another fine managerial candidate at the time was Phil Garner. He was a coach then, and he's done well as the manager in Milwaukee, putting together competitive teams for an organization that is always losing money. He would have accomplished a lot had he come to St. Louis.

Torre was a popular choice when he was hired and had a good run with the Cardinals. The team stalled, however, and Jocketty felt he had to make a move. He was so upset about having to fire Torre that when he went to Joe's house to tell him the news, Torre ended up comforting him and he gave Jocketty a bottle of wine when Walt left.

The St. Louis fans wanted Torre fired, rightly or wrongly. He was hamstrung by the brewery not giving Maxvill enough money and the authority to make deals that would have helped. Fans seem to forget when they want a manager fired that the team is going to have to hire a replacement, and the ranks are thin. The Cardinals were fortunate that LaRussa was available and Jocketty was able to get him. Of all the people who play baseball, very few are capable of being a manager, or really want the job. When you hire someone you don't know whether it's going to work or not.

The players knew that Torre was a better manager than the fans realized. He did control the ballclub. He fined players, he benched them when he thought it was necessary, but he never embarrassed them in public and always kept his cool. He went on to manage the Yankees in 1996, and led them to the World Championship. Oddly enough, all the people in St. Louis who had wanted him fired from the Cardinals were tickled that Torre won as skipper with the Yankees. Torre's brother Frank was able to receive a heart transplant the day before the Yankees clinched the World Series over Atlanta. It was a nice quinella for Joe.

One day in spring training, when Torre was with the Cardinals, I was sitting next to him on the bench and the team was working on situational drills. That's where you place runners on the bases, indicate a certain number of outs, and work on what to do when a ball is hit. I couldn't believe how many mistakes the major-league players made. You could have taken any nine kids from my old neighborhood in Holyoke and they would have played more correctly than those major-league players were doing. I was astounded.

It's not just the Cardinals who screw up. The quality of play in the major leagues has declined over the years, because of expansion and the lack of minor-league experience. I've decided when I go to the ballpark I'm not going to let those things bother me. I'm there to broadcast a game and have fun, and I try to leave it at that.

Should I care if George Hendrick wears his pants differently? Or if Ken Griffey wears his hat backwards? When players come out to take batting practice, they wear cut off windbreakers instead of warmup jerseys. I guess they are showing off their physiques. Nobody with any authority does anything about it, so I'm not going to let it bother me.

Earrings and necklaces used to bother me, but no longer. Dennis Eckersley doesn't need to wear his hair that long, but if that's the way he wants to look, it's OK by me. If he gets the hitters out, that's all that is important.

And it doesn't bother me how much money they make. If a .240 hitter makes $3 million, what can I do about it? Do I wish I made the money that Albert Belle makes? Yes.

Today's players receive a lot of criticism, but part of the blame rests with the fans, the writers and broadcasters. We expect a 20-year-old kid who becomes a baseball star to be a star person also, and they don't go hand-in-hand. If you back away from it, a lot of beautiful people have played the game, people like Musial, Gibson, Brock, Ozzie Smith, George Kell, Al Kaline, Dom DiMaggio, Bill Dickey, Yogi Berra, Robin Roberts, Dale Murphy, Henry Aaron, Roberto Clemente, Kirby Puckett and many others. There have been so many good ones that it's easy to ignore the bad guys.

Barry Bonds is one of the best players to ever play the game. He has a quirky personality, but it's not his fault if he doesn't please me. He doesn't care that he doesn't please me. I'm a panderer; I want people to like me. Harry Caray is not that way— he'd like people to like him, but he doesn't care if they don't. I have tried frequently to be friendly with Bonds, even just to visit without doing an interview, but he pays no attention. After a while my curtain comes down too. If he doesn't care, I don't care.

If Bonds is the example at one end of the spectrum today, the guy on the other end is Ken Griffey, Jr. He came to St. Louis with the Seattle Mariners for a pre-season game a few years ago, and I have never seen so much commotion over one baseball player in a strange town as I saw that day. He is probably the most charismatic player on the scene. His image is untainted. He smiles a lot and is a happy guy. When fans watch a game on television, they like to see a player they think would like them if the two ever met. People say that about Griffey.

Part of the reason some players act the way they do is money. They are going to get a lot of money for playing the game, no matter what else they do or don't do. The explosion in the collectibles market and the value of autographs and baseball cards has changed the way players act. Many won't sign autographs at the ballpark because they know they can go to a card show and be paid for it.

In Cincinnati a couple of years ago, I was staying across the street from a convention center card show where Mickey Mantle was signing autographs, and I went over to say hello. The dealers were charging $50 for Mickey's signature and he was limited to 700 autographs. He didn't have to talk to people, just sign his name. It was a Saturday afternoon, and for a couple of hours of signing his name he made $35,000. He caught a flight to Tulsa and had the same arrangement at another show that night. He made $70,000 that day.

When I leave the ballpark after a game, I see fans lined up waiting for the players. They want to see them and wave at them. Every once in a while a player will stop and sign some autographs, but it's rather rare. Ozzie Smith has signed as much as anybody, and he has set a good example for some of the younger Cardinal players, like Brian Jordan.

Jordan became a star player in 1996 and was the driving force of the team that won the division championship and almost upset the Braves to get into the World Series. I told Brian I saw some of Willie Mays in the way he played, and he thanked me for the compliment. He had a late start to his baseball career because he was also a pro football player, but what he does that reminds me of Mays is his desire to win, the dash and recklessness that it takes to be a player of Willie's caliber.

뢰

The 1996 Cardinals were a good team and probably went as far as they should have gone. LaRussa made certain everybody was rested during the season, but at the end of the playoffs they were out of gas. It took a while for the players and LaRussa to get on the same page, but everybody knew that was going to happen because of the adjustments first from Herzog to Torre and then to LaRussa.

When Herzog was the manager, he was the boss. Players did what they were told to do and didn't ask questions. Torre was 50 percent less intense than Whitey. If he had a good day's work at the ballpark and a nice bowl of spaghetti and meatballs, the day was a success for him. Then LaRussa came along, and I've never seen a manager work as hard as he did. In spring training, he was at the ballpark at 6:30 in the morning and he didn't leave until 6 o'clock at night. That's unheard of in baseball. He manages a baseball team the way a football coach does his work.

LaRussa is trying to make a science out of an unscientific game. He's always taking notes, and he and his coaches are always meeting. Usually, the more meetings you have with a baseball team the less effective those meetings become, and the more the players dislike it. Players don't think meetings are necessary, because it's an individual game, and they think in terms of doing their own thing. LaRussa has made a team game of it with his meetings with the hitters, then with the pitchers, and visits with each individual.

It works for LaRussa because he wins. If he approached it the way he does and didn't win, he'd drive the players crazy. He's like General Patton. Nobody makes a move unless they clear it with him, down to the tiniest detail.

Tony is intent on winning. He doesn't think there is any fun in baseball unless you win. He sells that same approach to his players and staff; he's a great salesman.

I know Tony has some outlets and releases, but he is so intense, I worry about his health. In Cincinnati late in 1996 there was a rumor he had suffered a heart attack. It wasn't true, but when I heard about it, I thought it was possible. I wish he could relax and find a way to be successful without being as intense as he is.

Some of the high-profile managers like Herzog, Tom Lasorda and Sparky Anderson have left in recent years, and many are coming out of the coaching ranks and taking over. The manager they should try to emulate is Felipe Alou in Montreal. If you pinned me down, leaving LaRussa out of it, I would say Alou is the best manager in the National League. He's always operating on a shoestring and always losing good players. He's one guy I wouldn't want to cross if I was a player. He reminds me a lot of Walter Alston, the longtime manager of the Dodgers. He was very quiet, but effective. He was fun to be around, an intelligent, friendly fellow.

I'm curious to see what sort of success Jim Leyland has in Florida with the Marlins. He was in an impossible situation in Pittsburgh. He's a loyal guy who hung on as long as he could, but he finally had to get out of there. Leyland's reputation has grown like Pinnochio's nose. I don't think anybody's *that* good, but I'm happy for Jim. Working for a team with more money to spend will give him a chance to finally make it to the World Series.

Managing is a difficult job because the players are so much in control of the game. The owners can't figure out what they want to do, starting with selecting a commissioner. Bud Selig is the owner of the Milwaukee Brewers. How can he be the commissioner of baseball? Donald Fehr, who heads the player's union, is really the commissioner. Whatever he wants to happen, will happen.

Fehr can't lose. He is in control of every aspect of the game, the schedule, the extra round of the playoffs, interleague play, and sharing the television money. Every time a dispute goes to court, the players win.

Personally I would never like to own a professional sports team, I couldn't bring myself to pay an athlete $20 million a year. That's beyond my capabilities.

Economics isn't the only problem in the game. The talent level has dropped because of expansion, and expansion also has brought about a decline in the quality of umpiring. The difference in the umpiring in the two leagues was apparent during the 1996 World Series, especially with regard to ball and strike calls. The umpires stubbornly protest that they are in control of the strike zone, but they're not. The leagues are different and each umpire is different and hitters are baffled by the difference. They would do well to hit the first pitch that's in their zone.

The lack of direction with regard to everything in baseball includes the umpires and umpiring is a very difficult job. Somebody should declare, "This is the strike zone. It goes from the bottom of the letters to the top of the knees. That's the strike zone." Nobody says that, because nobody in charge is willing to say it. Look at the presidents of the both leagues, Leonard Coleman and

Gene Budig, what do they know about umpiring? All they know is that they've inherited a mess. The strike zone won't change until Donald Fehr says to change it.

In 1996, Roberto Alomar was not properly punished because of the union. He spit in the face of an umpire, and Donald Fehr never said a word about it. You would think the head of the players' union would say how deplorable it was and that they would do something about it. All that was heard from the union was how Alomar shouldn't be suspended. That's the way they operate. The union is arrogant and strong. They say and do whatever they wish. Donald Fehr runs baseball.

You can't blame the umpires for being upset. A person would rather be kicked in the groin than have someone spit in their face. Most of the time, the umpires are arrogant and confrontational on the field, but this time they were right. Umpires have become too much of an entity. I have a lot of good friends in the umpiring ranks, but they shouldn't be as big a part of the game as they have become. There isn't enough room for another piece of the puzzle. The puzzle is perplexing enough without adding umpiring to the mix.

Another aspect of the game that isn't as good as it used to be is the quality of the broadcasters. Part of the reason for that is nobody asks for criticism or receives any help. I could help a lot of young announcers, so could Vin Scully or Al Michaels or some of the other veterans. Many people have helped get me where I am, including teachers who have written to me to correct my grammar. I appreciate it when I receive letters like that, and I acknowledge them on the air. I want to know my mistakes so I can correct them.

A teacher wrote to me once and asked me to please stop using the word "of" as in "the pitcher steps off of the rubber" or "the runner takes his lead off of first base." It was unnecessary, and just saying "the pitcher steps off the rubber" sounds better anyway. A correction I wish some broadcasters would make concerns the word "just." It's not pronounced "jest" as most of them say. Outfielders don't go "trottin" to the ball; they are "trotting." These are all minor points, but grammar and diction can positively or negatively affect the quality of the broadcast.

Someone from the Tampa Bay expansion ballclub called me and wanted some ideas about who they should hire as their announcer for 1998. That job has been wide open for someone with the talent to walk right in and take over. It would be a wonderful place to work. When they read off a list of the names they were thinking about, I wasn't impressed. I told them I didn't know anybody they should rush out to get.

Good announcers are hard to find. I don't know how you define the position, because more goes into it than most people know. The total package includes appearance, behavior, education, grammar plus the knowledge of the game. In a class of would-be sportscasters at the University of Missouri, you might have 100 students. If you handed each of them the book with the play-by-play sheet of a baseball game as was handed to me in 1949 and told them to go into a room and re-create the game, I wonder how many of them could do it? My guess would be one or two, maybe nobody. I'm not bragging, just pointing out how difficult it is to do the job.

Some broadcasters complain about former athletes getting jobs in our business. They get these jobs because they have a high profile and are easier to sell. The broadcasts have to be sponsored, and the bigger name you have on the broadcasts the easier it is to sell.

If an announcer is good enough, he will find a job. The other sports are easier—you can find a hockey announcer, a basketball announcer, a football play-by-play man. Baseball is more difficult, because the listening audience knows almost as much about the game as the announcer.

ò.

Things changed a lot when I stopped smoking in the early 1990s. Smoking had been a way of life for me. I smoked two packs of cigarettes a day for 53 years. Hank Stram used to joke that when he bought a new suit he bought an extra left sleeve because he knew I was going to burn a hole in his sleeve with a cigarette.

My mother smoked, my father smoked, my two older brothers smoked. I started smoking when I was 16, selling newspapers on the street corner. Then I went to work on the Great Lakes and everybody there smoked. In the Army everyone smoked. Smoking was a way of life in this country, before people were educated about cancer, emphysema, asthma, bronchitis and other problems that are caused by smoking. Carole used to smoke also, and now we sit in a restaurant and watch others smoke and think it's unbelievable that we were that crude and rude. People always lie about how much they smoke. If they say they smoke a pack a day, you can bet they smoke two. I know people who smoke four packs a day. You have to get up early and stay up late to do that. When I was a youngster, if a kid didn't smoke, they thought he was square. I've learned there's nothing wrong with being square. That's the topic of some of my talks to young people, that it's OK to be square.

One time when I quit, I counted how many cigarettes I didn't smoke. I went for a year and a half, and I was up to a couple of thousand cigarettes that I didn't smoke. Then I started to smoke cigars, and I tricked myself. Soon I was back smoking cigarettes regularly again.

I was in Florida a few years ago and got my annual bronchial infection, part asthma and part allergies. I just decided to quit. I had eight cigarettes left in a pack and I had that pack for a week. I said, "That takes care of that," and threw the pack away. I haven't had a cigarette since. People who say it's not addictive are kidding themselves. It's a need. It's a habit. It dictates your life. The phone rings, you light up. You have a drink, light up. You read the newspaper, light up. There's a story about a fellow who was trying to quit smoking. He lit the cigarettes, threw them down without taking a puff, stepped on them and died of cancer of the foot.

After conquering the smoking habit, there was another thing I wanted to do, and that was to skydive. When I was in the Army, I had the opportunity to join the paratroopers. I thought about it, but opted to stay on the ground. One thing I learned in the Army was not to stick my neck out and do something I didn't absolutely have to do.

Parachuting then was a risky proposition, but 50 years later, science has caught up with it. If you pay attention and do what the instructor says, landing is like jumping from a couch to the floor. It's easy.

Going around the country to different events, I saw people parachuting into stadiums and landing right on target. I was always intrigued, and wondered if I had the guts to do it. I thought about it again last summer because one of the Cardinals' trainers, Brad Henderson, went skydiving in San Diego and showed me the pictures. I thought, "I'm going to do it."

I looked in the Yellow Pages and found a listing for Quantum Leap in Sullivan, Missouri, called them and asked if it was a good day to come out. They said yes, so I had lunch and drove out to

Sullivan, about an hour and 20 minutes from downtown St. Louis. Carole had always told me that if I did skydive, not to tell her, so I didn't.

The instructor talked to me for a while, then I watched a video, and I was ready to go, after I paid the $189. I joke about the fact that they don't take checks, because the first thing that happens if you die is that your family closes your checking account.

I put on a jump suit and in a twin-engine plane went up to 14,500 feet. The instructor was hooked to my back, and he had the parachute on his back. I was standing at the door of the plane, and at that point, I was screwed; I had to go. Another skydiver went before us to film our jump. With all of the flying I've done, I've never seen anybody just get up and step out of an airplane. It's a strange sight.

When I tumbled out the door, everything was a blur. Experienced skydivers are able to float because they know what they're doing. The wash of the airplane and the wind was traumatic and disorienting.

We free fell for 9,000 feet, travelling at 150 miles an hour. That took one minute, 10 seconds. Then I opened our chute. We floated down and only missed our target by three feet. When we touched down, I did drop to my knees, but that was all there was to it. I enjoyed the trip. I was a little sore the next day from hanging in the harness, but otherwise there was no problem.

I tried to call Carole after I finished the jump, but she wasn't home. I had to go on KMOX that night, and I mentioned the jump on the air and that was the first she knew about it. She thought I was nuts. All my kids thought I was nuts. I hadn't told anybody because I didn't know if I had the guts to go through with it. I guess I finally decided, "I'm 72, when am I going to do it? When I'm 80?" I could do it again, but I don't want to.

A lot of wonderful and exciting things have happened in my life. There isn't too much I would have done differently. I have no regrets. I've tried to live life to the fullest, and I'm not ready to stop. There are many more things I hope to do.

15

A Good Life

I don't know how much longer I will broadcast baseball. I am going to do the Cardinals' home games in 1997, but I expect either 1997 or 1998 to be my last year.

I will never completely walk away from the game because of my son, Joe Buck. I will listen to him broadcast, and I wonder how much I'm going to miss the game when I'm not there. I have finally reached the point that I can go out to dinner and still wonder how the Cardinals are doing, but don't have to know the score inning-by-inning.

When I stopped doing basketball and hockey, I didn't miss either sport. They came and went. The same with boxing, wrestling and bowling. When I stopped doing football, first on television and then on radio, there were no pangs; I didn't miss it. I don't think baseball will be as easy to give up.

I've been doing baseball since 1950, that's 46 years, minus the one year I worked in television in Columbus. The day of my retirement is coming. I will be 73 in 1997, and don't want to hang around too long. I go to stadiums and see old former announcers just sitting in the press box, hoping someone will stop and talk. I don't want to play that role.

When the Cardinals clinched the division title in Pittsburgh in 1996, Mark Lamping, the president of the team, wanted me to be there. He suggested I stay on the road with the team until it clinched, even though I wasn't scheduled to broadcast those games. I didn't go, because I thought it wouldn't be fair to my son Joe, and Mike

Shannon, who are there every day. In addition, I wanted Joe to do it. It was a first for him, and I sat home and listened to him call the final out. It was very emotional. The time to draw the curtain comes for everyone, and my time is near.

I missed the end of the National League Championship Series against Atlanta because of a problem with a sciatic nerve. I was in so much pain I didn't care if they played the games or not. Bob Carpenter filled in for me, and had the thrill of calling Brian Jordan's clutch homer in game four. I was happy for him; I've had a lot of those thrills.

I don't try to hide the fact I have the early symptoms of Parkinson's disease and I also have worn a Pacemaker for three years. I had a sweet young thing say to me not long ago, "What sort of work did you used to do?" That will take you down a peg. My ailments don't bother me. I have a firm grip on who I am, what I'm doing and where I'm going. That's no different now than it's been throughout my life.

I love my family, and have been fortunate to have a great relationship with all eight of my children. Alyce and I had six kids, and after we divorced I married Carole, and we had Joe and Julie.

They've been fortunate with their health, and they're all good kids, well-mannered, polite, kind, and nice to each other. When those girls get together, they have a ball. All eight have been to college, and I'm proud of all of them.

It was a thrill listening to Joe telecast the World Series in 1996. He has come a long way in a very short time, and he has a great career ahead of him.

Some think he is where he is today because of me, but that's not true. Having the same last name opened doors for him when he was starting, but he has thrived because of his talent. Joe and Bobby Knight, the basketball coach at Indiana, met last summer for the first time. Joe went to school at Indiana, but never went to say hello to Bobby looking for favors; that's not his way.

When Joe televises a Bears football game, he never mentions that his grandfather, his namesake Joe Lintzenich, holds the record for the longest punt in Bears history, 94 yards. He never brags about things like that.

When Joe was playing football at Country Day High School he hit another player head on. He had some tingling in his arm, and Carole checked that out with a doctor and he told her it could be serious. She went to school and yanked him off the practice field.

Can you imagine the hooting and hollering that was going on? The X-rays showed that Joe's neck was broken. Carole did the right thing.

When Joe was playing Little League football, he was a defensive lineman and confused about his responsibilities. Carole told him, "All you have to do is hit that guy across from you. That's the most important thing." Joe's response was, "But I like him." A Butkus he is not.

You have to marry a happy person. You can't make someone happy. Carole, or blondie as I call her, is my best friend.

She has a degree from Washington University in psychology and physical education. She was on Broadway with a starring role in "How to Succeed in Business Without Really Trying" and she loves me.

Carole's a nice person and helps more people than I could mention. She helps many of the elderly, and she never forgets her friends. She has a lot of energy, and puts in long days. She is involved with charities and Bible Study groups and has a program on KSIV, the Christian radio station.

One of the common desires we have is to help other people, and to take advantage of our name recognition to benefit as many charitable causes as possible. I visit many who are sick or injured, and when they recover I get a kick out of it. I've been very lucky in my life, and I'm glad I can share my good fortune with as many as possible.

I've been the campaign chairman for the local chapter of Cystic Fibrosis for more than 27 years. We've raised more than $1 million each year, and that has helped fund research into the cause of Cystic Fibrosis. The researchers are close to finding a cure. That would be the greatest thing to happen in my lifetime. Youngsters used to die from the incurable disease when they were 10 or 12 years old, but now they are living longer, getting married and having healthy kids of their own. A lot of progress has been made.

I've always had trouble saying no whenever people ask me to make appearances to speak or be a master of ceremonies. I can't turn them down. Over the years I did almost everything I was asked to do—the Mathews-Dickey Boys Club, the Police Department, the Cancer Society, Boys Town, Boys Hope, the Girl Scouts, Veterans Hospital, the Variety Club, and Cystic Fibrosis.

The point of all this isn't about Jack Buck. My job has given me the opportunity to be involved with the public and to help many causes. A lot of broadcasters don't make that commitment. Some use their job as an excuse not to do it, saying they are too busy. Every time I've thought about cutting back on my activities, I'll receive a call from the St. Louis Symphony or another group and I'll almost always say yes. I'll never change.

Frequently I've gone to hospitals to visit youngsters who are ill or injured. I tell them to get well, then come and see me in the booth at the ballpark. Many of them have done so, and it's always gratifying when they do.

There have been hundreds of kids over the years, but some stand out to me so much that I frequently tear up when I think about them.

A lady called from St. Charles and asked me to go to the hospital to see her son. He had touched a high tension wire and was going to have a leg amputated the next day. I went to the hospital and saw him, tried to encourage him and told him to come see me in the future.

Toward the end of that year I received a message that he was at the ballpark and I brought him into the booth. He was wearing his Little League uniform and walking with a wooden leg. He hit over .400 that year in Little League. Kids are tough.

Red Schoendienst's wife, Mary, asked me to go see a youngster who had been burned. His name is John O'Leary. He was fooling around with some gasoline in the garage and started a fire. He had been burned so severely that all I could see when I visited were his eyes and his lips. I visited him frequently and asked others, such as Ozzie Smith and football coach Gene Stallings, to do the same. John suffered tremendously. Finally he got well enough to come to the ballpark and I took him down to the clubhouse and into the dugout to meet the players. I needed a bath towel to mop up my tears. He lost some of his fingers, but later played soccer and now he's attending St. Louis University. During the playoffs in 1996, a friend of his saw me at the ballpark and said he was there with John, who was inside trying to buy tickets for the World Series. I told him if the Cardinals got to the Series to call me.

Mike Frey and I first met in the Veterans Hospital. He was shot in Vietnam in 1969 and paralyzed from the neck down. That was 28 years ago. He comes to the ballpark occasionally, when the weather is just right, or he'll call and ask me to get him an autographed ball or whatever. He finally was able to leave the hospital and move into his own home. He's fortunate to have found some good people over the years who take care of him. We're still friends, and I'll always do anything he wants me to do.

After all the years I've been in the Cardinals' broadcasting booth, the most memorable event had nothing to do with a game on the field. A 13-year-old boy by the name of Lance Holzhauser was a victim of Cystic Fibrosis. He didn't have much time to live when he came to a game in 1979 and sat in the booth. He was so ill he had to wear an oxygen mask connected to a tank that his father carried.

He was sitting in the back row of the booth with his parents, and a foul ball was hit toward the adjacent booth. The ball hit a cable holding up the screen and ricochetted into our booth. There was a cardboard box on the counter in front of Lance's father. The ball struck the box, then rolled and stopped in front of Lance. He picked it up, and his eyes were like saucers. Later Stan Musial autographed the ball, and inscribed, "What a catch!" In my 31 years at Busch Stadium, that's the only ball that ever landed in the back row of our broadcast booth. Never before, and not since. That ball was delivered to Lance by— you know who.

Lance died a month later, a week shy of his 14th birthday. Our birthdays were on the same day, August 21. Visiting the funeral home was one of the most difficult things I've ever done. His parents still have that baseball in a plastic case, along with a ticket stub from the game. These days, Lance's sister, Denise, occasionally comes to the games with her child. His name is Lance. He's healthy and handsome.

Most recently, a youngster from Cape Girardeau, Missouri, Dustin McKinniss, has been coming to visit. He's 12 years old and has had more than 90 operations. He has a lung that continues to collapse and doctors don't know why. He is in the hospital more than he is out. He was in the booth during a game, and the Cardinals were ahead by four runs with two out in the ninth. I brought him down to the microphone and told him he was going to broadcast the final out.

He started to do the play-by-play. He has trouble breathing, and I told him to make certain he saved something for the end and to say, "That's a Winner!" There were two strikes on the batter, who then got a base hit. The next hitter got two strikes, and then he also got a hit. I told him, "Dustin, you're blowing it." I said, "You've only got one more chance. If this guy gets on, and the tying run comes to the plate, you're finito. You understand? Can you get this guy out?" He looked at me and said, "I hope so."

Dustin said, "Here's the pitch, ground ball to second, out at first and that's a winner!" We gave him the tape of his play-by-play. I don't think the broadcast is that holy that you can't do those things. The broadcast should be fun, it's not the most important thing in the world.

If and when I retire, I'm still going to be involved with as many charities as possible. I want to travel a lot—I want to visit the Northwest, see Montana, the Dakotas, and Wyoming. I want to visit western Canada, go to Alaska and Scandinavia. I want to go through the Panama Canal, and I'd like to see the Pyramids.

Carole says the best place she has ever visited was Venice, Italy. I wasn't on that trip with her. We'd like to go together.

I've been to the Masters golf tournament, the Kentucky Derby and Wimbledon. I've never been to the Indy 500 or to the Olympics.

I still intend to go to spring training every year, because that's the best part of the baseball season, unless your team is involved in postseason play. The entire baseball fraternity gears up for the season when the calendar turns to February. Everyone asks, "When are you leaving for Florida?" It's a big deal, packing your bags and going to Florida or Arizona for a month or six weeks. It's a grand time. You see all your old friends, watch baseball games, go to dinner and the dog track, and play golf. When you read in the newspaper that it's snowing in St. Louis, you're happy to be sitting on the beach. It's an inspiring time, but soon you've had enough of that also, and you're ready for the season to begin. You look at the schedule. Where do you open? Chicago, April 4, man, it's going to be cold! This year, April 1 in Montreal.

When I look back on my career and my life, I think of my father. He died in 1939 at age 49. I frequently say he never would have believed what followed. Our family never had an automobile. When I bought that Plymouth in 1950, I was the first one in our family to ever own a car.

My life has covered an intriguing span of years, starting with sleeping three in a bed. I still call a refrigerator an ice box, and remember putting a sign in the window to tell the delivery man how much ice we wanted. We also put a sign in the window when we were able to afford to buy coal in the winter. Clothes were hung outdoors on a line to dry. Carpets were cleaned with a carpet beater.

I can't think of any other period in history when I would have rather lived. Would I have enjoyed the Westward movement? I don't think so. I'm too much of a comfort creature. I don't mind roughing it, but I always enjoy a hot shower and a warm bed. I appreciate what I have now. Born into the Depression, we had very little. People stayed in their hometowns, never went anywhere and very few thought about college. World War II changed all that. If you lived through the war, your life was forever changed.

When I was 10 years old living in Holyoke, the odds of me going to college and later broadcasting Cardinals baseball were incalculable.

I thought I could be a baseball announcer when I was 15 years old, and I went out and did it. That's what I'm most proud of. I've helped my fair share of people. I hope that's what I'm remembered for.

A few years ago, my lawyer, Art Friedman, called to offer congratulations and told me I had been selected to receive the Horatio Alger award, the rags to riches award. I said, "Oh really? Tell them I don't want it."

Perhaps it was stupid on my part, but I thought that award would have reflected poorly on my parents. That award is to honor people who have come from nothing and have become a success. That would imply that my mother and father were worthless. I could never accept an award based on that premise.

When I was a boy, I received a Mickey Mouse watch one Christmas. I cried. My parents thought I cried because I was happy, but I cried because I knew they couldn't afford to buy the watch. I told that story to one of my children, and they told their kids. The next Christmas, I had a new Mickey Mouse watch from my grandchildren. I cried again.

I used to dream of owning a boat, but I've discarded that dream. I have a friend who has a boat, and that's better. I'll be happy to go on a trip with him anytime.

On our trips to Ireland, I learned how important it was to slow down. I went to buy a newspaper, and the clerk asked if I wanted yesterday's or today's. Of course I said today's, and he said, "Come back tomorrow."

Taking life a little slower has already been enjoyable for me. One time I told someone I thought I would die in the broadcast booth in the ninth inning of a game with the bases loaded. The next day, when someone told the story that I died, the response probably would have been, "That's too bad. Who won?"

Carole once asked me what I would say if I met the Lord, and my answer then is the same as it is now: I want to ask Him why He was so good to me.